OCT 7 '86	DATE DUE		
JAN 5 '87			
			ra

CREATIVE PLAYS
AND PROGRAMS
for
HOLIDAYS

Creative Plays
and Programs
for
Holidays

*Royalty-free plays, playlets, group readings,
and poems for holiday and seasonal
programs for boys and girls*

By

ROWENA BENNETT

Publishers   PLAYS, INC.   *Boston*

Acknowledgments

Grateful acknowledgment is made to the following, which first published some of the material in this book: *Child Life, Children's Activities, The Christian Science Monitor,* The Dramatic Publishing Company, Follett Publishing Company, *Grade Teacher, Highlights for Children, The Instructor, Jack and Jill,* Methodist Publishing House, *Plays: The Drama Magazine for Young People,* Row, Peterson Company, Clayton F. Summy Company, *Story Parade,* Whitman Publishing Company.

TABLE OF

CONTENTS

CREATIVE PLAYS
AND PROGRAMS
for
HOLIDAYS

PART ONE

Holiday Time

Holiday Time

The squares upon the calendar
  Are mostly black and white
For Father Time thinks only
  Of marking day and night;
But there were Pilgrim Fathers
  And heroes long since dead
Who made so brave a land for us
  We mark their births in red.
And Christmas is a red day, too,
  With hearthstones all ablaze!
What fun it is to celebrate
  Good things in special ways!
I love to have my calendar
  Fill up with HOLIDAYS!

Out of the Clock

Characters

MOUSE
CAT
DOG
FATHER TIME, *an old man*
LITTLE NEW YEAR, *a young girl*

TIME: *New Year's Eve.*
SETTING: *A living room.*
AT RISE: FATHER TIME *is sleeping by the fire, in the chimney corner right, and the grandfather clock, up center, is ticking loudly. Nothing happens for a moment or two, then* MOUSE *runs in from left, and knocks on the door of the clock.*

MOUSE (*In sing-song as he knocks*):
   Knickety-knock, knickety-knock.
   I am the mouse that ran up the clock.
   Little New Year won't you kindly unlock
   The pretty brown door of your tickety-tock?
FATHER TIME (*Roused from his nap*):
   Shoo! little mousie-kin, why do you claw

3

At the door of the clock with your prickly gray paw?

MOUSE (*Beginning to sob*):
Boo-hoo-hoo! What shall I do?
The cat will be here in a minute or two
To chase me and catch me . . . Oh, boo-hoo-hoo!

FATHER TIME: But how can the Little New Year help
   you?

MOUSE:
As soon as she comes, I have heard people tell,
The bothersome cat will behave very well;
For everyone tries to be good, I hear,
Whenever it's time for the Little New Year.
Oh, please blow a whistle or rattle a drum
So the Little New Year will come, come, come!

FATHER TIME:
I'm sorry. It may not be quite to your liking;
She cannot come out till the clock starts its striking.

CAT (*Offstage*): Mew, mew . . .

MOUSE (*Trembling*): What shall I do?

FATHER TIME:
You'd better be hiding behind that big chair
And maybe the kitty won't find you there.

MOUSE: Yes, yes, I'll be hiding behind this big chair . . .
   (*He hides behind a chair, left. Again there is silence,
   except for the clock's ticking.* FATHER TIME *dozes.*
   MOUSE *trembles.* CAT *enters stealthily, creeping on quiet
   paws.*)

CAT (*In stage whisper*):
Where is that mouse? *Where* is that mouse?
I'll find him if I have to tear up the house.
   (*She pokes about, sniffing and snooping.*)
They'll send me away at the first of the year
On a holiday trip . . . but before I leave here
I want to catch mousie-kin right by the ear . . .
   (*She is about to discover the* MOUSE *behind the chair*

when a bark is heard offstage.)

DOG (*Offstage*): Bow-wow-wow, bow-wow-wow!

CAT (*Suddenly frightened*):

There is that dog! He's big as a cow.

What shall I do to save myself now? (*She rushes over to the clock and knocks on it. In a sing-song as she knocks*)

Knickety-knock, knickety-knock.

I am the kitten who sits by the clock.

Little New Year won't you kindly unlock

The pretty brown door of the tickety-tock?

Knickety-knock, knickety-knock . . .

FATHER TIME (*Roused from his nap*):

Shoo! little kitty-kin, why do you claw

At the door of the clock with your prickly white paw?

CAT (*Crying*):

Boo-hoo-hoo! What shall I do?

The dog will be here in a minute or two

To chase me and catch me . . . Oh, boo-hoo-hoo!

FATHER TIME: But how can the Little New Year help *you?*

CAT:

As soon as she comes, I have heard people tell,

The bothersome dog will behave very well.

For everyone tries to be good, I hear,

Whenever it's time for the Little New Year.

Oh please blow a whistle or rattle a drum!

So the Little New Year will come, come, come.

FATHER TIME:

Although I'm afraid it is not to your liking,

I can't let her out till the clock starts its striking . . .

DOG (*Offstage*): Bow-wow!

CAT (*Frantic*): He's coming now . . .

FATHER TIME:

You'd better be hiding behind that big chair

And maybe the puppy will not find you there.

CAT (*Running*): Yes, yes, I will hide here, behind this big chair. (*She hides behind second chair.* DOG *enters noisily.*)

DOG (*In a gruff voice*):

Where is that cat? Where is that cat?

I'll look under every pillow and mat. (*He sniffs about.*)

I'll find her before she can skittle or scat.

They'll send me away at the first of the year

For a holiday trip . . . but before I leave here

I want to catch kitty-kin right by the ear . . .

(*He suddenly comes upon the* CAT *behind the chair. At the same moment the* CAT *sees the* MOUSE.) The cat!

CAT: The mouse!

MOUSE: LET ME OUT OF THIS HOUSE! (MOUSE *runs around in a circle in the center of the stage. The* CAT *runs after the* MOUSE. *The* DOG *runs after the* CAT. *They go round and round and round. All at once the clock strikes. The animals stop, stock-still.* FATHER TIME *opens the door of the clock. Out steps* LITTLE NEW YEAR.)

LITTLE NEW YEAR: A HAPPY NEW YEAR, EVERYONE.

ANIMALS (*Hanging their heads and mumbling*): A happy New Year to *you*.

LITTLE NEW YEAR (*Holding up three beautiful calendars*):

See what I brought you, one and all!

Beautiful days of spring and fall,

Beautiful days of winter and summer . . .

Are you not glad of a friend and newcomer?

(*She hands a calendar to each of the animals.*)

ANIMALS (*Delighted*): Do you mean that you *give* us these beautiful days?

LITTLE NEW YEAR (*Nodding*): To use as you please in a hundred nice ways.

DOG:

I want to do something that's special with mine.

I'll never waste time on a growl or whine.
I'll practice high jumping and learn to run faster
And think of new ways to take care of my master . . .

CAT (*To* DOG, *warily*): You will not go chasing a poor little cat?

DOG (*Decidedly*): No. Only a bully would choose to do that.

CAT: Then I shall go purring all over the house . . .

MOUSE: You will not go chasing a poor little mouse? (*Sniffs.*)

CAT: Of course not, you silly. Go wipe off your tear.

MOUSE (*Smiling*): How good it will seem to be free from all fear!

ANIMALS (*In chorus*): Oh, this will be surely a Happy New Year! (*They grab the* LITTLE NEW YEAR *and* FATHER TIME *by the hand and all dance in a circle.*)

ALL (*As the curtain falls*): A HAPPY NEW YEAR! A HAPPY NEW YEAR! A HAPPY NEW YEAR!

THE END

On New Year's Eve

Characters

Two Boys
Two Girls
Little New Year
Six Minute Fairies
Hours
Days

TIME: *New Year's Eve at midnight.*
SETTING: *A living room with a grandfather clock standing in corner.*
AT RISE: Two Boys *and* Two Girls *enter from left.*

1st GIRL (*Looking around*):
  Oh, where is the clock that talks in rhyme?
  Telling the time . . . telling the time!
1st BOY (*Gesturing*):
  Oh, here is the clock that is telling the time.
  It's going to strike, and it's going to chime.
  Pull up a chair and sit right here.
  The midnight hour is drawing near.
  (*They pull up chairs and as they sit down facing clock, it begins to chime and strike.*)
Boys *and* Girls (*Together*):
  Come out of the clock, O little New Year!

8

The midnight hour is near . . . is here!
Come out of the clock, O little New Year!
(*The clock door opens and* LITTLE NEW YEAR, *a dainty little girl in a party dress and gay ribbons, comes out, holding a wand. She curtsies to* BOYS *and* GIRLS *in turn and waves her wand with a flourish.*)

LITTLE NEW YEAR:

A happy New Year to you, each girl and boy.
Let me give you a present . . .

2ND BOY:

Oh, is it a toy?

2ND GIRL:

Or is it some candy or cookies or flowers?

LITTLE NEW YEAR:

It's minutes and days and seasons and hours.
(*She taps the clock with her wand and out of the door comes a very small* MINUTE FAIRY.)

MINUTE FAIRY:

I am a little minute.
I come and go in haste.
I'm really much too valuable
To throw away or waste.
(LITTLE NEW YEAR *opens the clock door again, and out troop five other small* MINUTE FAIRIES.)

MINUTE FAIRIES (*Together*):

We, too, are little minutes. . . .
(*Each then speaks in turn, bowing.*)
One . . . two . . . three . . . four . . . five. . . .
(*Then, in unison, swaying rhythmically.*)
We tick and tock, and tick and tock,
And keep the clock alive.
(*They toss balloons and confetti over* BOYS *and* GIRLS *and dance around them. Then* MINUTE FAIRIES *sit down on either side of clock.* LITTLE NEW YEAR *taps clock with wand and clock door opens. Onstage come the*

Hours, *carrying trays of flowers. They are much taller than the* Minute Fairies. *They circle stage, then bow to* Boys *and* Girls.)

Hours:

We are the passing hours.

Beautiful things we bring—

If you like, we shall toss you flowers

And dance for you in a ring.

Boys *and* Girls:

Oh, yes, please toss us flowers

And dance for us in a ring.

(*The* Hours *dance around stage, throwing flowers about, then take places near* Minute Fairies. Little New Year *steps forward and again taps the clock door with her wand. The* Days, *who are taller than the* Hours, *step out of clock dressed in Grecian robes of rainbow colors and carrying balls and small musical instruments.*)

Days (*Bowing to* Boys *and* Girls):

We are the coming days,

Here are the gifts we bring—

(*Holding up balls*)

Balls if you wish to play,

(*Holding up instruments*)

Or tunes if you wish to sing.

Boys *and* Girls (*Running forward and taking instruments*):

We wish to sing!

All (*Ad lib*): Yes, we want to sing! Give me a drum! Let's sing a song about winter. (*Etc.*) (*Everyone begins to sing a winter song or a song about clocks, children with instruments keep time on drums, triangles, etc., as the curtain falls.*)

THE END

Good Cheer! New Year!

*(A reading for two children, each with a
bell of a different tone.)*

1ST CHILD: The bell in the belfry
                  Is calling, "Good cheer!"
               It knows that this day
                  Is the first in the year.

2ND CHILD: I like to rise early
                  On New Year's to hear
               The bell in the belfry
                  Cry out far and near,
                     (Rings bell)
               Good cheer! New Year!

1ST CHILD *(Ringing bell)*: New Year! Good cheer!

Belfry Brownies

*(Two choral groups, one on each side of stage, alternate
reading, to the accompaniment of bells.)*

1st Chorus: There were some belfry brownies, once,
              Who were so shy of people

2nd Chorus: They built their little brownie nest
              High in the highest steeple.

1st Chorus: There they could see the sights of town
              By craning necks and looking down.

2nd Chorus: They played at hide-and-seek with bats,
              All night they liked to play.

1st Chorus: They rode astride the weathercock
              As soon as it was day.

All *(Together, ring bells softly as the following lines are
spoken)*:

              But most of all they liked to ride
              On chiming bells at New Year's tide!

(All ring bells loudly, as they march off stage.)

12

LINCOLN'S BIRTHDAY

Visitors for Nancy Hanks

Characters

NANCY HANKS LINCOLN
MISS FORTUNE
DAME DESPAIR
MADAM WANT

TIME: *A stormy afternoon in February 1809, about two weeks after the birth of Abraham Lincoln.*
SETTING: *Interior of the crude Kentucky log cabin which was Lincoln's birthplace.*
AT RISE: NANCY HANKS LINCOLN *is seated by the side of little Abe's cradle. She is sewing and rocking the cradle with her foot, humming as she sews.*

NANCY (*Pausing in her humming, she peers cautiously over the edge of the cradle*): What? Not asleep yet? I never saw such wide-open eyes! They look as though they'd like to swallow the whole room. What are you thinking about, Abe darling? About the days when you'll be grown up? (*She adjusts his covers tenderly.*) I like to think about those days, too. I like to look into the fire and see a picture of you there. (*She leans back*

13

in her chair and gazes dreamily at the burning log.) It
seems so wonderful that a little bundle like you will
some day grow up into a big, tall man! (*She bends over
cradle.*) You're going to be a *great* man, too, Abe . . .
not just a tall one. A *great* one! I *know* it. I'm *sure* of it.
I saw it in your eyes the day you were born . . . (*She
studies the burning log.*) and now, now I see it in the
fire. The fire has a way of making pictures, Abe, pictures of things that are going to happen. If you just
close your eyes halfway and squint a little at the em-
bers . . . then the pictures come . . . Now it's mostly
hands I see . . . They're reaching . . . reaching for
something out of sight. They're clasping, too. There's
a dark hand clasping a strong ruddy one. See? (*She tips
the cradle toward the fire.*) The ruddy hand is yours,
Abe, I know it is. It's so manly and powerful . . . and
the dark hand . . . it must belong to someone you're
helping . . . someone you're lifting . . . And there's
always another hand, Abe. I've seen it so many times—
a hand with a wreath in it. The wreath is green flame
that flutters like green leaves. It's the kind of wreath
great men wear . . . in pictures . . . and on statues
. . . it's the kind of wreath . . . (*There is a sudden
rattling of the door.* NANCY *stands up quickly.*) What's
that? Is someone there? (*She hurries over to the window and looks out. There is a flash of lightning and
a rumble of thunder. The wind whistles.* NANCY *draws
back. She looks startled, but smiles reassuringly as she
turns toward the cradle.*) I think it's only the wind, Abe,
and the rain. It's dreadfully stormy out. (*The rattling
sound comes again, and again* NANCY *looks out the
window.*) Oh, no! There *is* someone there! Someone is
standing on the doorstep. (*In surprise*) Why! It's three
old women . . . huddled together . . . (*There is a
loud rattling which is more like knocking this time.*)

Oh, dear, Abe! What shall I do? They're horrid-looking old crones. They must be the gossips who live out on the barrens. Nosy old things! (*She runs back to the cradle and puts her hand on the hood protectively, her eyes on the door as she speaks.*) They've come to see you, Abe. Why must old women always be curious about new babies? I can't bear to have them touch you. They're so ugly, so dirty, so . . . (*She leans forward over the cradle and peers in.*) Oh! Sound asleep. (*She breathes a sigh of relief.*) Smart boy! You know what to do at the right time, don't you? (*The knocking is repeated, this time insistently.* NANCY *runs to the door on tiptoe and speaks in a stage whisper.*) Yes, yes, I'm coming. Don't wake the baby. . . . (*She opens the door. Crash of thunder is heard, and flashes of lightning may be seen.* MISS FORTUNE, MADAM WANT *and* DAME DESPAIR *enter.* MADAM WANT *carries a workbag and* DAME DESPAIR, *a basket.*)

MISS FORTUNE (*Fussily*): Dear, dear! We thought you weren't home!

MADAM WANT (*Peevishly*): It's a wet day to be standing on the doorstep.

NANCY (*Kindly*): I'm sorry. I didn't mean to be inhospitable. The baby was just dropping off to sleep. You're my new neighbors, I s'pose?

DAME DESPAIR: Yes. We live out on the barrens, just over the way. (*She gestures vaguely.*) Perhaps you've heard of us, Mrs. Lincoln. This is Miss Fortune, here and Madam Want, there, and I am Dame DeSpair.

NANCY (*Nervously, as she shakes hands*): Yes. I have heard of you. I can't think where . . .

MISS FORTUNE (*Over-sweetly*): We came to see the baby and to give him our blessing.

NANCY: That's very kind of you, but . . .

DAME DESPAIR (*Firmly, insistently*): We'll have a look at him right now.

OTHER TWO: Yes, come . . . (*The three start toward the cradle, but* NANCY *steps quickly in front of them, barring the way with outstretched arms.*)

NANCY (*Using her outstretched arms to indicate chairs*): Won't you sit down a while first? He's sleeping now. Besides, you're cold and wet. The fire will warm you. (*She helps them move chairs near the hearth. She herself sits a little apart to keep an eye on the baby.*)

MISS FORTUNE (*Gushingly*): This is very kind of you, Mrs. Lincoln. Such a nice blaze as you have, too. Just the thing for a stormy day.

NANCY: I have to keep it extra warm for the baby, of course.

MADAM WANT: Just like a young mother! Always coddling her first-born! It's a pity old folks don't get the coddling babies do. They need it more than the young 'uns.

DAME DESPAIR: Yes. You mustn't be spoiling your boy, Mrs. Lincoln. What did you say his name is?

NANCY: Abraham. We call him "Abe."

DAME DESPAIR: Abe? Abe! (*Considering it carefully*) It's a good name for a *poor* boy . . . not too fancy . . .

NANCY (*Surprised and hurt*): But I never think of him as a *poor* boy. He has his father and me to look after him. It isn't as though . . .

MISS FORTUNE (*Curiously*): His father's away, I take it?

NANCY: Yes, for a day or two on business.

DAME DESPAIR: A very good time for a call, sisters. (*She looks at the other two meaningfully.*)

MISS FORTUNE *and* MADAM WANT (*Maliciously*): A *mighty* good time for a call.

NANCY (*With sudden foreboding*): Why do you say that?

MISS FORTUNE (*Smoothly*): Because we cannot bear to have

you lonely, my dear. A woman needs company when her husband's gone. . . . She—

NANCY (*Quickly*): But I have my baby. How can I be lonely with little Abe for company?

MADAM WANT (*Touchily*): Dear! Dear! I guess we're not wanted. (*She rises.*) You don't think much of your neighbors, do you, Mrs. Lincoln? (*She starts toward the door.*) Here we come on a stormy day, just to cheer you up and . . .

MISS FORTUNE (*Also rising*): . . . and this is all the thanks we get!

NANCY (*Apologetically*): Oh, I didn't mean it *that* way! Not at all . . . I only meant . . .

DAME DESPAIR: Yes, yes, I know. You mustn't mind my sisters, Mrs. Lincoln. They're always taking offense at nothing. They think because you haven't offered them a cup of tea that you don't approve of them as neighbors . . .

NANCY (*Upset*): I'm so sorry. I should have thought of tea at once, after your long, cold walk . . . Please sit down again. I'll have the water boiling in no time . . . (*She swings the teakettle over the burning log and pokes up the fire.*)

MADAM WANT (*Seating herself and watching the preparations greedily*): It isn't the tea, of course. It's the hospitality . . .

MISS FORTUNE: Yes. We can't bear to intrude where we're not wanted . . .

DAME DESPAIR: They're so sensitive, you know . . .

NANCY (*As she hurries from hearth to cupboard, from cupboard to table, setting out the tea things*): You must forgive me. (*She puts a hoecake on the hearth to warm.*) I've been so busy since the baby came, and my strength hasn't quite come back . . . I'm a little weak and faint at times . . .

DAME DESPAIR: Of course you are! Poor child! (*She turns to her sisters*) Aren't you ashamed! Misjudging Mrs. Lincoln so! All because of your touchiness!

MISS FORTUNE: We apologize, Mrs. Lincoln. You're hospitality itself. (*She turns to* MADAM WANT) Isn't she, sister?

MADAM WANT: Looks as if she is—from the way that meal's shapin' up. (*She scans the table greedily.*)

DAME DESPAIR: Then let's change the subject right now. Just what's taking your husband out of town, Mrs. Lincoln?

NANCY: He hopes to make some extra money on . . .

MISS FORTUNE (*Who has been pretending to look for something*): Good gracious me! I've lost it!

NANCY: Lost what?

MISS FORTUNE: My workbag.

NANCY: But I don't think you had one with you when you came in.

MADAM WANT: Oh, yes, she did, leastways she was carryin' it on the road.

MISS FORTUNE: I must have set it down when I jumped that puddle . . . and forgot to pick it up. Oh, dear! And I had a jar of jelly in it, too!

MADAM WANT: Oh, yes, she did, leastways she was carryin' bringing to Mrs. Lincoln?

MISS FORTUNE: Of course. (*To* NANCY) It was just a little delicacy to help a young mother get her strength back. (*She beams.*)

NANCY: How very kind of you! I love jelly, and I'm all out of it. We didn't have much of a fruit crop last fall and . . . and . . .

MISS FORTUNE: I'd go back to the road and fetch it this minute, if my feet weren't so cold . . .

NANCY: Why, *I'll* get it. (*She raises her shawl from her shoulders to her head and grasps it tightly under her chin. She looks around at the others hesitantly.*) If you

three don't mind keeping an eye on the kettle and seeing that the hoecake doesn't burn . . .

OTHERS (*Ad lib*): Of course. We'd be glad to. No trouble
at all. (*Etc.*) (*They exchange triumphant glances.* NANCY
*starts toward the door, but as she passes the cradle, the
baby coughs. She goes to him at once, in concern.*)

NANCY: Why Abe, darling, what are you coughing about?
(*To others, who look disgruntled by this interruption*)
Oh, dear! I hope he's not catching cold. I don't think
I'd better leave him, not even for a minute. (*She leans
over the cradle and, taking her own shawl off, tucks it
around the baby.*) I'm afraid he didn't have enough covers. I've been short of blankets . . . that is . . . it's
been such an unusually damp winter . . .

DAME DESPAIR (*Brightly*): Now if that isn't a coincidence!
We brought you a blanket this very day. We took turns
knitting it for the baby . . .

NANCY (*Delighted*): Really! How wonderful!

DAME DESPAIR: We weren't going to say a word about it.
We just planned to leave it here as a surprise when we
left. But if you need it now . . . (*She fumbles about in
her basket.*)

NANCY (*Running over to her eagerly*): Oh, I'd love it! I
can't tell you how touched I am! It's so thoughtful . . .
so neighborly . . . so—

DAME DESPAIR (*Giving up her search and turning to* MISS
FORTUNE): Dear! Dear! I must have tucked it into *your*
bag, sister.

MISS FORTUNE: I should *hope* not . . .

DAME DESPAIR: Yes, I remember, now, I wrapped it round
the jelly so the jar wouldn't break . . .

MADAM WANT: Then it'll be soaking wet . . .

MISS FORTUNE: But it can be dried out . . .

NANCY (*Happily*): Of course! I'll get it and hang it by the
fire right away . . . (*She rushes out without stopping*

for a wrap, calling back over her shoulder) Be careful not to wake Abe. I'll be right back. (*As soon as she has gone, the three women look at one another with malicious triumph and rise quickly.*)

MISS FORTUNE: At last! I thought we'd never get her out of here.

MADAM WANT: She is a stubborn one all right, not wanting to leave that baby.

DAME DESPAIR: Mothers are always the hardest people to get the better of.

MADAM WANT (*Going toward cupboard*): We must set to work. She'll be back any minute.

MISS FORTUNE: Yes, yes, she'll be back any minute. (*They bustle about purposefully.* MISS FORTUNE *lifts the tea-kettle off the crane and begins pouring water over the fire.* MADAM WANT *opens the cupboard and, taking the meager supplies from the shelves, stuffs food into her mouth and what is left, into her pockets.* DAME DESPAIR *goes over to the cradle and pulls the blankets off baby. Thunder and lightning make the scene unusually sinister.* MISS FORTUNE *laughs as she puts out the fire*) With the fire out and the cupboard bare, Miss Fortune and Madam Want are mistresses of any house. Ha, ha, ha!

MADAM WANT: She'll be takin' orders from us now, instead of our bowin' and scrapin' to her.

MISS FORTUNE (*With mock haughtiness*): We'll make an indefinite visit . . .

DAME DESPAIR: Don't get so cocky, you two. You can't move in here till Nancy Hanks gives up—till she admits that want and misfortune have gotten the better of her.

MADAM WANT: She won't be long admitting *that*. We've gotten the best of most folks we've called on, eh, sister?

MISS FORTUNE: Of course. A bare cupboard and a cold hearth work wonders. She'll never get this fire started.

The wood outside's all wet, and I hid the tinderbox. Ha, ha, ha. That idea of mine about the jelly was a good one, too, if I do say so! Ha, ha, ha!

MADAM WANT: It was *my* idea, not yours. Leastways I told you, comin' over, that these women can always be tempted with victuals . . .

DAME DESPAIR: Humph! As though the jelly would have got her out of the house! You'd both have bungled things if I hadn't been here. She wouldn't have budged an inch for herself, but for the baby's sake . . . well! I don't understand these *mothers* but that's the way they are. They'll do anything for their children . . . that's why they're so tricky to handle. They won't knuckle under, sometimes not even for want or misfortune, sometimes not even for . . . (*There is a sound of running feet outside.*)

MISS FORTUNE: Sh-h-h! Here she comes!

MADAM WANT: I can't get this cupboard shut. (*She pounds it with her fist.*) There!

DAME DESPAIR: Promise me you won't try to boss her *yet*. We have to fawn a little longer . . .

MISS FORTUNE: All right, we'd better be sure of her. We can't make any slips.

DAME DESPAIR: Quick! Back to your places! (*They all sit down in a hurry just before the door opens. As* NANCY *enters, they begin rocking back and forth, moaning and wringing their hands.* NANCY *is wet and wind-blown.*)

NANCY (*Breathlessly*): The bag's not there. The wind must have . . . (*She looks about her in bewilderment at the disheveled room and the weeping women.*) What's the matter? What's happened? (*She rushes over to the baby's cradle*) Oh, Abe, Abe, are you all right? (*She starts at sight of the tumbled blankets*) Why! You're all uncovered! You poor darling! And your little feet—they're getting blue! (*She looks at the old hags suspiciously—angrily.*) How did this happen? (*She studies them severely as she tucks the blankets about the baby.*)

DAME DESPAIR (*Moaning*): It was that wind. It came down the chimney like a hurricane.

MADAM WANT (*Groaning*): It brought the rain with it . . .

MISS FORTUNE: . . . and put out the fire . . . (*She weeps hysterically.*)

DAME DESPAIR: It tore the room to pieces.

MISS FORTUNE: It almost blew the house down. (*They rock back and forth, wailing.*)

NANCY (*Considering, for a moment*): Yes. It *was* frightful. I could hardly get to the house. It kept driving me back, but it must have been worse here. You must have been in the heart of the storm . . .

OTHERS: Oh, we were! We were! (*They moan and groan more loudly than ever.*)

NANCY: Hush! Hush! I'm sure it was a shock. But you mustn't carry on so. After all, others have been through hurricanes before. We must *do* something about it, not just sit and moan. The first thing's the fire. We'll have to rebuild it at once so little Abe won't get chilled.

MISS FORTUNE: How can we? The wood's outside, and it's all wet. Besides, there's not a red ember left.

NANCY: No ember? (*She rakes the coals.*) But there is! Look! Just one!

MISS FORTUNE (*Gasping*): Where?

NANCY: Here! We must feed it. (*She jumps up and grasps some branches of dry leaves that hang by the chimney. She breaks them up and tosses them onto the fire.*)

MADAM WANT (*Aside to* MISS FORTUNE, *angrily*): I thought you said there would be no slips.

MISS FORTUNE (*In stage whisper*): I can't understand it. I could have sworn I'd quenched every coal . . . It's supernatural. (*She looks frightened.*) Anyway, she can't budge the log.

DAME DESPAIR: Sh-h-h!

NANCY (*Throwing the last of the leaves and twigs into the flame*): Oh, how glad I am I gathered these! I did it just because they looked so pretty, but now—now they're the only dry things I have to burn, these, and this log. (*She indicates the rude bench*) If I can only get this log on. . . . (*She moves toward it.*)

MISS FORTUNE: Oh, but you can't, you can't! You're too little to lift it. Only a man could move it.

MADAM WANT: Remember, you haven't your strength back yet. You said so yourself. It would be dreadful even to *try* to lift it. You'd be strainin' your back in no time.

DAME DESPAIR: If we weren't so old and helpless, we could give you a hand.

NANCY (*Who has been straining and tugging at the log during the above warnings, now straightens and leans against the chimney panting, exhausted*): I can't budge it. (*She sighs wearily, and, for a moment, looks defeated. Then she rallies.*) Let me think. Let me think. There must be a way.

MADAM WANT (*Irritably*): There *is* no way.

NANCY: There's always a way, if one can just think of it. (*With sudden inspiration*) I know! I'll *roll* it. A log doesn't have to be lifted. It can be rolled. (*She pushes the log painfully forward. As it moves the three old women watch nervously. It is evident they are hoping against hope that NANCY will not achieve her objective. MISS FORTUNE and MADAM WANT exchange fearful glances. When, at last, the great log actually rolls onto the fire, they sigh loudly, defeated.*)

DAME DESPAIR (*Trying to divert NANCY's attention from her sisters*): Hurrah, my dear! You've done it! Who would have thought a frail woman like yourself . . .

NANCY (*Still panting, but triumphant*): Thank goodness, oh, thank goodness! That will keep us warm till I can dry out some smaller pieces from the pile outside. I asked my husband when we first moved here to put that great log by the hearth for a bench, but in my heart I thought how it might help us sometime in an emergency . . .

DAME DESPAIR: You are a very clever woman, Mrs. Lincoln, very clever! (*While* NANCY *and* DAME DESPAIR *are engaged in conversation,* MADAM WANT *and* MISS FORTUNE *move to the front of the stage and talk together in stage whispers.*)

MADAM WANT: She's gotten the best of us, curse the woman!

MISS FORTUNE: And we laid our plans so well!

MADAM WANT: She's one of the tougher cases that we have to leave to DeSpair . . .

MISS FORTUNE: Yes, and you're right about going. We'd better be getting along before she discovers your thieving . . . (*They go toward the door noiselessly and tiptoe out.*)

NANCY (*Putting the finishing touches on the fire; sweeping up the hearth, etc.*): We can have the tea now. It won't take the water long to boil with a blaze like that. (*She picks up the teakettle.*) Why, it's empty! The kettle's empty! (*She looks around in bewilderment.*) And the others—the two women, your sisters—where are they?

DAME DESPAIR: They've gone, Mrs. Lincoln, but don't you fret. I'll keep you company.

NANCY (*Puzzled*): Did I offend them again?

DAME DESPAIR: No, no, I'm sure you didn't. They're just a queer pair, if I do say so. But *I* shan't walk out on you like that. Come, let's have our tea and a cozy chat together . . .

NANCY: Of course. I'll get some more hoecake. The other's all soggy. (*She goes to the cupboard and opens it. When she sees it is bare she lets out a little cry.*) I—I've been robbed!

DAME DESPAIR (*Shaking her head gloomily*): It must have been when my back was turned. Those sisters of mine! They almost drive me mad.

NANCY: You mean they—

DAME DESPAIR: Yes. Madam Want is a bit light-fingered— an unfortunate case, a disease, you know . . . and . . .

NANCY (*Angrily*): So that's it! And who was it emptied the teakettle onto the hearth and put out the fire?

DAME DESPAIR: That was Miss Fortune. She's addleheaded and rattle-brained. The storm upset her. Neither of them is responsible, poor dears.

NANCY: Then why didn't you warn me about them?

DAME DESPAIR: I thought I could stave off any trouble— I thought . . .

NANCY (*Unheeding*): I'm beginning to see through it all now. The workbag dropped in the road! Why! There wasn't any such bag at all! And there wasn't a hurricane either! . . . And who pulled the baby's blankets off? (*She points an accusing finger at* DAME DESPAIR.) It must have been you, Dame DeSpair. The others were too busy with tricking and thieving, but you were worse than they. You wanted Abe to catch cold. You wanted him to die.

DAME DESPAIR: Hush! Hush! What nonsense! I only wanted to protect him from the future. Isn't death better than poverty and . . .

NANCY (*Only half hearing*): What do *you* know about Abe's future? Are you a prophet?

DAME DESPAIR: Yes, Mrs. Lincoln. I am a prophet. (*For once she sounds convincing.*)

NANCY (*Eagerly*): Then tell me about Abe. Tell me what he will do—what he will be.

DAME DESPAIR: Since you ask me, I will tell you. He will lose his mother early in life . . .

NANCY (*Drawing back as though struck*): You—you m-mean I will die young?

DAME DESPAIR (*With authority*): You will die young, Mrs. Lincoln. That is your fate.

NANCY: That may be *my* fate, but it's not *Abe's*. Oh, tell me that Abe will not die! Tell me that he will grow up to be a man!

DAME DESPAIR (*Grudgingly*): Yes. He will grow up to be a man.

NANCY: Then what does it matter about me? My life is nothing. But Abe's life will be a great one.

DAME DESPAIR: Not so fast, Mrs. Lincoln. I said he would grow up. I did not say he would grow up to be a great man.

NANCY (*Frightened*): But he will. I know he will. Oh, say that he will!

DAME DESPAIR: Tut, tut. Every mother thinks her son will grow up to be great. But how many do? I ask you that?

NANCY: Not many, I suppose. (*Musing*) Yet Abe is different.

DAME DESPAIR (*Laughing*): That's what all the mothers say. Use your common sense, Mrs. Lincoln. How can a poor boy, born in a log cabin, raised without schooling, forced to sweat for his bread—how can he be great? How can he stand up next to the rich and famous?

NANCY (*Defiantly*): I will see that he goes to school. I will see . . .

DAME DESPAIR: Oh, no you won't! Remember, his mother will die young.

NANCY: But his father . . .

DAME DESPAIR: His father will always be poor . . .

NANCY: No, no! Do not doom us to endless poverty! Do not doom my boy to—

DAME DESPAIR (*With malicious triumph*): Never mind, Mrs. Lincoln, you will have *me* to cheer you. I shall not desert you. I shall sit by your hearthstone always.

NANCY (*Desperately*): No! No! Go 'way, you dreadful woman!

DAME DESPAIR (*With glee she cannot hide*): You got the best of my two sisters, but you shan't get the best of me. Struggle and labor may defeat want and misfortune. But what shall defeat despair?

NANCY (*Going to the cradle and weeping as she bends over her child*): Little Abe! Oh, my little Abe! Why should you never have your due? I know it was greatness I saw in your eyes that first day, the day you were born, and I have seen it since. I *felt* it, too, when your heart beat beneath my heart. And what of the dreams I saw in the fire? (*She turns toward the hearth.*) They were so real. There were the reaching hands . . . and the clasping ones. (*In excitement*) But see! They have come back again! The dark one . . . and the ruddy . . . (*She moves toward the hearth as in a trance, her eyes glued to the flames. DAME DESPAIR rises and moves slowly backward toward the door as NANCY moves forward toward the hearth. Each seems drawn by an irresistible force.*) They are clasping, as in friendship; and there, above them, rises the other hand . . . the one with the wreath. How green the wreath is, and how glowing!

DAME DESPAIR: Stop! Stop! I can't stand it! Your words torture me!

NANCY (*Coming to suddenly and seeing the old hag move toward the door*): You are going? (*She is incredulous.*)

DAME DESPAIR: Yes. I can never stand up against a woman who sees visions—a mother who dreams dreams for her child . . .

NANCY: Then you admit your prophecy was false?

DAME DESPAIR: I admit your child will be great. (*She goes out.*)

NANCY (*Running on light feet to the cradle and looking down at her baby, her face radiant*): Oh, Abe, little Abe, you shall be great! You shall be great! (*Curtain falls.*)

THE END

A Bit of Book Earning

(The choral groups and the solos may be grouped in semi-circle. They speak alternately.)

1ST CHORUS:

> Oh, did you know that Lincoln,
>> When he was just a boy,
> Would rather have a book to read
>> Than have a game or toy?

1ST SOLO:

> He read at night by firelight
>> Such books as he could borrow.
> He had no volumes of his own,
>> Much to his secret sorrow.

2ND CHORUS:

> But once he left a borrowed book,
>> "The Life of Washington",
> Where winds blew through the cabin cracks;
>> And it was rained upon.

2ND SOLO:

> Most bitterly he blamed himself
>> And, giving up all fun,
> For three long days he shucked the corn
>> To pay for damage done.

29

3RD SOLO:

> Then, to his very great delight,
> The man who made the loan
> Of that prized book told Honest Abe
> To keep it for his own.

3RD CHORUS:

> Oh, happy day! Oh, happy hour!
> Such treasure brought new pride.
> The crumpled covers mattered not
> For *wealth* there was inside!

Prairie Growth

The young lad, Lincoln, was long and lank and lean
And clumsy as the bay colt that grazed the prairie's green;
But, oh, the wonder of his eyes,
As grave and gray as prairie skies!

The young lad, Lincoln, was schooled by firelight.
A wooden shovel was the slate whereon he learned to write;
And books became his friends, folk say,
They pushed his cabin walls away
And showed him what he'd longed to find:
The wider prairies of the mind.

A Boy's Wish

I wish that I'd known Lincoln
  When he was just a boy,
Before he roamed the prairies
  Of early Illinois.

We would have played together
  In woodland or in clearing,
And young Abe would have taught me
  The ways of pioneering.

But most of all, I should have liked
  To sit with country folks
Around the campfire and to laugh
  At Lincoln's endless jokes.

The Strong Man

Abe Lincoln? He was three times strong:
  He had the strength of limb
That splitting rails and hauling wood
  Had builded up in him.
He had the strength of thought that comes
  To every book-fed mind;
But, best of all, his heart grew strong
  By loving all mankind.

The Nickname

Abe Lincoln clerked in a country store
  And a very good clerk was he.
He sold bright bolts of calico,
  Matches, molasses and tea:
And talk traveled 'round in a wide, wide range
How Abe was fussy with money and change:
"Why! He walked three miles to return three cents
To old widow Jones at her own front fence . . ."
"And a fourth pound of tea (he had measured it short)
He delivered next morning." "He's just that sort!"
So "Honest Abe" was the name he bore
In New Salem town when he ran that store.

Lincoln

So long he looked on prairie lands
  That ran to reach the skies
He came to have a free, far-reaching
  Look within his eyes.

So long he lay by firelight
  (When he was lank and young)
To read the words of wonder that
  The Bible bards had sung
He came to have an eloquence
  Upon his country tongue.

So long he labored in the law
  To champion the right
He grew to have that moral strength
  That is the hero's might.

Such faith he had in human beings—
  Their dignity, their place—
The fates themselves selected him
  To liberate a race.

The Shovel Slate

When good Abe Lincoln
  Was just a little boy
He couldn't buy a plaything,
  He couldn't buy a toy.
He hadn't any money,
  There wasn't any shop
Where little Abe Lincoln
  Could buy a ball or top;
Of course he made some things himself
  But not just to amuse,
In those days people thought that toys
  Should be things you could use.
And Lincoln liked his shovel best
  For, though it had been made
To stoke the fire and dig the dirt,
  Upon its wooden blade
(All whittled clean) the eager boy
  Could do his sums and writing.
His shovel-slate, of all his toys,
  He found the most exciting.

The Prince of Hearts

Characters

GROOM OF THE BACKSTAIRS
LORD HIGH CHAMBERLAIN
PRINCE FAINTHEART
THREE PEDDLERS
PRINCESS
LION

TIME: *Long ago, on Valentine's Day.*
SETTING: *The throne room of Prince Faintheart's castle in the Kingdom of Hearts.*
AT RISE: *The* GROOM OF THE BACKSTAIRS *is dusting the room.*

GROOM:
    I don't mind dusting up the chairs
    Or polishing the table,
    Or helping grooms in other rooms
    Or even in the stable;
    But working for a foolish prince
    Who hasn't any bravery—
    Oh, that's a curse! And really worse

37

Than being known for knavery.
(*The* Lord High Chamberlain *enters from left.*)
Chamberlain (*Clapping his hands*):
 The Prince is going to the Fair!
 Bring out the cape that he will wear.
Groom (*In astonishment*):
 The Prince is going to the Fair?
 But what if he should have a scare?
Chamberlain (*Sighing*):
 Yes, what if he should have a scare?
 He's not been out to take the air
 For seven months. He doesn't dare
 For fear that he will have a scare.
 (*He sits down sorrowfully on a stool and wipes his eyes
 with his handkerchief.*)
 I never saw, before or since,
 So cowardly a king or prince.
 (*The* Groom *squeezes onto the stool with him and also
 wipes his eyes.*)
Groom *and* Chamberlain:
 To think that we should have to serve
 A prince who hasn't any nerve.
Prince (*Offstage*):
 Ow! Wow! Help! Help! (*The* Groom *and the* Cham-
 berlain *look at each other helplessly.*)
Groom (*Shaking his head sadly*):
 He's probably 'fraid of his fingers and thumbs.
Chamberlain:
 Hush! He may hear you.
 His Majesty comes.
 (*Sound of running feet is heard offstage.* Groom *and*
 Chamberlain *rise and stand at attention.*)
Prince (*Entering from left in a panic*):
 Ow! Wow! Help! Help!

(*He runs around in a circle, looking behind him at his shadow.*)
Take off, take off this dreadful thing!
It must be tied on with a string.

CHAMBERLAIN (*Bowing*):
That's just your shadow, noble sir.
It only moves because you stir.

PRINCE (*Standing still and looking down at his feet*):
Why, so it is! I guess you're right!
My shadow gave me such a fright.

(*The* GROOM *and the* CHAMBERLAIN *look at each other and shake their heads in despair. The* PRINCE *sees them as he climbs on throne.*)
I see your looks. I know you're tearful
Because you have a prince who's fearful.
Boo hoo, boo hoo! This must not be.
Can't someone make a man of me?

CHAMBERLAIN *and* GROOM:
Boo hoo, boo hoo! This will not do.
We'll have to make a man of you.

PRINCE (*Sadly*):
I did so want to see the Fair.
I've heard I might meet someone there
Who'd sell to me a heart that's brave.
A prince should know how to behave!
But I cannot go to the Fair.
My shadow gave me such a scare,
I'm 'fraid of going anywhere.

CHAMBERLAIN (*Suddenly businesslike*):
We'll bring the Fair, then, to this room.
Go out into the street, Sir Groom,
Send off the beggars and the meddlers,
Call in the bargainers and peddlers.

(*The* GROOM *smiles and bows, exits.*)

PRINCE:

Hurrah! I may find courage yet;
And if I do, I won't forget
The man who helped me seek the cure.

CHAMBERLAIN (*Bowing*):

Your Majesty is kind, I'm sure.

(GROOM *enters up center with* THREE PEDDLERS.)

GROOM:

Here are the peddlers with their wares.

(*He lines them up before the throne. They bow.*)

PRINCE:

A prize of gold and jewels there'll be
For him who makes a man of me.

(*To* 1ST PEDDLER)

What have you in that bag of yours?

1ST PEDDLER (*Taking out helmet*):

A helmet, sir, the best of cures,
For when you wear it, you will feel
As safe as stone, as strong as steel.

PRINCE:

No, no. I'd rather far be dead
Than wear that thing upon my head.

(PRINCE *motions* 1ST PEDDLER *to step to one side.* GROOM *and* CHAMBERLAIN *sigh and shake their heads. To* 2ND PEDDLER)

Have you the charm I deeply crave
To change my fearful heart to brave?

2ND PEDDLER (*Holding up a sword*):

I have a sword with such a blade
It cuts through anything that's made.

(*He flourishes it before the* PRINCE, *who shrinks back, trembling. He motions* 2ND PEDDLER *to one side.*)

PRINCE:

No. Put that sword upon the shelf.
I fear that I may cut myself.

(GROOM *and* CHAMBERLAIN *sigh and shake their heads.*
To 3RD PEDDLER)
I hope that you have something better.
If so, I shall become your debtor.
3RD PEDDLER (*Holding up a heart-shaped shield*):
I have a mighty shield, my lord,
That will protect you from the sword.
Your enemies will have to yield
Because they cannot pierce this shield.
PRINCE:
They cannot pierce it, but (confound it!)
I'm sure that they can get around it.
(*He motions* 3RD PEDDLER *to step to one side.* GROOM
and CHAMBERLAIN *sigh and shake their heads.*)
CHAMBERLAIN (*Aside to* GROOM):
Can no one find a remedy
For his absurd timidity?
(PRINCESS *screams offstage.*)
ALL (*Startled*): What's that? (PRINCESS *enters up center.*
She is runing and looks terrified. She rushes to the throne
and throws herself at PRINCE'S *feet.*)
GROOM: A stranger!
CHAMBERLAIN (*Irritably*): A beggar!
PRINCE (*Admiringly*): A princess!
PRINCESS (*Wringing her hands*):
Oh, save me, Prince! A dreadful beast
Would like to have me for his feast.
PRINCE:
A princess! Though she's splashed with mud,
I know that she's of royal blood.
(LION *roars offstage*)
CHAMBERLAIN (*To* GROOM):
A lion comes! A lion roars!
Go quick, Sir Groom, and shut the doors.
GROOM (*His knees knocking together*):

I c-c-can't. It's not my job
To bolt a door or turn a knob.

CHAMBERLAIN (*Trembling and looking imploringly at the*
PEDDLERS):

Won't someone go? Some serf or vassal?

(LION *appears at door, up center, roaring.*)

GROOM, CHAMBERLAIN, *and* PEDDLERS:

Too late! He's here, inside the castle.

(*As they speak, they all run and hide behind chairs. The*
LION *makes straight for the* PRINCESS. *She screams. The*
PRINCE, *forgetting himself, picks up the shield and*
rushes angrily at the LION *and shoos him away from the*
PRINCESS.)

PRINCE:

Go 'way. Go 'way, you wicked cat!
No one should treat a girl like that.

(*The* LION *snarls and tries to pounce on the* PRINCE,
who is protecting the PRINCESS *with the shield. He*
hands the shield to her and begins to wrestle with the
LION, *while the others shiver and shake behind their*
chairs. The struggle is violent, but in the end the PRINCE
overcomes the LION, *and the beast falls to the floor.*
PRINCE *speaks to* LION *as he shoves him out of the room*
up center and shuts the door.)

There! That will teach you and your sort
How you must act when you're in court
Before a lady whom I mean
To ask right now to be my queen.

(*He goes over to the* PRINCESS, *takes her hand, and whis-*
pers something to her. She smiles and nods. He takes
off his crown and puts it on her head, then leads her to
the throne and seats her upon it.)

1ST PEDDLER (*Aside to others*):
　No helmet, sword, or even shield
　Could make that roaring lion yield.
2ND PEDDLER:
　Our Prince had courage from the start
　'Twas hidden in his loving heart.
3RD PEDDLER:
　But he grew valiant at the sight
　Of the poor princess and her plight.
PRINCESS (*Looking up at* PRINCE):
　O Prince, you are so wonderful,
　And powerful, and thunderful!
　You are the strongest of the strong.
CHAMBERLAIN *and* GROOM (*Coming forward and bowing*):
　Your Majesty, we did you wrong.
　We thought you were a fool or knave,
　But you're the bravest of the brave.
PRINCE:
　I was a fool. But I suspect
　I needed someone to protect;
　And, since my strength is so high-powered,
　I never more shall be a coward.
　A prince or any royal scion
　Who saves a princess from a lion
　Can also keep his subjects safe
　From burgomaster down to waif;
　And so I'll be the best of kings
　Now that I'm not afraid of things.
　And since I'm known for bravery,
　No more Prince Faintheart will I be.
　(*He walks around, thoughtfully.*)
　I'll change my name—what should I choose?
　(*He claps his hands.*)

Prince Strongheart is the name I'll use!
(*He picks up the heart-shaped shield.*)
Though it was not this mighty shield
That made the dreadful lion yield,
I'll keep it always close at hand
To show Prince Strongheart rules the land.

ALL:

Long live the Prince! Long live his bride!
Long may they rule this countryside!
Hurrah! Hurrah! (*Curtain*)

THE END

The Littlest Artist

Characters

BENJAMIN BRAGG
SYLVIA SMART
JACK FROST
KING WINTER
ELVES

TIME: *The eve of St. Valentine's Day.*
SETTING: *Benjamin Bragg's playroom.*
AT RISE: BENJAMIN BRAGG *is seated at his desk, cutting and pasting. He whistles as he works.* SYLVIA SMART *appears at the window behind him. She is bundled up in winter clothes and carries a workbag on her arm. She knocks at the window and calls to* BENJAMIN. *He starts, and looks around.*

SYLVIA:
　　What are you doing, O Benjamin Bragg,
　　With scissors and cardboard and little paint rag,
　　What are you doing, O Benjamin Bragg?
BENJAMIN (*Holding up his work for her to see*):
　　I'm cutting a heart and I'm pasting on lace;
　　And I'm drawing a cupid with chubby, round face.
　　For the King of the Winter, at quarter to nine,
　　Is giving a prize for the best Valentine.

SYLVIA:

> Oh, is it too late for me to begin
> To work for the prize?

BENJAMIN: Of course not, come in. (*He beckons to her and she passes the window, entering from right.*)

SYLVIA (*Taking off her wraps and seating herself in the rocker*):

> I'll have to get busy to try for the prize.
> I know what I'll do! I'll be clever and wise.
> (*She takes sewing things from her workbag*)
> I'll make a fine pin-cushion, just the right size.
> I'll cut out my cloth in the shape of a heart
> And the prize will be given to Sylvia Smart.

BENJAMIN (*Laughing*):

> I don't mind your making a cushion at all,
> Or whether it's large, or whether it's small;
> But as for the prize, that's "all in the bag."
> Old Winter will give it to Benjamin Bragg.

SYLVIA:

> Now don't be too sure. It's *time* that will tell.
> You know *that* yourself and you know it right well.
> Let's hum as we work, and work as we hum
> So time will go quickly and evening will come.
> (*They hum a tune together. As they do so, a small figure passes the window behind them. There is a knock at the door.*)

BENJAMIN:

> Hello! Who is knocking? Come in, if you please,
> And shut the door after, or else we will freeze.
> (*JACK FROST enters, disguised as a small child. He carries a suitcase labeled "Water Colors".*)

SYLVIA: Dear me! Who are *you*?

> You're only a baby.

BENJAMIN: He lives in the new house that's down the street, maybe . . .

JACK FROST:
> I've come to try out for the Valentine prize
> And please do not judge me at all by my size.

BENJAMIN (*With a scornful laugh*):
> You poor little fellow, you surely don't think
> We'll let you have paper or scissors or ink—

SYLVIA: Or satins for sewing. I'm 'fraid you would soil them.

BENJAMIN: We can't lend you such things, because you would *spoil* them.

JACK FROST:
> I'm not here to borrow. I have my own paint-box
> And brushes and palette all packed in this quaint-box.
> I'll use for a canvas that wide windowpane.
> I'll sketch in a mountain and etch in a plain—

BENJAMIN (*Aside to* SYLVIA):
> He's not just a baby. He can't be quite sane
> Painting the glass of a cold windowpane.
> With weak water colors that trickle and dribble—

SYLVIA: Oh, let him alone! We can wash off his scribble.

JACK FROST (*Running eagerly to window and opening his paint box*): I really won't bother you two while I try it— (*He pulls the window curtains almost shut and stands in the crack between them. Then he works with his brushes, back to the audience, so that the audience can see him working, but cannot see his work, which is hidden from view by the draperies.*)

BENJAMIN: All right, little boy, if you'll only be quiet. (*All three work silently for a while. The twilight deepens. Outside sleigh bells ring and "Jingle Bells" is heard in the distance.*)

SYLVIA (*Picking up the song and adapting her own words to the chorus*):
> Valentines, Valentines, oh, what fun they are!

Cut from lace and shaped like hearts or pointed like a
star—
Valentines, Valentines, oh what fun to send
Valentines in envelopes that will surprise a friend.
(BENJAMIN *repeats the song.*)

SYLVIA:

There! My Valentine is done!
Isn't it a pretty one?

BENJAMIN:

Very pretty! But I'm afraid
Mine is really better made
Don't feel badly if I win—
(*He holds his up for her to see. There is a sound of
trumpets outside.*)

SYLVIA: Quick! King Winter's coming in. (*They run
around picking up scraps and clearing the room.*)

JACK FROST (*Stepping back and closing the curtains*):

I will keep my picture hidden
Till the time when I am bidden
By King Wintertime to show it—
He will like it then. I know it!

SYLVIA (*Aside to* BENJAMIN):

No one wants to see his picture—
It will be a silly mixture
Made of scribbling and of scrawling—
But we mustn't start him bawling.
(*To* JACK FROST)
Come and help us greet King Winter,
Little neighbor.
(*A knocking is heard.*)

BENJAMIN (*Opening the door*):

Won't you enter,
Noble monarch of the snow time,
You shall see our work in no time.
(KING WINTER *enters with his attendants, who are* ELVES.)

KING:

> Ah! Good evening, everyone.
> Though the day is past and done
> We have not found 'neath the sun
> Any Valentine of size
> That is worthy in our eyes
> Of King Winter's annual prize.

SYLVIA AND BENJAMIN (*Together as they hold up their Valentines*):

> Here's a Valentine of size
> That is worth King Winter's prize.
>
> (*Each tries to push the other aside. They poke their Valentines almost into his face.*)

KING:

> Very nice, quite nice indeed!
> But there surely is no need
> Of this pushing and this poking
> It is really quite provoking—
> (*He sees* JACK FROST)
> Who's this patient little fellow
> In a muffler, red and yellow,
> Have you made a picture for me?

JACK FROST (*Quaintly*):

> Yes, Old Winter, it is for thee,
> It will show that I adore thee!
> Come and see it, I implore thee.
>
> (*He runs to the window and pulls back the curtains. A glittering frost picture is revealed.*)

EVERYBODY (*Delighted*): Oh! Oh!

> (JACK FROST *throws off his hat and coat and stands before the others in a white, spangled elf costume.*)

KING (*In astonishment*): Jack Frost!

JACK FROST: I trust you like my strange surprise—

KING: Yes, you've won King Winter's prize. (*He puts a silver chain around* JACK's *neck.*)

SYLVIA AND BENJAMIN:
  Yes, you've won King Winter's prize!
  Just to think so small a boy
  Can give everyone such joy
  Painting pictures like a master . . .
KING: No one ever painted faster!
BENJAMIN (*Thoughtfully*):
  It is not so very wise,
  Judging people by their size.
SYLVIA:
  No, it's not so very wise
  Judging people by their size.
KING:
  Never did a friend of mine
  Make so fair a Valentine.
ALL (*Except* JACK):
  Give a cheer for Jackie Frost
  May his talents not be lost!
  May our windows be embossed
  Every year by Jackie Frost!
  Hurrah!
  (*Curtain*)

THE END

A Valentine for Mary

Characters

MARY
PUSS
THREE FROST FAIRIES
OFFSTAGE VOICE

TIME: *The evening before Valentine's Day.*
SETTING: *The living room of Mary's home.*
AT RISE: MARY *is sitting at a table near the window, making valentines.* PUSS *lies at her feet on the floor.*

MARY (*Putting down her scissors*): There! I've finished the last valentine. (*She licks the envelope, then picks up a pile of other envelopes, and holds them up triumphantly.*) See, Puss, they're all done.
PUSS: Meow!
MARY (*Counting them over*): There's one for Daddy, and one for Mother, and one for each of my cousins.
PUSS: Mew!
MARY: Oh, Puss, do you think I'll get a valentine, myself? I'm awfully afraid I won't. You see, Mother and Daddy went off in such a hurry to Cousin Martha's wedding. They won't even *think* about Valentine's Day tomorrow.
PUSS (*As if to say, "Won't they?"*): Me-ow?
MARY: No, they won't. And my cousins will be at the

51

wedding, too, so I guess they'll forget about valentines. A wedding in the family just makes *everybody* forget *everything*.

PUSS: Mew, mew, mew!

MARY: And I don't know *any* children in this *new* neighborhood. I really don't think I'll get a single, solitary valentine. Wouldn't that be terrible?

PUSS (*Indignantly*): Meeeee-ow!

MARY: Oh, dear! Why can't you say something besides "Meow" and "Mew"? If only you were a *fairy cat* you could talk. Perhaps you could even make me a valentine.

PUSS: Purr, purr, purr.

MARY: Sometimes I almost think you *are* a fairy cat. You go off so mysteriously every night. And once, last summer, when you came out of the woods, you were wearing a firefly on your forehead.

PUSS: Purrrrrrrrrrr!

MARY: Just as though you'd been to a fairy ball in all your best jewelry.

PUSS (*Almost trilling*): Purr-r-r! Purr-r!

MARY: Daddy says you're nothing but an alley cat, though. (*She sighs*) I suppose he's right.

PUSS (*Angrily*): Meow! Meow!

VOICE (*Offstage*): Mary! Mary, come to bed now.

MARY: There's Mrs. Brown calling. I suppose I *have* to go.

PUSS (*Sadly*): Mew, mew.

MARY (*Rising and patting* PUSS): Good night, Puss. I don't so much mind going to bed. But I *do* hate the thought of waking up in the morning and not finding any valentines.

PUSS (*Sympathetically*): Me-ow, me-ow. (MARY *goes out.* PUSS *pads around the room, checking the corners to make sure no one is about. Then she comes forward and talks to audience.*)

Puss:

Nobody knows I'm a fairy cat,
Born in a fairy wood.
I keep my secret all to myself
As every fairy should.
Mew, mew, mew.

(Puss *stamps her foot three times, and then claps her hands. The* Three Frost Fairies *enter, dressed in white and silver. Blunt kindergarten scissors are tied to a ribbon and hang at the waist of each fairy, to be used in the "cutting-out" scene. The* 3rd Fairy *carries a scroll.*)

Fairies: Did you call us?

Puss:

Yes, I must have a valentine—
A valentine for Mary.
Oh, it must be all silver-white
And fashioned by a fairy.

1st Fairy: Well, there's nothing a frost fairy likes better than making valentines.

2nd Fairy: Where is that scroll of silver frost?

3rd Fairy (*Handing her the scroll, a roll of white or silver paper in which cutouts are concealed*): Here it is!
(1st Fairy *unrolls the scroll just enough to take out a star, which she then pretends to trim with her scissors.* 2nd Fairy *unrolls the scroll a little more and takes out a row of roses, which she "trims", and then* 3rd Fairy *takes out some lace.* Puss *may really cut out a white heart from the paper on* Mary's *table, while the others are saying their verses.*)

1st Fairy (*As she pretends to cut out a star*):

I'll cut a star all silver-white
And paste it up here at the right.

(*The* 1st Fairy *pastes the star on the windowpane, using* Mary's *paste to do so.*)

2ND FAIRY:

I'll make some roses white as snow

And paste them on here in a row.

(*The* 2ND FAIRY *pastes her cutting on the windowpane.*)

3RD FAIRY:

I'll paste some fluffy fairy lace

Right in the middle of this space.

(*The* 3RD FAIRY *does so. They continue to work until the windowpane is covered.* PUSS *contributes a big white heart. The cutouts should be planned to make a balanced and attractive window-picture when they are all assembled.*)

PUSS (*Capering about, after the task is finished*):

Bravo! Bravo! Thank you, Frost Fairies.

There never was a valentine as pretty as Mary's!

1ST FAIRY: And here comes the sun to give it sparkle. We must run before Mary wakes up. (*The* THREE FROST FAIRIES *run out.* PUSS *then curls up in a corner and pretends to sleep. The lights may dim for a moment to indicate the passing of time. They come up again. A bright light now shines beyond the window.* MARY *enters.*)

MARY (*Seeing the valentine at once*): Oooh! What a beautiful valentine! A frost valentine! I've never seen anything like it in all my life! Wake up, Puss, and see my valentine!

PUSS (*Yawning and stretching*): Meow!

MARY: Look, lazybones! Did you ever see such silvery stars and flowers? How did they get there . . . on the windowpane? (*To* PUSS) *You* ought to know. You've been here all night.

PUSS (*Innocently*): Mew, mew, mew, mew!

MARY: That's right. Pretend you don't know anything about it. But I can see a mysterious look in your eyes. I believe you *are* a fairy cat, after all. (*She takes* PUSS *in her arms.*) I think you know all about my beautiful frost valentine. I think it's your valentine to me. Thank you, Puss. Happy Valentine's Day! (*She pats* Puss *as the curtains close.*)

THE END

Valentine People

(*The* LADY *and the* CAVALIER *stand at center. They may
be in costumes. The children sit at either side and read
from books decorated with red hearts.*)

1ST CHILD:
>   There was a lovely ladykin,
>   No bigger than a minute,
>   Who sat and played a minuet
>   Upon a tiny spinet;
>   Her hair was powdered white as snow,
>   She wore a dress of long ago
>   With satin flowers on it.
>   She lived upon a valentine
>   Behind a paper shutter,
>   And, though she played so charmingly,
>   Her spinet did not utter
>   A single sound—but as she sat
>   Her heart was all a-flutter.

2ND CHILD:
>   For just outside her window
>   Stood a cavalier in yellow.
>   He was a very handsome and
>   A chivalrous young fellow.
>   He stood with tricorn hat in hand
>   In attitude most charming

And listened to the music with
A rapture quite alarming,
Considering no music stirred
Except the soft repeating
Of his own heart, which played a tune
In very rapid beating.

CAVALIER:

Alas, I know it isn't right
To blame one's own creator,
And mine a lady artist, too;
But truly, I do hate her!

LADY:

To think that she should have no heart
And paint us two so far apart!
It really would have done no harm
To show us standing arm in arm.

CAVALIER:

But there she is, inside the folder,
And through the window I behold her.

LADY:

We cannot go and get acquainted;
Our knees are far too stiffly painted.

CAVALIER:

And it would be my own undoing
Were I to shout my words of wooing.

3RD CHILD:

And so he stood with pulses burning
The while the lady sat in yearning,

And thus they might have stayed forever
If fate had not been quite so clever.

4TH CHILD:

One day there came with skip and hop
A laddie to the ten-cent shop
And bought the very valentine
Whereon the lovers seemed to pine.
He sealed it up, the reckless scamp,
And mailed it with a postage stamp.
The postman took it to the gate
Of Mary Jane, a lass of eight. (MARY *comes in, claps
her hands together when she sees the* LADY *and the*
CAVALIER, *then pantomimes the actions described in
the verses.*)

5TH CHILD:

You should have seen her two eyes shine
When she beheld that valentine!
And being equal to her years,
She promptly went to fetch the shears.
Then, with a most triumphant shout,
She cut our lovely lady out.

6TH CHILD:

Her mother sighed and gently told her
It was a shame to spoil the folder;
But Mary thought it was no folly
To have so nice a paper dolly,
And straightway trimmed the cavalier
(Her scissors just escaped his ear).
And, though this was of course a trial,
He bore it with a beaming smile,
For now his barrier was scissored.
Then Mary, like a knowing wizard,

The couple to her dolls' house carried
And in great splendor had them married. (MARY *leads
the* LADY *and* CAVALIER *forward.*)

LADY:

And there we lived in love and laughter.

CAVALIER:

A happy couple ever after! (*They bow to each other.*)

The Valentine Vendor

(A reading for a CHORUS *and* TWO SOLOS. *If desired, three children may act this out in pantomime.)*

CHORUS:
> The Valentine Vendor, all dressed up in splendor,
> > Went running to call on the king, king, king.
> He'd been working for hours with hearts and with
> > flowers
> > Designing a wonderful thing, thing, thing.
> By the light of long tapers he'd cut out of papers
> Some wonderful laces and paper doll faces
> > And pretty white doves on the wing, wing, wing.
> So . . . being elated at what he'd created,
> > He ran off to call on the king, king, king.

1ST SOLO:
> But the king was no spender. He said to the vendor:
> > "Oh, why should I purchase such trash, trash, trash?
> The thing is too silly and lacy and frilly.
> I don't like the cupid. He looks a bit stupid
> > All dressed up in bowknot and sash, sash, sash."

2ND SOLO:
> Then the queen came in quickly. She'd been some-
> > what sickly
> > But, seeing the Valentine lace, lace, lace

60

With its ribbon and posy, she turned very rosy
And dimples crept into her face, face, face.
She cried, "King of mine, what a sweet Valentine!
Have you bought it to brighten this place, place, place?
A dingy old castle needs ribbon and tassel
And Cupid and dove—*and a great deal of love*—
Oh, let's hang it up in this space, space, space."

CHORUS:
So . . . over the throne, without grumble or groan,
The king hung the trivial trash, trash, trash;
And he felt so serene over pleasing his queen
That he paid up the vendor in cash, cash, cash!

Making A Valentine

(A group reading for TWO CHORUSES)

BOYS AND GIRLS (*Together*):
   We made a pretty Valentine,
     We made a heart of red.
   "Snip-snap, snip-snap,"
     Our noisy scissors said.
   (*They make scissor motions with their first two fingers.*)
GIRLS (*Pretending to draw, cut and paste*):
   We drew a pretty little girl
     All dressed in ruffles fine.
   We cut her out and pasted her
     Upon the Valentine.
BOYS (*Pretending to draw*):
   We drew a jolly little boy
     With cheeks all rosy red.
   "Squeak-squeak, squeak-squeak,"
     Our busy pencils said.
BOYS AND GIRLS (*Together*):
   We took our pretty Valentines
     And sealed them all away
   (*They make the motions of sealing and stamping enve-*
    lopes.)
   And gave them to our mothers
     On St. Valentine's Day.
   (*All walk through audience and give valentines to*
    mothers.)

Snow Valentines

Secretly and silently
  All through the winter's night
The snow once fashioned valentines.
  She chalked them all in white.
She made a ribbon of a wire,
  And ruffles of a tree;
And even rusty latticework
  She turned to filigree.
She hung her feathers on the wind,
  Made velvet out of bars.
Her filmy bits of lace she pinned
  With fragile, patterned stars.
All night she worked and yet she dropped
  No clippings on her floor;
And in the morning everyone
  Found pictures at his door.

George Washington Calls on Betsy Ross

BETSY ROSS (*Pretending to open a door*):
Who lifts the knocker of my door?
Who comes with sword and gun
To call upon a seamstress poor?

WASHINGTON (*Bowing*):
It's General Washington.

BETSY ROSS:
Come in, come in, good gentleman,
I'm honored by your calling!
I'm here to serve a patriot
Who keeps this land from falling.

WASHINGTON:
Oh, have you made our country's flag
That's never flown before?
I wish to take it off with me
To cheer the boys at war.

BETSY ROSS (*Holding up flag*):
I've made a flag of stars and stripes
And sewed it with a cord.

A woman's needle now will have
The power of a sword.

TOGETHER (*Displaying flag*):
And may this flag forever be
A symbol of man's liberty.

Victory Ball

GIRLS:
  With candlelight, with candlelight,
    So long and long ago,
  The windows of Mount Vernon,
    All running in a row,
  Lit up the pillared porch and gave
    The grass beyond a glow.

BOYS:
  The silhouettes of folk inside
    Who danced on polished floors
  Were seen by those who came and went
    Or watched from out-of-doors.
  The laughter that came floating forth
    Was hale, they say, and hearty;
  The victory ball was not at all
    Like Boston's grim tea party.

GIRLS:
  But those who sat to laugh and chat
    Or rest from minueting
  Spoke low to General Washington.

1ST BOY:
  They said, We're not forgetting
  The way you weathered Valley Forge,
    The way you fought each battle.

1st Girl:
   We're not forgetting anything
   No matter how we prattle.

2nd Girl:
   No matter how we dance about
   And have our bit of fun—

2nd Boy:
   We know that we would not be free
   To celebrate our victory
   Except for Washington.

All:
   We know that we would not be free
   To celebrate our victory
   Except for Washington!

Picture People

George and Martha Washington
   Are smiling in our hall.
They look down from a picture frame
   That hangs upon the wall,
And yet they do not seem to me
   Like picture folk at all
But more like friends or neighbors who
   Have come to make a call.
I half believe they would step down
   And dance most any minute
If I should play a minuet
   Upon an old-time spinet.

The Leprechaun

It happened on St. Patrick's Day—
  St. Patrick's Day in the mornin'—
I met a little leprechaun
  Without a mite o' warnin',
And he was thin as any wraith
  And wee as any child
And in his eyes there was a look
  All wary-wild.

"How came you to America?"
  I asked as there he sat,
A bag of gold clutched in his hand,
  A buckle on his hat.
He only grinned an impish grin.
  He wouldn't answer that.

"You stowed away in Bridget's bags,"
  I said, "as like as not.
Your bag of gold you've just dug up
  From Bridget's shamrock pot."
He looked at me in wide surprise.
  "I've found him out," I thought.

69

And so I made a grab for him.
He uttered laughter weird
And in my very hands he shrank
And slowly disappeared.
Since then I've never seen his like,
But every year in March
I half expect to find his gold
Beneath the rainbow's arch.

The First Easter Eggs

Characters

RABBIT
HEN
TURKEY
GOOSE
DUCK
HERALD
LITTLE BIRD
KING
ATTENDANTS

SETTING: *The King's barnyard.*

AT RISE: HEN, TURKEY, GOOSE *and* DUCK *hop in, looking plump and important.* RABBIT *follows them, limping as though his feet were sore. He is dressed in neatly patched overalls, and carries a market basket.*

RABBIT (*Calling in a tired voice*):
Sweet cane to sell! And berry juice!
Come buy, oh hen and duck and goose.
Sweet sugar cane and berry juice.
(*The barnyard fowl turn and look at him scornfully.*)

HEN:

Go 'way, you bumpkin. Do not meddle
With hens and chickens. You cannot peddle
The juice or berries or sugar cane
To barnyard fowl so rich in grain.

TURKEY (*Haughtily*):

We've golden corn and golden meal.
You've naught at all that could appeal
To folks like us . . .

DUCK *and* GOOSE (*Together*):

Unless you sold
Something golder than corn is gold.

(*They all turn their backs on* RABBIT *and begin to pick-peck along the ground at the back of the stage. The tired* RABBIT *sits down on a stump looking very forlorn. He wipes away a tear with a big bandanna from his overall pocket. The* HERALD *enters. He stands at the extreme left of the stage, front, and blows a trumpet or rings a crier's bell.* HEN, DUCK, GOOSE *and* TURKEY *stop pecking and look up. The* RABBIT *becomes suddenly alert.*)

HERALD:

Oh, I am the herald of the king!
    Oh, hear ye, one and all!
The good king sends a message to
    His subjects, great and small.

TURKEY:

Hear! Hear! Hear!

HERALD (*Unrolling a long scroll and reading from it*):

The king is weary of water and wine,
    The king is tired of meat—
Of the wild boar's head and chicken legs,
And what he wants is some good fresh eggs,
    Some good fresh eggs to eat.

HEN (*Excitedly*): Hear! Hear! Hear!

HERALD:

> A good fresh egg is hard to get
> In the early spring when the fields are wet
> And this is the thing you must all be told:
> The good king offers a bag of gold
> To the one who brings him from east or west
> The finest eggs in the finest nest.

GOOSE (*To other fowl in a flutter of enthusiasm*):

> Did you hear *that,* friends?
> What a piece of luck!

TURKEY: Oh, gobble!

DUCK: Oh, quack!

HEN: Oh, cluck, cluck, cluck!

HERALD (*Crossing stage, front, and walking slowly*):

> To the one who brings from the north or south
> Eggs that will water a monarch's mouth
> Ere the Easter day begins to lag
> Will be given gold in a bulging bag.
> (*He exits.* DUCK, HEN, TURKEY *and* GOOSE *move to the front of the stage. The* RABBIT *follows but keeps his distance.*)

DUCK (*Exclaiming*): My! What a message!

TURKEY (*Grandly*):

> It makes me perky.
> There are no eggs like the eggs of the turkey.

GOOSE: You're going to do what the king has bidden?

TURKEY (*Nodding*):

> I'll get my eggs in the nest that's hidden
> Down by the hedgerow. Then under my wing
> I'll carry them safely straight to the king.
> I'm bound to be winning the bag of gold.
> I guess there's no one who needs to be told
> That the King's an epicure who knows what's best—
> And turkey eggs lead all the rest!

(TURKEY *exits haughtily, strutting as she goes.*)

RABBIT (*Looking after her and sighing hopelessly*):

My! What a barnyard snob *that* bird is!

DUCK (*To* HEN *and* GOOSE):

I really don't know how good her word is (*He gestures after* TURKEY.)

She *may* get the prize if she's *very* lucky.

Her eggs are big. But they just *aren't ducky.*

GOOSE (*To* DUCK):

You and I may be waders and wobblers . . .

But our eggs are better than that old gobbler's.

HEN:

And so are mine. I'm all in a flurry

To get my eggs to the king in a hurry. (*They start off stage but the* RABBIT *intervenes.*)

RABBIT:

I've just one question. Please let me ask it.

When you've won the gold, will you buy from my basket?

DUCK:

Oh, don't be silly!

GOOSE:

We'll be too grand . . .

HEN:

To talk to a peddler and poor farm hand. (*They go off, heads in air.*)

RABBIT (*Bursting into tears and sobbing loudly*): Oh, isn't there some one to understand? (LITTLE BIRD *enters. He hops around* RABBIT *once or twice looking very concerned.*)

BIRD (*As he hops*):

Oh, dear! Oh, dear! What have we here?

Please, little rabbit, dry your tear. (*He pats the* RABBIT *on the shoulder with his wing.*)

RABBIT (*Between sobs*):

There are no beans stored up in our beanery,

And the good spring greens haven't come with their
  greenery . . .
BIRD (*Sympathetically*):
  I know. And the snow still chills the scenery.
RABBIT:
  My mommy is working her hands to blisters
  Trying to care for my brothers and sisters
  But our rabbit hole, from cellar to garret,
  Holds nary a nibble of cabbage or carrot.
  And the barnyard fowl, they put on such airs
  That I just can't sell my poor little wares.
BIRD:
  Then why not try for the bag of gold
  The king has offered (for eggs, I'm told)
  It would rescue your family from hunger and cold.
RABBIT:
  Oh I'd love to try, but it's quite absurd.
  I can't lay an egg, for I'm not a bird.
  I can't do a thing for the prize, I'm 'fraid;
  Eggs are a product that must be *laid*.
BIRD:
  Nonsense! They're something that can be *made*.
  Nowadays it's all in the making
  Whether it's brewing, or boiling, or baking;
  Whether it's welded, or glued, or cemented,
  There's nothing that cannot be *made* or *invented*.
RABBIT:
  I see what you mean. I get your suggestion.
  Oh, what can *I* make?
BIRD:
  Yes. That is the question.
RABBIT:
  Well, I know of *one* thing at which I am handy.
  It's making a panful of good sugar candy.

BIRD:

Hurrah! Just the thing. Now get up, and cheer up.
Do you see, over yonder, that kettle of syrup? (*He points offstage.*)

RABBIT:

I see it quite clearly. (You've made things so plain.)
I'll make *candy* eggs of my sweetening cane.

BIRD:

And add maple syrup not spoiled by the rain.

RABBIT (*Excitedly*):

I'll color them gaily with berry juice stain.
What fun it will be! (*He dances about.*)

BIRD:

I hope it will bring
Pleasure for you and a prize from the king.

(RABBIT *and* BIRD *exit. There is a short silence, and then a tumult of quacks, honks, clucks and gobbles is heard offstage. The* DUCK, GOOSE, HEN *and* TURKEY *enter quarreling. Each of them carries a nest of eggs, and they talk so fast that they all seem to be talking at once.*)

DUCK:

My nest is best . . .

GOOSE:

My eggs are whitest.

HEN:

Mine shine the most . . .

TURKEY:

No, mine are brightest. (*They begin shouting and squawking at each other.*)

DUCK:

Don't shout, you clout . . .

HEN:

Don't talk so loud. (*They begin pushing and bumping each other*)

GOOSE:
Don't rush!
DUCK:
Don't push!
HEN:
Don't crush!
TURKEY:
Don't crowd! (*They are getting rougher and rougher.*)
GOOSE (*Half crying*):
You've hurt my wings.
TURKEY (*Angrily*):
You've bruised my legs!
(*They all drop their nests and the eggs break.*)
HEN (*Wailing*):
Oh, my! There go our precious eggs!
(KING, HERALD and ATTENDANTS *enter.*)
KING (*Looking at broken nests and eggs*):
What's this? What's this? I never saw
Such rioting. It is the law
To make arrests of those who riot
So *next* time *none* of them will try it.
(*He starts to summon soldiers.*)
DUCK:
Please, sir, we tried to suit your diet,
By fetching, as we ran or rambled,
The best fresh eggs—but *now* they're *scrambled!*
KING (*Angrily*):
I don't like scrambled eggs at all.
Why did you ever let them fall?
(DUCK, GOOSE, HEN and TURKEY *hang their heads in shame.*)
RABBIT (*Entering and dancing up to* KING, *bowing happily*):
I've overcome my rabbit shyness
To bring these eggs, Your Royal Highness

KING (*Taking the pretty nest that is filled with beautiful colored eggs*):

> What eggs are these? I've never seen
> Bright colored ones, all red and green
> And blue and gray, on Easter Day. (*He takes one and nibbles it, then bites it.*
> Upon my word! The taste is *sweet!*
> They're good to see, and good to eat. (*He samples more.*)
> Friend rabbit, let's not be too hasty,
> Tell me what makes these eggs so tasty.

RABBIT (*Hopping and skipping about*):

> They're made with sweetest sugar cane
> And maple sugar (smoothest grain)
> And colored with a berry stain.

KING:

> Some day you'll have to tell to me
> The very secret recipe.

RABBIT:

> Oh, do not praise, and do not scold me—
> It was *a little bird who told me.*

KING:

> At any rate, my thanks, tenfold;
> And here, sir, is your bag of gold.

RABBIT (*He takes bag of gold and bows to* KING, *then dances about, wildly happy*):

> My mother and my little sisters
> No more will wear their paws to blisters,
> And rich will be my little brothers,
> My aunts, my cousins and the others.
> Our rabbit holes and all our garrets,
> Will overflow with peas and carrots. (RABBIT *throws coins to downcast* HEN, TURKEY, DUCK, *and* GOOSE *who look happier as they pick up money.*)

KING (*To* RABBIT *who dances toward door*):
  I like your eggs; they're sweet as honey.
  Come back next year, good Easter Bunny.
  (*All cheer and dance around* RABBIT *as the curtain falls.*)

THE END

Good Morning, Mr. Rabbit

Characters

EASTER RABBIT
FOUR GIRLS
FOUR BOYS

TIME: *Easter morning, at dawn.*
SETTING: *A clearing in the woods.*
AT RISE: EASTER RABBIT *enters left;* GIRLS *and* BOYS *enter right. They meet and bow.*

1ST BOY:
Good morning, Mr. Rabbit.
1ST GIRL:
Good morning, snow-white bunny.
2ND BOY:
Why are you up so early,
Before the day is sunny?
2ND GIRL:
Why do you stand up on your toes,
And scratch your ears and twitch your nose?
Oh, do you think it's funny? (*She laughs.*)
EASTER RABBIT (*Bowing and doffing his hat*):
Good morning, lads and lassies;
Good morning, boys and girls.

You ask so many questions
My head just spins and whirls. (*He mops his brow with
a red bandanna, then counts on his paws.*)
Now first, I'm up so early
Because it's Easter dawn,
And I must leave surprises
On every field and lawn.
I scratch my ears and twitch my nose
And stand up on my tippy-toes (*He does so.*)
Just out of habit, I suppose.

3RD BOY:

What have you in your basket?
Some clover blooms and honey?

EASTER RABBIT (*Disgusted*):

No, no, you little silly,
I am the Easter Bunny! (*He thumps his chest.*)

3RD BOY (*In amazement*):

The real live Easter Bunny?

EASTER RABBIT: That's right! Today, on hopping legs
I'm rushing to deliver eggs
To every child in every city.

3RD GIRL (*Excitedly*):

Let's see the eggs! They must be pretty!

EASTER RABBIT (*Holding up the cover of the basket*):

A little peek I'll let you take,
But do not touch them, or they'll break. (*Children
move close to get a good look.*)

4TH BOY: Oh, see! They're yellow, red, and green!

4TH GIRL (*Pointing*):

And violet and tangerine!

1ST BOY (*Pointing*):

The prettiest eggs I've ever seen.

1ST GIRL:

For all these years, oh, what a task it
Must have been to take your basket,

And all alone to make the rounds
Of every house and all the grounds.

EASTER RABBIT:

It is a job, I must confess,
And yet it brings me happiness.
Besides, I have a magic potion (*He takes out a little
bottle, and pours some liquid from it onto his leg.*)
That helps me hop across the ocean. (*He takes a great
leap.*)
It makes my feet as light as feathers,
So I can skim through sands and heathers, (*He dances.*)
And brave all elements and weathers.

2ND GIRL:

Oh, won't you teach us how to hop,
And make a nest at every stop?

2ND BOY:

We'll follow you with scampering legs.

3RD GIRL:

And help you to deliver eggs!

EASTER RABBIT:

That would be wonderful for me.
I'm wearing out, as you can see.
But are you sure you won't be done-up?
With such hard work before it's sun-up?
You children mustn't have the notion
It's easy, even with the potion.

3RD BOY:

Oh, we are not afraid to try it.

EASTER RABBIT:

Then here's the stuff—you cannot buy it. (*He pours a
little liquid from the bottle onto their feet. The children wobble around the stage, and finally flop to the
ground.*)

4TH BOY:

Oh, dear! Oh, dear! There's something wrong.

4TH GIRL:

My legs feel weak instead of strong.

EASTER RABBIT (*Helping them to their feet*):

There, there! Don't be in such a hurry.

I should have told you not to worry,

If just at first you felt all swervy,

And upside down and topsy-turvy.

You'll have to practice with a will,

Until you've learned a little skill.

1ST GIRL (*Still a little wobbly*):

Yes, yes, we'll practice with a will.

But first, please help us to stand still.

EASTER RABBIT (*Steadying them with his outstretched paws*):

There! Now you're safe. Just do as I do.

3RD BOY (*Panting a little*):

All right! All right! We'll follow you.

EASTER RABBIT:

First crouch upon all fours and creep. (*He demonstrates.*)

Then, lift your forepaws for a leap. (*He sits on haunches, and children imitate him throughout.*)

1ST BOY:

First crouch upon all fours and creep.

Then, lift your forepaws for a leap. (*They almost lose their balance.*)

EASTER RABBIT (*On hind legs, dancing*):

Here's the way to dance and skip!

Step lightly, now, and do not trip.

2ND GIRL (*As children follow* RABBIT *in a dancing circle*):

Here's the way to skip and scurry.

(*Aside to other children*)

A rabbit's always in a hurry.

EASTER RABBIT (*Stopping and taking some grass out of his basket*):

I'll show you how to stop and weave
A little nest in which to leave
Some candy eggs for girls and boys—
The kind that *everyone* enjoys.
(*Children stop.*)
2ND BOY: Yes, yes, our feet have passed the test!
Now teach us how to make a nest.
EASTER RABBIT (*Making nest on the ground and filling it with eggs*):
Weave out, weave in, with grass that's thin—
Weave in, weave out, with grass that's stout;
And scatter clover blooms about (*He picks and scatters blossoms.*)
Don't let the little eggs roll out.
3RD GIRL (*As children imitate motions* RABBIT *makes and weave grass he gives them*):
Weave out, weave in, with grass that's thin—
Weave in, weave out, with grass that's stout;
And scatter clover blooms about. (*They take eggs from the basket and put them in nests.*)
We will not let the eggs roll out.
3RD BOY:
I'd like to hear the children shout
When they hunt from east to west,
And find each little hidden nest.
EASTER RABBIT:
Oh, you'll hear them! Wait and see!
We'll hide behind the nearest tree.
But hurry, now you've learned my trade—
How rabbits run, how nests are made.
It's getting later, I'm afraid.
4TH GIRL:
Oh, yes, the sun will soon be rising.
EASTER RABBIT:
In half a wink, in time surprising

We'll make the trip on tippy-toe. (*He takes the children by the hand, and they dance.*)

ALL:

Now off we go! Now off we go! From Santa Fe to Buffalo. (*They begin to run in a circle.*)

Oh, see us run! Oh, see us run,

From Albany to Washington!

With nests and eggs, all bright and gay,

We'll bring a happy Easter Day. (*They run and jump offstage as the curtain falls.*)

THE END

A Rhyme for Easter

CHILDREN (*Resting cheeks on hands, as though sleeping*):
We are the children who dream in bed
Of a hidden treasure of gold and red—
On Easter Eve.

BUNNIES (*Hopping around for a moment, hands held like paws, before speaking*):
We are the bunnies that nest in the night
And scamper away in the morning light—
Guess what we leave!

ROOSTERS (*Flapping arms like wings*):
We are the cocks that wake to tell
The yellow chicks to come out of the shell
To peck and play.

STEEPLE (*Head in cardboard "tower"*):
I am the steeple that pricks the sun
And rings a bell for everyone,
On Easter Day.

ALL:
Ding . . . dong, ding . . . dong, *ding!* (*Everyone marches out, swinging arms as though pulling ropes to ring bells.*)
Ding . . . dong, ding . . . dong, *ding!*

One Easter Morning Early

CHORUS:
> There was an Easter Rabbit
>> Who walked on quiet feet
> One Easter morning early,
>> Along the village street.

GIRL:
> And on his arm a basket,
>> All filled with eggs to eat,
> Swung merrily
> While cheerily
>> The birds above his head
> All sang the Easter sun up
>> And chirped folks out of bed.

CHORUS:
> The rabbit tiptoed lightly
>> About the waking town
> And little nests he fashioned
>> Of greening grass or brown.

GIRL:
> While merrily
> And cheerily
>> The knowing birds looked down.

BOY:
>He built nests in the back yard,
>He wove them in the front—
>In bushes and in branches
>Wherever children hunt.

CHORUS:
>But when the hunt was started
>And morning turned to day
>The rabbit and the rabbit tracks
>Had vanished all away.

Easter Bonnets

The mushroom wears a brown beret,
The jonquil wears a bonnet,
The primrose likes a picture hat
With a golden crown upon it.

The dandelion, old and pale,
Ties round her head a gray silk veil,
While willow twigs wear soft gray caps
(They need the furry warmth, perhaps).

Early Easter

Before the crocuses were up,
  Before the daffodils,
When spring winds piled the late snow high
  Upon the purple hills,
I saw a little garden plot
  Out in the chilly air.
And roses red and violets blue
  Were blooming brightly there.

Where did I see a garden plot
  On a cold spring day like that?
Why, it was going down the street
  Upon my mother's hat!

The Garden Hat Shop

A meadow mouse with a long tail on it
Went out to shop for an Easter bonnet.
The shop of Madam Mole she chose
Because it advertised: CHAPEAUX,
IN EVERY COLOR FROM BLUE TO ROSE.

She tried a bluebell on for size
But found it did not suit her eyes.
She tried a crocus on for shape
But saw it did not match her cape.

She said, "I do not want a quill,
They're much too stiff. Have you a frill?"
The mole brought out a daffodil
With little golden ruffles on it.
"Oh, what a lovely Easter bonnet!"
Exclaimed the mouse, "It's just the thing
To make me feel in style this spring."

She paid the mole a pennywort
And went off looking pleased and pert.

An Adventure in April

A rabbit came to my house once
  With furry, stretched-out ears.
His nose was full of wriggles, and
  His eyes were full of tears.
I said, "Why do you twitch your nose?
  Is that a bunny-habit?
And are you called the 'March Hare,'
  Or named the 'Easter Rabbit?' "
He never said a word; but bounced
  Away on pushing legs;
But, oh, he left behind a nest
  Of colored Easter eggs!

Maypole Dance

(*As* READER *recites, any number of children enter carrying baskets of flowers. They dance around stage—which should have a Maypole at center—tossing flowers about as they dance.*)

READER (*Beckoning children from offstage*):

Come Maying, come playing, dear lassies blithe and fair!
The bud has burst, the leaf is green. There is no time
    to spare,
For May has walked across the hills
And scattered them with daffodils!

(*Children dance onstage, tossing flowers about.*)

Bring garlands, spring garlands, to strew the waiting
    street,
And let none pipe who can't impart the magic to our
    feet;
And let none sing who cannot sing sweetly as Pierrot
For Mother loves the old-time songs, the songs of long
    ago.

ALL (*As they dance around Maypole*):

So out and in, and out and in,

We'll dance as light as Harlequin.
And on a throne of Lincoln Green
'Tis Mother who will be our queen.

(They bow and run through audience, passing flowers from their baskets to mothers.)

For Mother on Mother's Day

An anteater is mostly nose.
(He likes to smell things, I suppose.)
An owl, of course, is mostly eyes
And that's what makes him look so wise.
A monkey? He is mostly tail.
He likes to swing upon a rail.
And ostriches are largely neck
Since they are tall and like to peck.
A beagle hound has big long ears—
I don't know what strange sounds he hears.
An alligator's mostly mouth
(I'm glad he's living 'way down south).
But as for you, Mom, there's a part
Of you that has a special art.
I love you 'cause you're mostly *heart*.

A Gift in May

What would Mother like to get
    As a gift in May?
"Something that you make yourself."
    (That's what *she* would say.)

So I'll color and I'll paste,
    Or I'll cut and sew,
And I'll make a special gift
    And tie it with a bow.

(Then I'll hide it all away
Till it's time for Mother's Day.)

Then, at breakfast, by her place,
    I shall put the gift.
She'll take the ribbons off the box
    And give the lid a lift;

And she'll smile, and both her eyes
    Will open very wide
When she sees the secret thing
    I have put inside.

A Bouquet for Mother

I wove a little basket
   (The kind they use in May)
And took it to the wildwood
   To fill for Mother's Day.
I picked some hawthorn blossoms
   And a violet or two
And a handful of hepaticas,
   Both lavender and blue,
And put them in the basket
   With a bit of meadow rue.
I met some pussy willows, all
   Cuddly-soft and fat,
And thought how Mother would delight
   To fondle one and pat
Its fluffy fur.
So, just for her,
   I picked a pussycat.

How Mother loved her basket!
   She knew each flower-face;
She put them on the mantel
   In a shiny, crystal vase.

Homemade

The gift I give to Mother
I always make myself
And hide it in my closet
On the topmost shelf.
One year I made a pincushion
All stuffed with snowy cotton.
Next time I sewed an . . . oh, dear me!
I really have forgotten
The name of it; but this year
(Now that I am older)
I'm doing fancy stitching
On a real pot holder.

Oh, lots of people shop in stores
And (isn't it funny?)
They think the nicest presents always
Cost the mostest money.
But Mother says a homemade gift
Always means much more.
That's why she likes mine better
Than a present from the store.

Memorial Day Parade

Oh, we had a parade on Memorial Day
And we carried two flags for the Blue and the Gray
And the band made a music that thumped in our ears
While folks on the sidewalk made clappings and cheers;
But the music played softly, like prayers on the breeze,
As we entered the graveyard and stood beneath trees;
And the girls carried flowers to put on each stone
Of the boys who were sleeping, apart and alone.
And the sun was more shining and golden, perhaps,
Than the gold notes of bugles that sounded out taps.

Old Glory

Over the housetops Old Glory is flying—
Red as a sunset, white as a cloud,
Blue as the midnight where little stars crowd,
Over the housetops Old Glory is flying.

Up on the flagpole Old Glory is waving,
Waving to airplanes that sput-sputter by,
Waving to birds that wave back as they fly,
Up on the flagpole Old Glory is waving.

Never stop flying, never stop waving,
Hold up your head over housetop and tree!
As long as you do this, O beautiful banner,
All of my playmates and I shall be free!

FOURTH OF JULY

Fireworks

1st Boy:
"BANG!" said the firecracker, bursting on the lawn.
All he did was puff and pop—then he was gone.

2nd Boy:
"WHOOOOOOOOSH!" cried the sky rocket, spurting
into space,
"See! I'm shedding golden sparks over this place.
When I get above the town then I'll drop my meteors
down."

3rd Boy:
"POOH!" the Roman candle cried. "You are much too
quick.
All you do is rush and flash and turn into a stick.
Why should you drop down your stars, all of them at
once?
That is very foolhardy. You are just a dunce.
I prefer to toss my own, one star at a time . . ."
4th Boy:
"Tut!" the whirling pinwheel hissed. "Speed is not a
crime.

I go fastest of you all, yet there's not a doubt
I'm still turning, I'm still burning, when you've all
burned out."

NARRATOR:
All these words so glibly uttered
Died away as fire sputtered
   And was gone
   On the lawn.
Fireworks were broken—blasted.
Only stars in heaven lasted.

Balloons at the Fair

Come see the balloons that they have at the Fair.
They bob and they bounce on the waves of the air.
They look like a rainbow of color up there . . .
Each one is a bubble that's tied to a string.
It hasn't a feather. It hasn't a wing.
But if it were free, how far it could fly:
Up, up to the very tiptop of the sky!

My pockets are jingling with pennies to use
For popcorn and crackerjack if I should choose.
But oh, I believe I should much rather buy
A colored balloon that will dance in the sky.
Let's each pick a big one, all shiny and new,
See, here is a beauty! It's red, white and blue!
I want it to float like a bubble in air.
I'll buy a balloon from the man at the Fair.

COLUMBUS DAY

The Plot

Characters

QUEEN ISABELLA
KING FERDINAND
CHRISTOPHER COLUMBUS
FATHER PEREZ
CARLOS
ANTONIO
HERALD
GUARDS
COURT ATTENDANTS

TIME: *A day in April, 1492.*
SETTING: *Throne room in the castle of King Ferdinand and Queen Isabella of Spain.*
AT RISE: *The room is empty. Almost immediately* CARLOS *and* ANTONIO *enter.*

CARLOS: But this Christopher Columbus is such a determined fellow!
ANTONIO: A veritable demon!
CARLOS: At least we won't have to deal directly with him.
ANTONIO: As for King Ferdinand, we've cast enough doubts in his mind to sink a ship.

CARLOS: To sink a ship! That's a good one! (*They laugh.*) Only there mustn't be any ship. It's just a matter of persuading the Queen now. That ought to be easy. After all, she's only a woman.

ANTONIO: Don't fool yourself. She's not a fool. She's the brains and heart of Spain.

CARLOS: She was ready to throw away money on his venture the first time he asked for it.

ANTONIO: Luckily there wasn't much money five years ago. The war with the Moors was emptying the royal coffers fast.

CARLOS: But last year she encouraged Columbus again. She has secured funds to help him and is ready to sign papers authorizing his voyage.

ANTONIO: Not only that—she is making Columbus Admiral of the Ocean Sea, Viceroy, and governor over any islands he may discover.

CARLOS: What is your plan to prevent her signing?

ANTONIO: I have forged a letter to Isabella from Father Perez.

CARLOS: But Father Perez will be here!

ANTONIO: Not so fast, my dear Carlos. I overheard the Queen telling the King that Father Perez is on a secret mission. With him away, and this letter to damage the reputation of Columbus, all should be smooth sailing.

CARLOS: Smooth sailing? Ha, ha! For us, yes. But not for the great navigator. Ho, ho!

ANTONIO: After all, why should an Italian get favors when we who are good Spaniards can never receive a grant of money for any cause whatsoever?

CARLOS: What noble cause do you sponsor now?

ANTONIO: A monastery. The Queen is so religious she ought to rise to that bait.

CARLOS: Splendid! She'll grant more gold for that than she would for ships.

ANTONIO: And when we get it, we can go to England saying we want to consult with architects.

CARLOS: Excellent! Then we can set ourselves up in style at the English Court and trade a few of Ferdinand's secrets for titles and prestige.

ANTONIO: And live in luxury the rest of our lives. (*They both laugh, as they move left.* QUEEN ISABELLA *and* ATTENDANTS *enter right.*)

ISABELLA: Ah! Carlos and Antonio! You seem to be enjoying some joke. (*She smiles.*) You wish to see me? (*She goes to throne and sits.*)

CARLOS *and* ANTONIO (*Bowing very low*): Yes, Your Majesty.

ISABELLA: Can the King take care of it? I am expecting Columbus to arrive any minute to discuss some business with me.

ANTONIO: It is about this very man that we wish to speak.

CARLOS: And you seem more interested in his cause than the King, who has no time for minor matters.

ISABELLA: But this is not a minor matter. This concerns wide seas and far lands and the carrying of Christianity to heathen hearts.

ANTONIO: Ah, Your Majesty, you are mistaken. This man Columbus is but a freak and a fraud. He is not interested in converting the heathen. He is only interested in proving his foolish theory that the earth is round.

CARLOS: And surely Your Majesty can see with your own eyes that it is flat.

ANTONIO: His nautical maps prove only on paper that a ship can reach the East by sailing West.

ISABELLA: Father Perez says he believes Columbus can prove it not only on paper but with ships.

ANTONIO: But think of what ships will cost!

CARLOS: Besides, the ships would no doubt be devoured by sea monsters.

ANTONIO: Or drop off the edge of the earth into oblivion.

ISABELLA: That is not what great scientists say.

ANTONIO: Surely you don't believe this glib Italian is a great scientist? (HERALD *enters.*)

HERALD (*Announcing in a loud voice*): Christopher Columbus! (HERALD *bows and exits, as* COLUMBUS *enters and approaches the throne.*)

ISABELLA: Now he can answer for himself.

COLUMBUS (*Bowing and kissing* ISABELLA's *hand*): The great day has come at last, Your Majesty. I am here not only for the signing of the papers but also to speak my gratitude to a gracious Queen.

CARLOS (*Stepping forward angrily*): Do not think, sir, to flatter the Queen with fine words.

ANTONIO (*Taking letter from his pocket*): We have proof of your fraud and your chicanery.

COLUMBUS (*Excitedly*): How can there be proof of something that does not exist?

ANTONIO (*Handing letter to* ISABELLA): Here is the proof. It is for you, my Queen, to examine.

ISABELLA (*Opening letter*): What? A letter from Father Perez?

CARLOS: Read it aloud, Your Majesty.

ISABELLA (*Reading*): "My great and gracious sovereign, Queen Isabella of Spain: May God sustain you as you read this message. Proof positive has recently been put into my hands of the fraudulent intentions of one named Christopher Columbus . . ."

COLUMBUS (*Stunned*): Father Perez says that?

ISABELLA (*Continuing*): "He is accused of plotting and planning to obtain money under false pretenses from Spain. He is further accused . . ." (HERALD *enters.*)

HERALD (*In a loud voice*): His Majesty, King Ferdinand. (KING FERDINAND *enters with* ATTENDANTS. HERALD *exits, bowing.*)

FERDINAND (*To* ISABELLA): Ah! I see you are reading the letter which I have already read. It is from Perez and was brought to me by two of my trusted advisers. Show it to Columbus.

COLUMBUS (*Taking letter*): It is in the good Father's own hand. But he must be mad! (*He looks at* CARLOS *and* ANTONIO.) Or perhaps it was written at sword's point. (*To* ISABELLA) Has he not always encouraged my enterprise? It was he who first secured me an audience with you; he who understood my maps and charts because of his great knowledge of astronomy and geography. He was always my true friend.

ISABELLA: And mine.

COLUMBUS: He would never do this to me.

FERDINAND (*Sternly*): Not unless he knew you were guilty.

ISABELLA: My Lord, had you ever thought of a forgery? There have been several forgeries committed in the kingdom of late.

FERDINAND (*Thoughtfully*): Hm-m-m! If only Perez were here to own or disclaim this letter!

ISABELLA (*Raising her voice*): He is here. (*Calling*) Father, come forward. (FATHER PEREZ *enters quickly.*)

ANTONIO (*To* CARLOS): We had better get out. (*They slink toward door.*)

FERDINAND (*Calling*): Guards, arrest those two men! (GUARDS *enter and take hold of* ANTONIO *and* CARLOS.) And now, perhaps, we can get this matter straightened out.

PEREZ: It is very simple, Your Majesty. These two men wished to discredit Columbus, so that they could get a large grant of gold, presumably for a monastery, but actually for their own pockets.

FERDINAND: And how could a prior in seclusion have learned of such things?

ISABELLA: It was I who told him. I heard Antonio and

Carlos plotting when they did not know I was near. I guessed at once that they were the two rascals who have been forging royal papers—the men whom you have been seeking.

FERDINAND: Praise be for so clever a Queen!

PEREZ: Well may Your Majesty say that! It was your Queen who laid the trap. She suggested I pretend to be away on a secret mission so that they would show their hands.

FERDINAND (*Smiling*): Yes, and their handwriting, too. (*He turns to* COLUMBUS.) My wife knew your worth from the beginning, she and the good Father. (ISABELLA *rises and goes to table, where she picks up a scroll.*)

ISABELLA (*Spreading scroll on the table*): Then you will sign the order for the ships, dear King? I, myself, have already signed it.

FERDINAND: Gladly. (*She hands him a quill pen and he signs.*) And now I must go and see that these traitors get comfortable seats in prison. (FERDINAND *exits, prodding* ANTONIO *and* CARLOS *with his scepter as they march ahead,* GUARDS *on either side.* ATTENDANTS *follow.*)

ISABELLA (*Handing* COLUMBUS *scroll*): And this is your assurance of ships and men for perhaps the greatest adventure a mariner has ever known.

COLUMBUS (*Bowing*): Father Perez has told me how you helped to make this great adventure possible. Of all the queens in history, you shall be remembered as the most generous and the most farsighted. (*He kneels and kisses* ISABELLA's *hand, then goes out.*)

PEREZ: There goes a truly great sailor!

ISABELLA: A great sailor and a greater man. He is the hope of Spain . . . nay, of the whole world! (*Curtain*)

THE END

Three Caravels

The *Niña*, the *Pinta*, the *Santa Maria*,
   Oh they were the caravels three!
With wings like gulls and wooden hulls
   And prows that pushed the sea;
And long ago they set their sails
   To find a far countree . . .
The *Niña*, the *Pinta*, the *Santa Maria!*

They left the sunny shores of Spain
   To view a vast unknown
Where ships had never raised their masts
   And sails had never flown;
And far beyond the mist they found
   New harbors of their own . . .
The *Niña*, the *Pinta*, the *Santa Maria!*

Oh ships may sail from East to West
   And buck the brittle rain!
But there will never be a ship
   To bounce the seas again
More brave than those from Palos port,
   From Palos port in Spain . . .
The *Niña*, the *Pinta*, the *Santa Maria.*

United Nations Day

Hang high the flags of many lands—
The banner and the streamer—
Let nations shake each other's hands!
Let doer and let dreamer
Draw strength and hope from one another.
Let each man bear the name of brother!

Write documents and sheathe the sabers!
Let laws for us and for our neighbors
Be just and fair. Let understanding
Reach overseas from land to landing!

A world of lightning-hate and thunder
Will only crash and fall asunder;
But worlds of unity and peace
Shall shine in orbit without cease.
Hang high the flags!

HALLOWEEN

The Scarecrow and the Witch

Characters

WITCH
SMALL FAIRY (*Cat*)
SCARECROW
FAIRY QUEEN
CLOWNS
ELVES
SPRITES
FAIRIES

TIME: *Halloween.*
SETTING: *A field.*
BEFORE RISE: *The* CLOWNS, ELVES, SPRITES, FAIRY QUEEN, SMALL FAIRY *and other* FAIRIES *march or snake-dance onto the stage in front of the curtain. They recite in chorus.*

ALL:
This is the eve, the wonderful eve,
Of fairies and brownies and make-believe;
When the pumpkin-moon rolls over the sky,
Pushed by the wind that's hurrying by,

Carrying the leaves with their withery crackle,
Sounding like laughter or witches' cackle.

This is the night, the mysterious night,
When Jack-O'-Lantern is winking his light.
When witches are riding their runaway brooms
And ghosts are a-gliding right out of their tombs.
When frolic and rollick and games-on-the-run
Make-up and shape-up the Halloween fun.

CLOWN (*Stepping forward*):
I am a goblin turned into a clown.
I make people giggle by tumbling down. (*He turns a somersault or cartwheel, then returns to his place.*)

ELF (*Stepping forward*):
I was a wizard. I lived by myself.
I hated my looks so I changed to an elf.
(*He does a little jig and returns to his place.*)

SPRITE (*Coming forward*):
I was a witch who grew tired of badness.
Now I like laughter and dancing and gladness. (*She laughs and dances about, then returns to place.*)

FAIRY QUEEN (*Coming forward*):
Evil and badness are over and done.
This is the time for Halloween fun.

SMALL FAIRY (*Running forward*): No, no, no! I've met a witch who is still very bad.

ALL (*Shocked*): Oh-h-h! No-o-o!

FAIRY QUEEN: When? Where?

SMALL FAIRY:
Over in the pumpkin field near the corn and bean.
She dances with a scarecrow there every Halloween.

FAIRY QUEEN:
Can you go and find her? And teach her better things?

SMALL FAIRY:
Yes, oh, yes, I'll try, my queen. I want to earn my wings.

FAIRY QUEEN (*Handing cat costume to* SMALL FAIRY):
Then wear this little catskin.
Put on this kitten face.
(*She hands her a mask.*)
And send the witch's cat away.
So you can take her place. (*She helps* SMALL FAIRY *dress as she talks.*)

SMALL FAIRY (*Padding about*): Mew, mew! (*She licks a paw with her tongue.*) Meow, meow! (*She picks up her tail and twitches it.*) Purr, purr! (*She struts about proudly.*)

ALL: Oh, what a wonderful cat!

FAIRY QUEEN (*Kissing* SMALL FAIRY *on the forehead*):
I wish that I could help you face that dreadful witch;
But, since you know the right from wrong, go teach her which is which.

ALL (*As* SMALL FAIRY *walks slowly offstage*):
Yes, go into the world, dear puss,
With mews, and meows, and purrs;
A fairy-child must win her wings
   The way a man wins spurs.
(*All wave goodbye, as* SMALL FAIRY *exits. Then they form a snake-line, single file, hands upon one another's shoulders, and repeat the opening verses as they exit.*)

*   *   *   *   *

AT RISE: *The stage is semi-dark, with a harvest moon shining. The* SCARECROW *is leaning against the fence in a lifeless way. Clock off-stage strikes midnight, and the* WITCH *enters, straddling broomstick.*

WITCH (*Chanting as she gallops about stage*):
Lippity-clippity, here I go
Over the pumpkins, to and fro,
Hippity-hoppity, high and low,

Ride-away, glide-away, fast or slow—
Lippity-clippity, here I go!
Wearing a cape, all flippity-flap,
Wearing a mighty and magical hat,
Riding along with my big black cat . . .
(*She stops suddenly and looks around.*)
Where *is* that cat?
(*She walks to the edge of the stage, and calls angrily*).
Come here, you Shadow, come out of the gloom.
What do you mean, jumping off my broom? (CAT, *who
is really* SMALL FAIRY, *enters.*)
CAT (*Meekly*): Me-ow.
WITCH (*Getting off broomstick she hands it to* CAT):
Here, tie up my broom. Do as I say.
Don't let that broomstick gallop away.
CAT: Me-ow, me-ow-wow-wow. (*She moves to right with
broom and ties it to a corn shock.*)
WITCH:
And now I'll waken my friend the scarecrow
I'll give him a magic to make his hair grow.
(*She takes a pepper shaker from her pocket, and with a
cackling laugh approaches the* SCARECROW. *She waves
her arms wildly in front of him and sprinkles him with
powder.*)
Mumble-y, bumble-y, glimmery-glance
Tuck in your shirt-tail and brush off your pants,
The hour has come for our Halloween dance—
Mumble-y, bumble-y, glimmery-glance!
(*The* SCARECROW *moves, yawns, stretches. The* WITCH
cackles with delight. The CAT *mews plaintively.*)
SCARECROW (*Rubbing his eyes and looking at* WITCH *in
disgust*): Oh! So it's you, is it? Same old ragged cape!
Same old pointed hat! Same old dirty face! I've been
dancing with you every Halloween for the last hundred
years. Why can't I have another partner?

WITCH (*Angrily*):
  You ought to be glad that I brought you to life,
  Not only to dance, but to give you a wife.
  The Queen of the Witches will mend up your britches.
SCARECROW: *You* for a *wife?* Ha, ha, ha! Mend me up,
  would you? He, he, he! You never took a stitch in your
  life. Look at the rags you're wearing!
WITCH:
  My raggedy cape is a part of my riches.
  The magic comes out of the holes when it twitches.
  But as for your britches
  I'll take lots of stitches
  And after I've finished with all of the mending,
  They'll never rip out with your bowing and bending.
SCARECROW: It all sounds very good. Perhaps you *can* sew
  and I daresay you can sweep since you're always carry-
  ing a broom. But—can you cook? That's what I'd like
  to know.
WITCH (*Grinning*):
  Can I cook? I'll show my mettle. (*She turns to* CAT.)
  Shadow, fetch water. I want my kettle. (CAT *exits.*)
  I'll make a very wondrous brew
  As only a proper witch can do.
  (CAT *enters with kettle. To* CAT, *pointing off-stage right*)
  Now fill the kettle with owl eyes
  And serpent tongues and wings of flies
  And cricket legs for cricket pies. (*She turns to* SCARE-
  CROW. CAT *remains at stage right.*)
  You'll praise my cooking to the skies!
SCARECROW: Ugh! I never could eat *that* stuff! (*He makes
  a face.*) I'm going to look for a *real* wife. (*He takes a few
  wobbly steps away from the fence.*) A wife who can dust
  and cook and sew. She has to be pretty, too, pretty and
  clean!

WITCH (*Cackling and shaking all over with laughter*):
No woman like that would call her own
A fellow who never could stand alone
And hadn't a hint of a real backbone.

SCARECROW (*Saddened*): No, you're right. I haven't any backbone. (*He leans back against the fence and his head droops.*)

WITCH (*Patting his arm*):
Never mind! I like you just as you are,
All wobbly and worried and harried.
I'll go and I'll fetch my magical charms
And then we'll take off and be married.
(*She straddles her broomstick and gallops off, left.*)

SCARECROW (*Miserably*): If only I could make myself over! (*He bursts into tears*) If only I could be a man!

CAT (*Suddenly running to him*): You mean that? You really want to be a man? (*She sets the kettle down near him.*)

SCARECROW (*Blinking and looking around*): Who's talking?

CAT: I am. I learned to talk long ago, but I never let the witch know it.

SCARECROW: Well, of all things! You must have picked up quite a bit of magic, living with her.

CAT: Hm-m-m. I know only white magic. I don't like the black kind.

SCARECROW: Then perhaps you can help me.

CAT: Of course, I can! See that hawthorn tree over there? (*She points off-stage, right.*) One of those branches would make a wonderful backbone.

SCARECROW (*Shrinking a little*): Wouldn't it prickle?

CAT: It might. But anything good is worth suffering for. (*She runs to the right, "plucks" branch from off-stage and takes it to SCARECROW.*)

SCARECROW (*Handling it gingerly*): Oh, oh! Ouch!

CAT: Don't be a 'fraidy-cat. I may be a cat, but I'm not a 'fraidy one. See, I'll help you put your backbone in place. But you have to be brave about it or it will spoil everything.

SCARECROW: I'll try. I'll shut my eyes, and cover my ears and bite my lip. (*He does so. The* CAT *pushes the prickly stick down his back, under his shirt. He makes faces but manages not to cry out.*)

CAT (*Backing off and watching as* SCARECROW *straightens himself*): There! Open your eyes! You're already beginning to look like a man.

SCARECROW (*Delighted*): Am I? Oh, give me a mirror, quick!

CAT (*Picking a piece of tin up off the ground*): There! (*She holds it up for him.*)

SCARECROW (*Swelling with pride as he looks at himself*): Oh, I do look straight and tall! I do! I do! It must be magic!

CAT (*Goes behind corn shock and brings forth an armful of clothes*): But you need a better coat and hat. (*She helps him off with the old clothes and on with the new, and looks him over critically.*) Now take off that grin and give me a real smile.

SCARECROW (*Pulls off his mask and smiles radiantly as he looks in the tin mirror*):

Oh, I am a man, an honest man,
   I stand up all alone. (*He struts.*)
I need no fence to lean upon,
   For I've a real backbone!

(*He bows to* CAT *with a sweep of his hat.*)

CAT: You're wonderful. Now if only the poor witch would reform!

SCARECROW (*Thoughtfully*): Yes, I do feel sorry for her. I

think I'll go and see if I can find a little magic to help
her. (*He exits.*)

CAT (*Doing a triumphant dance and chanting*):
It never is magic and magic alone
That teaches a body to stand on his own.
You must *want* to be manly to earn a backbone.
(WITCH *enters. She is straddling the broom and is loaded
with bags, bundles and books. She looks around, be-
wildered.*)

WITCH: Now where is that scarecrow? He makes me pout.
He's slinking and hiding, I haven't a doubt.
(*She gets off her broom and pokes around with it behind
the fence and among the corn shocks.*)
He couldn't get far, since he's so slow,
Without my magic spell, I know.

CAT (*Coming up behind her*): Yes, he could! He's turned
into a *man.*

WITCH (*Wheeling about*): Who said that? It can't be the
cat.

CAT: Oh yes, it is! And it's true!

WITCH:
Who taught you to talk,
You foolish young gawk?

CAT (*Smoothly*):
I've always known how.

WITCH (*Sitting down suddenly on a big pumpkin and
bursting into sobs*):
Oh dear! Oh dear! It's really tragic!
What good are my charms?
(*She tosses away her bags and bundles.*)
What good is my magic?
(*Tosses away her books*)
My scarecrow has taught himself to walk,
And my cat has somehow learned to talk.

And I thought without my charm or spell
They couldn't do anything very well.
(*She wails and wrings her hands.*)
And now they'll leave me—my only friends!
Is that the way witchery always ends?

CAT (*Kindly*): Why don't you try making yourself over?
The way the scarecrow did! (*She fetches another set of clothes from behind corn shock.*)

WITCH (*Looking up hopefully*):
Oh, do you think I really could?
I'll throw off my cape and my conical hood.
(*She casts the old clothes away and puts on the new. The CAT meanwhile fetches the kettle.*)

CAT: And you'll wash your face and you'll wash your hands.

WITCH (*Turning her back to audience and going through the motions of washing over the kettle, but really removing her mask*): And I'll make some wonderful, beautiful plans.

CAT: What plans?

WITCH:
I'll go to the scarecrow and tell him he's wise,
And say that I want to apologize.

CAT: Very good! You can do it right now, because here he comes. (SCARECROW *enters proudly.* WITCH *runs toward him and he looks at her in amazement.*)

SCARECROW (*Admiringly*):
What a change in you, dear friend of mine!
I never dreamed you could look so fine.
You're pretty and clean, and you'd make a good wife—

WITCH (*Ecstatically*):
You really mean it?
(*She throws her arms around him.*)
I'm yours for life!

CAT (*Running to front of stage and winking at audience*):

And nobody knows, unless he's wise,
That I am a fairy dressed in disguise!
(FAIRY QUEEN *comes on stage followed by* CLOWNS,
ELVES, SPRITES *and* FAIRIES *who weave in and out of corn
shocks and form a semicircle around main characters.*)
FAIRY QUEEN (*Running up to* CAT, WITCH *and* SCARE-
CROW *and shaking hands with each in turn, introducing
them to her followers as she does so*):
Here is the cat, the wonderful cat
Who reformed a witch—just think of that!
ALL: Just think of that! (*They bow to the* CAT *and the*
CAT *returns bow.*)
FAIRY QUEEN:
And here is the witch who's discarded her hat
And all her black magic—now just think of that!
ALL (*Bowing to* WITCH *who returns bow*): Just think of
that!
FAIRY QUEEN:
And here is the scarecrow who stands on his own,
Manly and tall, with a big backbone.
ALL: Hurrah! Hurrah! For the big backbone. (*They bow
to* SCARECROW, *who nods in return.*)
WITCH (*To* CAT):
And you are a fairy disguised as a cat!
FAIRY QUEEN (*Helping* SMALL FAIRY *take off her cat skin*):
Yes, just think of that!
ALL: Oh, just think of that!
FAIRY QUEEN (*As* SMALL FAIRY *emerges from cat skin*):
And now, for your good deed you've earned your two
wings.
(*One of chorus members hands wings to* FAIRY QUEEN
who pins them on SMALL FAIRY.)
WITCH *and* SCARECROW (*With eyes popping*): Well, of all
things!
ALL: Yes, of all things!

FAIRY QUEEN (*Taking* WITCH *and* SCARECROW *by the
hands*):
Now join our party, and dance to our tune,
Under the gold of the Halloween moon.
(*All join hands and weave in and out among the corn
shocks, chanting.*)
ALL:
Evil and badness are over and done.
This is the time for Halloween fun.
Evil and badness are over and done.
(*They chant, as the curtain falls.*)

THE END

In the Witch's House

Characters

WITCH
CAT (*Little Girl*)
BOY

SETTING: *The interior of the Witch's house.*
AT RISE: *The* WITCH *is standing at the table mixing something in a big bowl. Her black* CAT *sits near her feet. As she moves to reach a spice can at the far end of the table she stumbles over the* CAT.

WITCH (*Irritably*): Get out of my way, Midnight. You're always under my feet.

CAT (*Saucily*): I'm not in your way. You're in mine.

WITCH (*Going on with mixing*): Impudence! Why didn't I take away your voice when I turned you into a cat? You can say the sauciest things!

CAT: Why in the world did I ever come to live with you? That's what I'd like to know.

WITCH (*Laughing*): Heh, heh, heh! So you don't like being a witch cat, eh? Well, I'm not going to change you back to a little girl, no matter how much you whine.

CAT: Don't worry. I won't whine. I've gotten over that. I know better than to expect favors from you.

This play may easily be adapted for presentation with hand puppets.

WITCH: You're well fed and housed, aren't you?

CAT: If you call sour milk, food, and a dirty house, a home.

WITCH: You don't know when you're well off . . . (*Whistling is heard from outside.*) Listen! Do you hear somebody coming?

CAT (*Excitedly*): It sounds like a boy whistling. I used to whistle, once, when I was a girl. Wonder if I could do it now? (*She puckers up lips and tries, but only succeeds in making cat noises.*) MEOW! MEOW! MEOW! (*Whistling grows louder.*)

WITCH: Hush! It's a boy. He's coming here. You'll scare him away with all your meowing.

CAT: That's just what I want to do. (*She runs to closed door and calls through crack*) Go 'way, boy. Go 'way! Meow, meow, meow!

WITCH (*Going to door and pushing* CAT *aside with her foot*): Very well, Smarty, if you won't invite folks in, I'll go out and get them. (*She slips out and slams door behind her.* CAT *scratches at door but can't open it.*)

CAT (*Plaintively*): Meow, meow, meow. (*She runs over to window as though with sudden purpose. She pulls curtain back with her paw and looks out. Her back is now to door.*) Go 'way, boy! Go 'way! THIS IS A WITCH'S HOUSE. Where are you, boy? I can't see you. Do you hear me? THIS IS A WITCH'S HOUSE! (*Door opens cautiously, and* BOY *peeks in.*)

BOY: Who called me?

CAT (*Turning around in surprise*): I did.

BOY (*Puzzled*): I don't see anyone but a cat.

CAT: You've never heard a cat talk, I suppose?

BOY (*Excitedly*): Was it really you? You must be a *magic* cat.

CAT: I'm a witch cat. Didn't you hear me say this is a witch's house?

BOY: A witch cat! How exciting! May I come in and pet you?

CAT: I wouldn't if I were you. If you once get in you may never get out.

BOY: But the witch has gone away. I saw her take the path to town.

CAT: It may be a trick. She may only be pretending to go to town.

BOY: No. I'm sure she went. Anyway, I'm coming in. I've always wanted to see the inside of a witch's house. (BOY *enters. As he gets to center of room, the door bangs shut. He and* CAT *jump.*)

CAT: What did I tell you?

BOY: It was only the wind.

CAT: I don't think so. Just try getting out. (BOY *runs to door and tries it. It won't open. He beats on it, kicks it in vain, looks around at* CAT *in despair.*)

BOY: I guess you were right.

CAT (*Sadly*): I guess I was.

BOY (*Trembling*): O-o-o-h! It's dark in here, and dirty, and smelly.

CAT: Did you think it would be like the outside? All frosting and gingerbread?

BOY: I thought it would be something better . . . ice cream, or pudding, or pie . . .

CAT: That's what *all* the children think.

BOY (*Trembling again*): W-what will the witch do with me?

CAT: Make you into gingerbread, most likely. (*She motions toward oven.*)

BOY: Ugh! I shouldn't like that.

CAT: First she'll leave you here a while to get you good and scared.

BOY (*Bristling*): Oh, is that so? Thinks she can scare me,

does she? Well, just let her try it! (*Clenches fists and spars in the air.*)

CAT: Bravo! You're a *regular* boy.

BOY (*Encouraged*): She's not going to turn me into ginger-bread, either. I'll find a way out.

CAT (*Sighing*): I wish I could help you. I've been trying to think of a way out myself for years . . .

BOY: You have? You want to get away from here, too?

CAT: Of course. It's no fun being a witch cat.

BOY: What made you one?

CAT (*Hanging her head*): I guess it was my own fault. I was a little girl, once. But I didn't like bothering to brush my teeth or wash my face. I thought it would be much nicer to be an animal and not have to worry about manners or dressing up . . .

BOY: But how did you get changed?

CAT: I was coming to that. You see, I used to run away and play in the alley all the time. Well, one day I met a witch there. She seemed to know just what I was thinking. She said if I'd let her change me into a cat, I could come home and live with her and never have to do any work or wash my hands and face . . .

BOY: And you're sorry now?

CAT: Of course. *Playing* in a dirty place was *one* thing. But *living* in it is another. I spend most of my time giving myself a bath with my tongue, so I won't get to look like the witch. *She* never washes, you know, and her hair is all snarly.

BOY: But why don't you run home?

CAT: I can't. She keeps me locked in for company. She only takes me out when she can go, too and watch me.

BOY: There ought to be a way to fool her—to take away her magic power . . .

CAT: Yes. If she lost her power I'd be a little girl again. (*Almost crying*) Oh, how I wish I were a little girl! I'd just love taking hot baths and brushing my teeth . . .

BOY: I have it! I have a plan! (*Footsteps are heard outside*)

CAT: Tell it to me, quick. Here comes the witch. (BOY *whispers and gestures, first toward oven then toward rain barrel.*) It sounds good. I hope it works. (*She and the* BOY *run to oven.* CAT *locks it, takes out key; gives it to* BOY. *He runs to rain barrel and drops key in. They have both withdrawn hastily to middle of room when* WITCH *enters.*)

WITCH (*Speaking to* CAT, *but looking at* BOY): Well, well, well. You seem to have company, Midnight.

CAT (*Sulkily*): I guess you knew it.

BOY (*Politely*): How do you do, Mrs. Witch?

WITCH (*Surprised*): Got some manners, haven't you? That's more than I can say for *most* boys. (*Turns to* CAT) He ought to make real *sweet* gingerbread, eh, Midnight?

CAT: He might. If there were an oven to bake him in.

WITCH (*Pointing to oven*): What do you call that?

CAT: I—I mean if you could open it.

WITCH: Open it? Of course I can open it. (*Runs to do so and discovers key is missing.*) Oh, ho! So that's it! Someone's been hiding my key . . .

CAT: Well, you see, I knew you'd want to use the oven. But the key was pretty sticky . . . and needed washing . . . and . . . and . . .

WITCH (*Crossly*): And so you tried to wash it, eh? Silly cat! What makes you want things so clean? I suppose you dropped it in the rain barrel. (CAT *and* BOY *say nothing, but hang heads guiltily. On the sly, however, they look at each other, knowingly.* WITCH *goes to rain barrel*) You needn't bother to answer. I can see for myself. (*Leans over barrel, hands locked behind her, and peers in.* CAT *grabs her hands and holds them tight.* BOY *begins to wash her face with a clean handkerchief from his pocket. WITCH sputters and tries to get away from* BOY *and* CAT.) Ow! Ow! Ow! Ow! HELP! HELP! HELP!

BOY (*Soothingly*): There, there! It's only soap and water. It won't hurt you a bit.

WITCH: Let me go. LET ME GO! Water's to drink, not to wash in. Help me, Midnight. Help me. Think of all I've done for you. You know I hate water. Help me! (*She faints, draping herself limply over rain barrel.*)

CAT: Well, I declare! She's fainted.

BOY: Help me get her over to that chair. We'll fix up her hair, too. (*They put* WITCH *in chair at front of stage, a towel over her face. Her head lolls back.* CAT *runs and gets comb. She begins to comb* WITCH's *hair.*)

CAT (*Nervously, as she combs*): I hope it works, I hope it works, I hope, hope, hope it works. (*Repeats in a mumble*)

BOY (*In sing-song*): It's got to work, it's got to work. It's got to, got to, got to work. (*Repeats.* WITCH *stirs.*)

CAT: There! That's done. Bring a mirror quick. She's coming to.

BOY (*Bringing mirror*): Take off the towel. (*WITCH opens her eyes. They hold the mirror up before her. She looks pretty and young.*)

WITCH: What's this? Who is it? Who's that pretty girl?

CAT *and* BOY: That's *you*.

WITCH (*Pathetically*): You're making fun of me. I wish— I wish I did look like that . . .

CAT *and* BOY: You *do*. This is just a mirror, see?

WITCH (*Amazed*): Why so it is! That's *my* face. Why! I *am* pretty . . . and young . . . and . . . and . . .

CAT (*Emphatically*): CLEAN.

BOY: You've been pretty and young all the time only you couldn't see your face through the dirt.

WITCH: How *wonderful!* I'm not a witch any more. (*She*

throws her arms around CAT.) And you're not going to be a cat any more. Here, let me take off your cat skin. (*She unbuttons the costume and takes off the mask. A* LITTLE GIRL *steps out of the cast-off clothes.*)

LITTLE GIRL: Oh, thank you! Thank you, witch!

WITCH: Thank *you!* And the boy, too. You are my best friends. (*She takes them by the hands and they all dance around in a circle as the* WITCH *says in sing-song rhythm.*)

Witchery, sorcery, magic and mumbo,
I am all through with their gibber and jumbo.
Hocus and pocus and pitter and patter!
What are they good for? What do they matter?
Murmur and mumble and singing of spells
They're nothing at all but mere bagatelles!
(*Curtain*)

THE END

The Three Terrors

Characters

PUMPKIN HEAD
SCARECROW   } *the three terrors*
WITCH
BOY
GIRL

SETTING: *A field, on Halloween.*

AT RISE: PUMPKIN HEAD, SCARECROW, *and* WITCH *are dancing around a caldron at center, mumbling and muttering in a kind of chant.*

PUMPKIN HEAD:
   We are the three, the fearful three
      Of whom the world's afraid.
SCARECROW:
   There never was a gang so bold
      Or bad as our brigade.
WITCH:
   We are the three, the fearful three
      Of whom the world's afraid.
PUMPKIN HEAD (*Breaking away from other two and bowing to audience*):
   I am a pumpkin head called "Jack."
      I have a fiery face.

It's lots of fun to see folks run
When I begin to chase.
There's not a boy, there's not a girl,
But runs away from me.
Beware, beware, you'll get a scare.
I'm terrible to see.

BOY'S VOICE (*From audience*): Ho, ho, ho!

GIRL'S VOICE (*From audience*): Ha, ha, ha!

(BOY *and* GIRL *come dashing up onto the stage.*)

BOY *and* GIRL (*Together*):
We're not afraid of pumpkin heads,
For we are very wise.
We know that Jack-o'-lanterns can
Be turned to pumpkin pies.

PUMPKIN HEAD (*Aghast*):
What? You're not afraid of me?
Oh, dear, oh, dear! How can this be?
If I can't scare the likes of you
There's only one thing left to do:
Give up my spookiness and try
To turn myself to pumpkin pie.
(*He goes out, wailing.*)

SCARECROW (*Coming forward and speaking to audience*):
Of all the sillies I have met,
That pumpkin head's the silliest yet.
It's I who am the scariest one
As everybody knows,
A scarecrow's business is to scare
The everlasting crows.

BOY (*Giving him a playful poke*):
We're not afraid of you at all!
You're only made of straw;
And clothes can never make a man.
That is a well-known law.

SCARECROW (*Backing away a little*):

You're not afraid of staring eyes?
　　Or of my wicked grin?
　　Or of my flapping ragtag clothes . . .
Boy (*Scornfully*):
　　They only need a pin.
　　That outfit doesn't scare the crows.
　　　Why should it bother me?
Scarecrow (*Pulling a large bandanna out of his pocket and weeping into it as he speaks*):
　　You're not afraid at all, I see . . .
　　I'm miserable as I can be.
Girl (*Comfortingly*):
　　There, there, old boy, don't sob and cry!
　　There isn't any reason why
　　You *must* scare people with your staring.
　　You're very nice, though not too daring.
　　(*She pats him on the back.*)
Scarecrow (*Wiping his eyes but still sobbing*):
　　Anyway, I'm through with scaring.
　　(*He goes out.*)
Witch (*Coming forward and facing audience*):
　　The scarecrow and the pumpkin head
　　　Have lived too long in error.
　　They thought they were ferocious folk,
　　　But *I'm* the only terror!
　　I am a witch, a frightful witch.
　　　I live up in a tree,
　　And everyone beneath the sun
　　　Quakes at the sight of me.
　　(*She rides up and down the stage on her broomstick, chanting.*)
　　I am a witch, a fearful witch.
　　　I like to leap and fly
　　Upon a broom, where there is room
　　　Up in the open sky.

(*She leaps and circles about.*)
The moon-man hides, the small stars shake
   When I go dashing by,
For there is not in all the world
   So wild a witch as I.
(*She stops, facing audience and teetering on her toes.*)
I am a witch, a frightful witch.
   I live up in a tree,
And everyone beneath the sun
   Quakes at the sight of me.

BOY (*Indicating audience*):
   Ha, ha! HO! HO! Of all assembled
   In the hall, not one has trembled.
   (*He and* GIRL *run up to* WITCH).

GIRL:
   Hello, old witch, we do not fear you.
   See! We dare to come quite near you!

WITCH (*Drawing back and waving her wand*):
   Hocus, pocus, keep your distance!
   This I say with great insistence.

BOY:
   Are you trying just to joke us?

GIRL:
   There's no sense to "hocus pocus".

WITCH (*Retreating with a few backward steps*):
   Don't you fear my hat and cape?
   Or my ugliness and shape?
   (*She points to caldron.*)
   Aren't you just a bit afraid
   Of the brew that I have made?
   Aren't you frightened of my magic?
   (*She is still moving backward and the children are
   bearing down upon her slowly but surely.*)
   This is getting very tragic.
   (*She begins to sniffle.*)

What on earth can witches do
When the children . . .

GIRL (*Pouncing upon* WITCH):

Just say, "BOO!"

(BOY *grabs* WITCH's *hat; the girl takes* WITCH's *broom.
They dance around* WITCH, *laughing gaily.*)

BOY:

This will show how much we fear you.

Let the others all come near you.

(*They beckon offstage to* PUMPKIN HEAD *and* SCARE-
CROW, *who come back on stage and join hands with the
children. All take hands and dance around* WITCH.)

Spooks and witches may be cunning

GIRL:

With their tricks and charms,

PUMPKIN HEAD:

But Halloween is made for funning—

SCARECROW:

Not for false alarms.

WITCH (*Suddenly nodding in approval, smiling and clapping her hands*):

Halloween is made for prancing.

Let me join you in your dancing!

(WITCH *joins circle. Everyone repeats the last two lines.
Then all dance around merrily, as the curtain falls.*)

THE END

The Magic Powder Can

(A group reading for FIVE SOLOS *and* THREE CHORUSES.*)*

1ST SOLO:
   Bob Besom was a witch's son—
      He was a mischief-maker.
   He spied a magic powder can
      (Just like a pepper shaker)
   Upon his mother's pantry shelf;
      And so Bob Besom helped himself.

2ND SOLO:
   For on the label he could read:
   "This is the powder witches need
   To turn a broomstick to a steed.
   It only works on Halloween
   When stars are pumpkin-gold or green."

3RD SOLO:
   So straightway (though you must excuse it)
   Bob thought of naughty ways to use it.
   (Since he was just a witch's son
   He knew no proper kind of fun.)

4TH SOLO:
   He gave the broom a scornful smile
   And tossed it on the refuse pile;

For airplanes had come into style
And they had left but little room
To gallop skyward on a broom.

5TH SOLO:

He hurried out into the night
Where every house had doused its light
And every child had said his prayers
And lay in bed asleep upstairs.
Bob found the playthings of the day
These children had not put away:

1ST CHORUS:

The tricycles,
The bicycles,
The wagon wheels,
The pushmobiles,

2ND CHORUS:

The barrel hoops,
Toy sailing sloops,
The roller skates
(Not always mates).

3RD CHORUS:

The kiddie cars,
The monkey bars,
The scooter,
The tooter
    and the long bean shooter. . . .

1ST SOLO:

All of these Bob Besom found
Strewn carelessly upon the ground;
And, with a mumbling sort of sound,

He made a hocus-pocus spell
(The kind his mother knew so well).

2ND SOLO:

He waved his arms and then began
To sprinkle powder from the can
On every kind of mobile toy
That's pushed or pumped by girl or boy;
And suddenly, with squeaks and squeals,
The toys rolled off upon their wheels.

1ST CHORUS:

With nobody to ride them,
   or guide them,
   or push them,
   or rush them,
   or pump them
   or bump them,
   or saddle them,
   or straddle them. . . .
Without the guidance of a child
The toys went rolling free and wild.

3RD SOLO:

The roller skates all swung on rails
Like monkeys with their straps for tails.
The barrel hoops made loop-the-loops
For tiny tanks that rolled in troops.
The tractors all set out to race.
The tricycles began to chase
The bicycles from place to place. . . .

2ND CHORUS:

The foghorns tooted,
The scooters scooted,

The sirens moaned,
The axles groaned,
The brakes all squealed,
The bike bells pealed,
The riot ran from street to field.
The riot ran from field to lawn
        Until the dawn. . . .

4TH SOLO:

And those who heard or raised their heads,
Or got up from their cozy beds
To look outdoors, saw such a sight
They turned and ran away in fright.
They jumped again into their beds
And pulled the blankets 'round their heads.

5TH SOLO:

But when the morning came at last
And no strange terrors hurried past,
They drank their coffee hot and steaming
And told what nonsense they'd been dreaming.
Only Bob, the witch's son,
Believed the nightmares, every one.

3RD CHORUS:

The moral of this tale, if any,
Is, whether you have few or many
Toys to play with on the green,
DON'T LEAVE THEM OUT THIS HALLOWEEN.

Who Would Ride a Broomstick?

(Four youngsters are straddling broomsticks, as they recite.)

1ST CHILD:
  Who would ride a broomstick
    As the witches do—
  Straight across the pebbly stars
    On a path of blue?
  (He prances.)

2ND CHILD:
  I would! I would!
    Oh, wouldn't you?
  (He neighs and rears.)

3RD CHILD:
  Who would take a wild cat
    With eyes all yellow-green
  To ride upon his broomstick
    Late on Halloween?
  (He circles stage.)

4TH CHILD:
  I would! I would!
    If Mother sat between.
  (He runs and hides, as all laugh and gallop about stage.)

139

Broomstick Time

On Halloween the witches fly
Like withered leaves across the sky,
Each with a broomstick for a steed
That gallops at tremendous speed.

Although I don't approve of witches
Who wear tall hats and live in ditches,
Still I am glad there is a day
When broomsticks have a chance to play.

Witch Cat

I want a little witch cat
   With eyes all yellow-green,
Who rides upon a broomstick
Every Halloween,
Who purrs when she is taking off,
   Just like a purring plane,
And doesn't mind a tailspin
   Even in the rain.

I want a cat who dares to light
   The candle of the moon
And set its jack-o'-lantern face
   A-laughing like a loon.

I want a cat who laps the milk
   Along the Milky Way,
A cat of spunk and character
   As daring as the day;
But gentle-looking kittens
   Are in the stores to sell
And which cat is a witch cat,
   I really cannot tell.

I Met a Witch

I met a witch, down in a ditch,
   Who wore a flapping cape.
She thought that she could scare me with
   Her funny twisted shape.
She waved her hands and muttered rhymes
   For nearly half an hour.
I only laughed and said, "These days
   Old witches have no power."

"I have a big grimalkin, though,"
   She said, "He's black and fat."
But I knew a grimalkin was
   A common alley cat.

She cried, "I'll ride my besom, strong,
   Right up into your room . . ."
But I replied, "A besom's just
   Another name for broom."

She said, "I guess I must give up
   Pretending I'm a witch."
She left her hat. She left her cape,
   And climbed up from the ditch.

She smoothed her dress and took a comb
  And combed her snarly hair.
"It's no use scaring folks," she sighed,
  "When nobody will scare."

At Goblin Time

(May be acted out with costume as recited.)

The way to scare a scarecrow
  Is to wear a sloppy coat
And tattered hat, and in your hair
  Stick wisps of hay and oat.

The way to scare a witch is
  To wear a flappy cape
And peakèd hat, and as you walk
  Stoop down and change your shape.

The way to scare most any spook
  From goblin down to elf
Is just to buy a funny face
  And be a spook yourself.

The Witch of Willowby Wood

There once was a witch of Willowby Wood,
And a weird wild witch was she,
With hair that was snarled and hands that were gnarled,
And a kickety, rickety knee.
She could jump, they say, to the moon and back,
But this I never did see.
Now Willowby Wood was near Sassafras Swamp,
Where there's never a road or rut,
And there by the singing witch hazel bush
The old woman builded her hut.
She built it with neither a hammer nor shovel.
She kneaded, she rolled out, she baked her brown hovel.
For *all* witches' houses, I've oft heard it said,
Are made of stick candy and fresh gingerbread.
But the shingles that shingled this old witch's roof
Were lollipop shingles and hurricane-proof,
Too hard to be pelted and melted by rain.
(Why this is important, I soon will explain.)

One day there came running to Sassafras Swamp
A dark little shadowy mouse.
He was noted for being a scoundrel and scamp,
And he gnawed at the old woman's house
Where the doorpost was weak and the doorpost was worn,
And when the witch scolded, he laughed her to scorn.

And when the witch chased him, he felt quite delighted.
She never could catch him for she was nearsighted.
And so, though she quibbled, he gnawed and he nibbled.
The witch said, "I won't have my house take a tumble.
I'll search in my magical book
For a spell I can weave and a charm I can mumble
To get you away from this nook.
It will be a good warning to other bad mice,
Who won't earn their bread but go stealing a slice."
"Your charms cannot hurt," said the mouse, looking pert.

Well, she looked in her book, and she waved her right arm,
And she said the most magical things.
Till the mouse, feeling strange, looked about in alarm,
And found he was growing some wings.
He flapped and he fluttered the longer she muttered.

"And now, my fine fellow, you'd best be aloof,"
Said the witch as he floundered around.
"You can't stay on earth and you can't gnaw my roof.
It's lollipop-hard and it's hurricane-proof.
So you'd better take off from the ground.
If you are wise, stay in the skies."
Then in went the woman of Willowby Wood,
In to her hearthstone and cat.
She put her old volume up high on the shelf,
And fanned her hot face with her hat.
Then she said, "That is that! I have just made a bat!"

On Halloween

One night I went out ghosting
   In pillowcase and sheet.
I thought I'd scare the big black cats
And whoo-ing owls and fluttering bats
   That lived along our street.
I thought I'd ring the doorbells, too,
   And spookily retreat.
But in a doorway, dim, there sat
   A mirror on a shelf.
Oh, how I screamed and ran away,
   For I had scared *myself!*

Halloween Magic

He came a-whistling down the street
On clumsy, clopping, clown-like feet.
He stopped and leaned upon a stile
And gave me quite a winning smile—
A smile that stretched across his face
And put his cheeks all out of place.

An early dusk had made the day
Melt into dark and fade away,
And yet I saw, to my dismay,
He was a scarecrow stuffed with hay.

"How can it be, sir," I said then,
"That scarecrows walk about like men?"
He winked his eye. (His eye was green.)
And said, "My dear, it's Halloween!"

Rumpelstiltskin

Characters

KING
MESSENGER
TWO SERVANTS
MARION, *the Miller's daughter*
RUMPELSTILTSKIN
COURTIERS

SCENE 1

TIME: *Long ago.*
SETTING: *Countinghouse in the King's castle.*
AT RISE: *The* KING *is sitting at his counting-house table counting out a very small pile of money. Great piles of unpaid bills are stacked around him. He thumbs through the top ones.*

KING (*To himself*):
  Bills from the hatters, bills from the tailors,
  Bills for outfitting my soldiers and sailors.
  Bills from the bakeries, markets and mills—
  Nothing but bills, no, *nothing but bills!*

149

(*He sweeps them from the table in an angry gesture and they flutter everywhere.*)

MESSENGER (*Entering from right, running hastily forward and kneeling before* KING): Oh, Your Royal Highness, I think I have found a way to pay the bills!

KING: What? Do you really mean it?

MESSENGER: I have found a miller's daughter who can spin straw into gold.

KING: Well, what are you waiting for? Bring her in. And tell my courtiers to come in, too. I want them to know the good news.

MESSENGER (*Rising and hurrying out*): I go at once. (TWO SERVANTS *enter left, carrying brooms, and sweep up the bills.*)

KING (*To* SERVANTS): Pile them up neatly this time. I'm going to pay them.

SERVANTS (*Ad lib*): Pay them? With what? How? (*Etc.*)

KING: You'll see. Just fetch me the last three bales of straw from the stable and a spinning wheel from the attic.

SERVANTS: Yes, Your Highness. (*They bow and go out as* COURTIERS *enter, right. They are talking excitedly to each other about the girl who can spin straw to gold.*)

KING (*As they all bow to him*): Well, I see you have heard the news . . . (*He looks offstage, right*) And here comes the magic maiden now. (MESSENGER *enters, right, with* MARION.)

COURTIERS (*Admiringly*): Oh-h!

KING (*As the girl bows before him*): I see you have spun your own hair to gold. Would you spin my straw for me —for the good of your country and mine? We must have gold or the land will be lost.

MARION (*Frantically*): Oh, Your Royal Highness, I should like nothing better! But I cannot work such magic.

MESSENGER: Your father tells me you can.

MARION: But my father likes nothing better than to brag

and boast about me. He thinks there is nothing I cannot do.

MESSENGER (*Aside to* KING): She is too modest.

KING: *That,* I can see.

COURTIERS (*As* SERVANTS *enter, carrying bales of straw and a spinning wheel and stool*): Ah-h!

KING (*As* SERVANTS *come forward*): Splendid! Put the bales in that closet over there, and the wheel in front of the door. (*He points toward the closet and* SERVANTS *obey.*)

MARION (*In panic*): Must I spin before all these people?

KING (*Kindly*): No, no. We shall leave the room. When the straw is spun to gold, we shall come back. (KING, COURTIERS, MESSENGER, *and* SERVANTS *exit. As the last one exits,* MARION *bursts into tears.* RUMPELSTILTSKIN *enters from left, on tiptoe.*)

MARION (*Crying, goes to the closet and looks at straw*): Oh dear, oh dear! What shall I do? I can't possibly spin straw into gold. Who in the world can?

RUMPELSTILTSKIN (*Running up to her*): *I* can.

MARION (*Looking around, startled*): You? Who are you?

RUMPELSTILTSKIN: Someone whose name you could never guess.

MARION: Wh-where did you come from?

RUMPELSTILTSKIN: From the end of the world, from the edge of nowhere.

MARION: But how did you get in here? The door is locked and . . . ·

RUMPELSTILTSKIN: I can get into any room, locked or not. What's more I can spin straw into gold.

MARION: I don't believe it.

RUMPELSTILTSKIN: Well, I can, and what's more I will! What will you give me if I spin these three bales for you?

MARION: Anything! Anything!

RUMPELSTILTSKIN: I must have one thing for each bale.

MARION: Well, here is my necklace for one. (*She hands it to him.*)

RUMPELSTILTSKIN (*Taking it*): Very well. It will do.

MARION: And here is my ring for another.

RUMPELSTILTSKIN: Yes. That is better. (*He slips it onto his own finger.*)

MARION (*Distressed*): I can't think of anything else to give.

RUMPELSTILTSKIN: Why not give a promise.

MARION (*Puzzled*): A promise?

RUMPELSTILTSKIN: Yes, promise you will give me your first-born baby when you become Queen.

MARION (*Laughing*): Oh, you funny little man. You're cheating yourself. A king would never marry a miller's daughter. I shall *never* be a queen.

RUMPELSTILTSKIN: I'll take a chance on it.

MARION: Very well. I promise. Only don't blame me if . . .

RUMPELSTILTSKIN (*Shutting closet door*): Ah, here goes, then! (*He seats himself at wheel and chants as he spins.*)
Whirr, whirr, spin, spin,
Gold is heavy and straw is thin.
Turn the wheel with a pixie-purr—
Spin, spin, whirr, whirr.
Oh, he who is versed in the Good Folk's law
Shall spin bright gold out of straw, straw, straw.
(*The wheel stops and the closet door flies open revealing three pails instead of three bales.*)

MARION (*Rushing over to closet and looking in*): Oh, it's done, done, done! (*She scoops up handfuls of gold from the pails and tosses the coins wildly into the air. They fall clinking to the floor.* RUMPELSTILTSKIN *tiptoes out, a sly look on his face.* MARION *dances about.*) Enough to save a kingdom. Gold! Gold! Gold!

KING (*Entering hurriedly from right*): What? Did you say "gold"? Is it spun already? (*He looks into pails.*) The magic is done! (COURTIERS *enter, running from all directions.*)

COURTIERS (*Ecstatically*): Oh-h!

KING (*Turning toward* MARION): But the most beautiful gold in all the world is the gold of this maiden's hair. Marion, the miller's daughter, shall be my queen.

COURTIERS (*Ad lib*): Hail to Marion, the miller's daughter! Long live the Queen. (*Etc.*)

MARION (*Amazed*): What? *I* shall be a queen?

CURTAIN

* * *

SCENE 2

TIME: *A year later.*

SETTING: *Same. A baby's cradle is at center.*

AT RISE: QUEEN MARION *is seated by the cradle, rocking it.*

MARION (*Singing*):
Hushabye, rockabye, little crowned head—
Safe in your cradle, snug in your bed—
Hushabye, rockabye, little crowned head,
Your mother's a queen and your father's a king—
They will protect you from any rude thing—
Sing, sing, sing . . .

RUMPELSTILTSKIN (*Tiptoeing in left and breaking into the song with a forward leap and an evil laugh*): I'm not so sure about that.

MARION (*Frightened*): Oh, dear, it's you! I'd forgotten all about you.

RUMPELSTILTSKIN: Forgotten about your promise? I've come for your baby.

MARION (*Throwing her arms about the cradle*): No, no!

I will give you anything else. Gold, jewels, *my* half of the kingdom . . .

RUMPELSTILTSKIN: But I have heard that none of these things is so precious as a baby.

MARION (*Sobbing*): You are asking me to pluck the moon out of the sky and live in shadow, to snatch away the sun and dwell in darkness. You are asking me to tear the heart out of my breast and . . . (*Her words dissolve into a moan.*)

RUMPELSTILTSKIN (*Stamping his foot and brushing a hand across his eyes*): Stop, stop! You'll have me crying, too, if you're not careful.

MARION (*Looking at him hopefully*): Oh, you do have mercy in your heart! You won't take my baby away?

RUMPELSTILTSKIN (*Uppishly*): I didn't say *that*. But I'll give you one more chance. (*He smiles slyly.*) If you guess my name by nightfall you may keep your baby.

MARION (*Delighted*): I shall start guessing at once.

MESSENGER (*Entering with a big book under his arm and bowing to* MARION): Your Majesty, I could not help hearing all that has been said, for the King, when he rode off to the hunt today, bade me never to go far from your door.

MARION: It is well.

MESSENGER: And I have brought you the great book of names—names collected from all over the kingdom. It may be of use to you now.

MARION: Good messenger, you shall be knighted for this. Come, we'll read off the names to the little man.

MESSENGER (*Opening book and beginning*):

Tom or John?
  Jake or Harry?
Bob or Rob?
  Lonnie, Larry?

(He pauses and looks at dwarf who shakes his head "No.")

MARION *(Coming over to MESSENGER and reading more from book)*:
James or Jim?
   Jack or Jerry?
Mike or Ike?
   Ted or Terry?
(She looks up at the dwarf expectantly.)

RUMPELSTILTSKIN:
No, no, no. Ho, ho, ho!
That's a book I happen to know.
You won't find it there. I'm telling you so!

MARION: It must be a very odd name, then, like Kataklump or Diddledop . . .

MESSENGER *(Closing book)*: Or Bandyback . . .

RUMPELSTILTSKIN *(Laughing harder than ever)*: No, no, you'll *never* guess it. I'll run out for afternoon tea and if you haven't guessed it by the time I get back . . .

MESSENGER: Very well, go along. It will give us a little time to look up more names.

MARION *(Looking doubtful)*: We can at least try.

RUMPELSTILTSKIN *(Singing as he goes off)*:
Today I'll brew, tomorrow I'll bake,
But now I'll go for tea and cake
And then the Queen's child I shall take. *(He dances off.)*

MARION *(To MESSENGER in stage whisper)*: Quick! Follow him. You may learn something.

MESSENGER *(Nodding)*: It's our only chance. *(He goes out on the run.)*

MARION *(Hurrying back to cradle)*: There, there! Don't cry. I will sing to you. *(She repeats lullaby with intermittent sighs and sobs. Suddenly MESSENGER re-enters. MARION goes to meet him)* What? Back so soon? I thought he lived at the edge of the earth.

MESSENGER: Perhaps he does, but he went only as far as the woods.

MARION: I think he forgot to put on his invisible cap. That's why you saw him.

MESSENGER: Well, he built a fire, for brewing tea, I suppose, or mischief. But he danced around it first, and sang.

MARION: That dreadful song about taking my child?

MESSENGER: Yes, but what do you think he added? (*He laughs.*)

MARION (*Hopefully*): Tell me. Oh, tell me quickly!

MESSENGER (*Singing and acting it out*):
Today I brew, tomorrow I bake,
Tonight the Queen's child I shall take—
She doesn't know, poor foolish dame,
That Rumpelstiltskin is my name.

MARION (*Clapping her hands in delight*): Rumpelstiltskin!

MESSENGER (*Looking offstage*): Sh! Here he comes. (RUMPELSTILTSKIN *enters left.*)

RUMPELSTILTSKIN (*Gleefully*): Do you know my name yet, my fair queen? I will give you three guesses.

MARION (*Hesitantly*): Well—could it be Woodleworm?

RUMPELSTILTSKIN (*Delighted*): No!

MARION: It's not Minimone, is it?

RUMPELSTILTSKIN (*Going near cradle and dancing about*): It is not! One more guess—and then the child is mine!

MARION (*Smiling a little*): Could your name be Rumpelstiltskin?

RUMPELSTILTSKIN (*Flying into a rage*): The fairies must have told you! The fairies must have told you. I have lost my chance forever! (*He runs from the room, screaming.*)

KING (*Rushing on, followed by* COURTIERS): What's happened? What was that noise?

MARION (*Going to cradle and rocking it*): The baby was frightened and cried a little. But everything is all right now. Yes, everything is all right. (*The* KING *and* COURTIERS *surround the cradle as the curtain falls.*)

THE END

Snow-White and Rose-Red

Characters

SNOW-WHITE
ROSE-RED
MOTHER
DWARF
BEAR
KING
TOWN CRIER
MINSTREL
ATTENDANTS

SCENE 1

TIME: *Winter.*

SETTING: *The cottage of Snow-White, Rose-Red, and their mother. There is a door up center, with a window on either side, each framing a bare rosebush, covered with snow. A third window is left, above a table set for supper, and a closet door is nearby. At right is a large fireplace.*

AT RISE: MOTHER *is seated at the table, reading aloud from a large book.* SNOW-WHITE *sits near the fireplace, spinning on her spinning wheel, and* ROSE-RED *is nearby, weaving at her loom.*

MOTHER (*Reading*): "And so it was that a prince came to the door; but because he was in disguise, no one knew him. For who could see under his rags the cloak of royal purple or the chain of gold? Only by the look in his eyes could one have guessed he was a king's son; and, indeed, no one guessed it. For most people did not take the trouble to look into his eyes."

ROSE-RED (*Pausing in her weaving*): I would! I would take the trouble to look into his eyes, no matter how ragged his cloak or how worn his shoes. I would know at once that he was a prince.

SNOW-WHITE (*Halting her spinning wheel*): So would I! I have never seen a real prince, but I'm sure I would know one, even in disguise.

MOTHER: I hope so. Yet it is not always as easy as one thinks to see things as they really are. (*There is a sound of tapping and scratching outside. A clawlike hand is seen, by the audience, at the window to the right of the door.*)

ROSE-RED (*Listening intently*): What was that? Was someone knocking?

SNOW-WHITE: I think it was only the wind, or the rose-bushes scratching the windows.

MOTHER: Yes, the wind is rising. What a terrible night! All blow and bluster!

ROSE-RED (*Rising and going to right window*): The snow is whirling and the rosebushes are bowing with the weight of it.

SNOW-WHITE (*Sighing*): The winter has come upon us all at once. Our four-footed friends of the forest are hidden away, the songbirds have flown, the insects no longer hum. It will be a long time before the roses bloom again. A long, long time! (*She gives a deep sigh and rises from her work, going to window at left of door. Great flakes of snow are whirling outside the windows. The girls gaze at them in silence.)*

MOTHER (*Rising from table and walking to girls*): Yes, a long time before the roses bloom. But since I have a red rose and a white one on my hearthstone, it will seem like summer to me. (*She draws her two daughters to her.*)

SNOW-WHITE: Did you really name us after the rosebushes, Mother?

MOTHER: Of course. On the very day you were born, you were as white as the roses that bloom on *that* bush. (*She indicates the bush seen through the window at left.*) And your sister was as rosy as the pink petals on *that* bush. (*She indicates bush seen through window at right.*) How should I otherwise have told my twins apart? (*They turn from windows and return to their work. The tapping noise is heard again.*)

ROSE-RED: There's that sound again! Somebody *must* be knocking.

SNOW-WHITE: I'll open the door and see.

MOTHER: Yes. Go quickly. We mustn't let anyone stand outside on a night like this. It may be some poor lost traveler. (SNOW-WHITE *runs to door and opens it.* DWARF *enters, scowling and stamping angrily. He carries a bulging sack over his shoulder.*)

DWARF (*Furiously*): Well, it's about time! I've been knocking and knocking, and nobody paid any attention.

SNOW-WHITE: I'm sorry. We thought at first it was only the rosebushes tapping and scratching at the window.

DWARF: Well, it wasn't. It was me! And I'm cold and wet and hungry. (*He sets down bundle by the door.*)

MOTHER (*Coming forward and ushering him to the fireplace*): Do come over here by the fire, sir. It will warm you and dry you off in no time. And Snow-White will give you a bowl of soup (*Walks to table*) while I cut you a little bread and cheese. Our fare is humble, but we never let a stranger go hungry. (*She hands* SNOW-WHITE *a bowl.* DWARF *seats himself by hearth.*)

SNOW-WHITE (*Going to hearth and bending over iron kettle*): I'll ladle you a little soup. The kettle is still on the fire and the soup is still hot. (SNOW-WHITE *hands him the bowl.*)

DWARF (*With a grumble*): Well, that's more like it! (*He eats greedily.*) And hurry up with the bread and cheese. I can't stay long. I have to get out of these woods and into the hills before midnight.

ROSE-RED (*Aside, to* SNOW-WHITE): Did you ever see such bad manners?

SNOW-WHITE: Never. But, then, the storm is enough to make anyone cross. (ROSE-RED *takes up her weaving at the loom.* SNOW-WHITE *goes to table and helps* MOTHER.)

DWARF (*To* ROSE-RED): Why don't you help your mother and sister?

ROSE-RED: Because I must finish my weaving before bedtime. A merchant is coming from the village this evening, just to buy this little scarf. He's such a nice man!

DWARF (*Scornfully*): He won't come in a storm like this.

MOTHER (*Proudly*): My daughters are noted for their spinning and weaving. Even the young prince orders his handkerchiefs from them. He sends the merchant to purchase them from us.

DWARF: Humph! Who knows but what the girls will fail some day.

MOTHER: You must not say such a thing. It is bad luck.

DWARF (*Impudently*): Very well. I won't talk at all. I'll just sit by the fire and sing. (*He begins a muttering singsong. The others go about their business and do not listen.*)

Wingle, wangle,
Spit and spangle.
How the thread

Gets in a tangle!
(*He waves his hands as though making magic.*)
How the needle
Starts to mangle
All the pattern
And to strangle
Half the thread
With horrid knots
So the cloth
Has lumpy spots.
(*He waves his hands again.*)

ROSE-RED (*With a sudden cry*): Oh dear! Look how my thread is knotted! And I've spoiled the pattern. It won't come out right! I'll have to do it over!

SNOW-WHITE (*Running to loom*): Good gracious! It *is* spoiled!

MOTHER (*Going to loom*): How did you ever get the thing in such a scramble?

ROSE-RED (*Despairingly*): I don't know! I don't know! (*She bursts into tears.*) What will the merchant think?

MOTHER (*Patting her shoulder*): There, there, don't cry! Snow-White will spin you some new thread.

SNOW-WHITE: Of course. You help Mother with the little man's supper, and I'll be done in no time.

ROSE-RED: Oh, thank you! Thank you! All I need is a very little thread. There's only an inch or two of the pattern to do over. (*She goes with* MOTHER *to table.* SNOW-WHITE *sits down at spinning wheel and begins to spin.*)

MOTHER (*To* ROSE-RED): Was it that song the dwarf was singing? Was *that* what bothered you?

ROSE-RED: I think so. It seemed to make me nervous. All I could hear was a mutter, but somehow it mixed me up. (*DWARF begins to hum and mutter and wave his hands once more.*)

MOTHER: Listen! He's going to sing again.

ROSE-RED: Oh, don't let him! He'll spoil the spinning! (*She starts to go toward* DWARF *but* MOTHER *holds her back.*)

MOTHER: No. Stay here. We mustn't let him know we're listening. Just go on setting the table.

ROSE-RED: But—but—

MOTHER: We mustn't accuse him unless we are *sure*.

ROSE-RED: Look what a sly smile he has!

MOTHER: And just hear those queer words he's singing!

DWARF:

Spin, spin!
You never can win.
The thread's too thick,
Or the thread's too thin.
It will never weave out,
It will never weave in.
It will only dangle and tangle and break.
Then, *what* can you make? Oh, *what* can you make?

SNOW-WHITE (*Jumping up with a despairing cry*): What *is* the matter with my wheel? I can't spin at all! The thread keeps snapping and raveling!

ROSE-RED (*Running to her and looking over her shoulder*): Why, the spinning's as bad as the weaving!

MOTHER (*Going to* DWARF *and shaking her finger at him*): This is all *your* fault. You had no business singing those songs. You did it just to get the girls mixed up.

DWARF (*Throwing back his head and laughing contemptuously*): Ha, ha, ha! If that isn't just like a mother! Ho, ho, ho! When her daughters can't weave or spin, she blames it on someone else. Ho, ho, ha, ha, ho, ho, ho! (*Suddenly, there is a loud growling sound outside, and the door rattles ominously.*)

ALL (*Startled*): What's that?

DWARF (*Suddenly trembling*): It—it sounds like an angry animal, a f-f-fierce growling animal. (*He runs frantically around the room.*) An animal! A wild animal! A big, bad beast! (*He tries to find an exit other than the front door.*) Let me out of here! Let me out!

MOTHER (*Calmly*): Hush, hush! Don't be a silly. It's only the storm. It's the thunder roaring and the wind shaking the door.

SNOW-WHITE: Of course!

ROSE-RED: It's only the storm.

DWARF (*Spying closet door and rushing toward it*): It's not the storm. It's an animal! It's a big, black beast! Let me out of here. Let me out! (*He flings the closet door open. When he sees it is not an exit, he bangs the door shut angrily and it closes on his beard. He dances up and down wildly, shouting and screaming.*) Oh, oh! I'm caught! I'm caught!

ROSE-RED (*Running to him*): Here, here! Don't jump about so. (*She tries to loosen the beard, but he continues to leap and gesture wildly.*)

SNOW-WHITE (*Going to* DWARF): Be still. You're only making things worse. (*She tries to pull the beard out of the crack in the door.*) It's no use. The door is stuck.

DWARF (*Angrily*): Well, *un*stick it then.

ROSE-RED (*Tugging on closet handle*): I can't unstick the door. It's jammed shut. (*The growling and banging is heard again at the door.*)

DWARF (*In a panic*): Get me out of here! Get me out! The beast is coming! The big, bad beast!

MOTHER: Don't be foolish. There are no big, bad beasts in *our* forest.

DWARF (*Stamping in rage*): Let me out, I say!

SNOW-WHITE (*Taking scissors from her apron pocket*): Here we are! This will set you free. (*She quickly snips off the end of the beard.*)

DWARF: How dare you? How dare you? You've clipped off my beautiful beard! (*He rushes at* SNOW-WHITE, *shaking his fist.*) You will pay for this. (*Knocking and growling are heard again at the door. The* DWARF *stops, then leaps on the table, scattering dishes and overturning stools, and exits through the window at left.* MOTHER *and girls rush to window and look out, then sigh with relief.*)

MOTHER: What a horrid little man! I'm glad we're rid of him. (*They begin to pick up scattered dishes and overturned stools.*)

SNOW-WHITE: He tried to frighten us with his silly songs.

ROSE-RED: But he was so frightened himself, he forgot his bundle!

SNOW-WHITE: Look! He left his sack right there by the door.

MOTHER: I'll just put the bundle away for safekeeping. Maybe he'll come back for it. (*She pulls closet door open and puts bundle inside.*) You don't suppose there really *was* someone at the door, do you?

ROSE-RED: Maybe there was!

SNOW-WHITE: He acted as though someone was after him.

ROSE-RED: But he said it was a wild beast.

MOTHER: I'd rather take in a wild beast than that little man! (*A sudden loud, clear knocking is heard.*)

ALL: There *is* someone knocking!

MOTHER (*To* SNOW-WHITE): Open the door, dear. It may be the village merchant. (SNOW-WHITE *opens the door, and a huge black* BEAR *enters. The girls scream.* SNOW-WHITE *hides under the table, and* ROSE-RED *runs to closet.* MOTHER *takes poker from the chimney place.*)

BEAR (*Advancing toward* MOTHER *and bowing politely*): Good evening, madam. Don't be afraid. I will not harm you. But I have lost my way in this blinding blizzard and I am nearly frozen. I ask only to warm myself for a few moments by your fire.

MOTHER (*Recovering herself and hiding poker behind her*): Of course, of course. We were just startled for a

moment. We were expecting a merchant who was coming to buy some of my daughters' handiwork.

BEAR (*Laughing*): And you hardly expected a bear at the
door?

MOTHER: Well, it *is* a little unusual, you know. (*They both
laugh.*)

ROSE-RED (*Coming out of closet*): A talking bear! How
wonderful! How exciting!

SNOW-WHITE (*Coming out from under the table*): We love
all the animals of the forest. They are our friends. But
we have never met any bears before.

BEAR: No, I suppose I am the only one in these woods. I
am quite new here. I hope you will consider *me* a friend,
too.

SNOW-WHITE: Of course we will.

MOTHER (*To* ROSE-RED): Bring the broom, dear. I should
like to sweep off Sir Bruin's coat. He is covered with
snow and see how he's shivering!

ROSE-RED (*Fetching broom from fireplace and handing it
to* MOTHER, *who brushes off* BEAR): Are you the kind of
bear that does circus tricks?

SNOW-WHITE: Can you dance for us?

BEAR: Of course. I can even carry you both on my back.

MOTHER: But first, girls, you must let him dry himself by
the fire. (*She takes him by a paw and leads him to the
fireplace.*) Would you like a bowl of porridge, Sir Bruin?

BEAR: Yes, thank you. Indeed I would. Porridge has been
a favorite with bears ever since the days of Goldilocks.
(*They laugh.* MOTHER *brings him food, while* ROSE-RED
ties a napkin under his chin, and SNOW-WHITE *combs
his hair.*)

ROSE-RED: I hope you can stay with us all winter.

SNOW-WHITE: Yes. It looks as though the weather is going
to be pretty bad this year. We may all be snowed in.

MOTHER: And we'd certainly enjoy company.

BEAR: I'd be delighted to spend the winter here. Sitting with friends by a fire like this would be far better than hibernating alone in a cold cave. Besides, I could help you with the work—chop wood, build fires, shovel snow, carry water and . . .

MOTHER: Think of having a pet animal that can do all that!

ROSE-RED: He's not just a pet, he's a playmate.

SNOW-WHITE: He's not just a playmate—he's a friend.

ROSE-RED: Well, anyway, he'll play games with us! (*She pulls his ear playfully.*)

BEAR: Of course I will. I'm going to play a game with you right now. (*He swallows the rest of his porridge in one big gulp.*) Just sing me a tune and clap the time.

ROSE-RED (*Excitedly*): How about "A-tisket, A-tasket?" Come, Mother, help us make a circle. (*They link hands, and sing "A-tisket, A-tasket."*)

BEAR: I guess that leaves me to drop the handkerchief. (*He pulls from a hidden pocket a large handkerchief, then trots around the circle. He goes twice around and on the third time drops the handkerchief at* SNOW-WHITE's *feet. She picks it up and chases him round and round.* ROSE-RED *joins the chase.*)

MOTHER (*Clapping her hands*): That's enough! That's enough! You'll all get dizzy. (*The girls and* BEAR *halt, laughing and panting.*) We forgot Sir Bruin hasn't had his dessert. (*She moves to table pulling* BEAR *along.*) See! Wild blackberry jam and a currant bun!

BEAR (*Seating himself at table*): Yum! (*As he eats,* SNOW-WHITE *draws* ROSE-RED *aside to the fireplace. She shakes out the handkerchief which she is still holding.*)

SNOW-WHITE: Just look at this handkerchief! It's royal purple and gold.

ROSE-RED (*Pointing*): And see the crown in the corner!

SNOW-WHITE: Do you recognize the spinning and weaving?

ROSE-RED (*Looking closely*): Why, it's the handkerchief we made for the prince! There is our mark on it! (*She points.*)

SNOW-WHITE: What can it mean?

ROSE-RED: Maybe the bear found it in the forest. The king and prince often hunt there.

SNOW-WHITE (*Dreamily*): Yes, he may have found it in the forest. But, when I look into his eyes, I can't help wondering about him. (*She looks thoughtfully at* BEAR. *Then both girls shrug, laugh, and run to sit at* BEAR'S *feet.*)

CURTAIN

* * *

SCENE 2

TIME: *Spring.*

SETTING: *The same. The rosebushes outside the windows are now covered with blossoms, white at left, red at right. The front door is open.*

AT RISE: *The* BEAR *is curled up beside the fireplace asleep.* SNOW-WHITE *and* ROSE-RED *are sweeping and dusting the room in a dreamy manner.*

ROSE-RED (*Pausing in her work to stand at door and look out*): Isn't it wonderful? Did you ever see such a spring? The world is running over with blossom and song!

SNOW-WHITE (*Sighing and continuing to sweep*): Yes, it's all very beautiful.

ROSE-RED: But it doesn't seem to make you feel as gay as I do.

SNOW-WHITE: The spring has always made me feel gay, but somehow, this year, it is different.

ROSE-RED: Is it because Sir Bruin will be going away now?

SNOW-WHITE (*Sighing again*): Yes, I suppose it is. No more dancing, no more games, no more stories by the fireside.

ROSE-RED: I don't see why he has to go.

SNOW-WHITE: Neither do I. But wild things are restless in spring, and hibernation time is over.

ROSE-RED: Surely he could come here evenings and sleep on the hearth in summer as well as winter. The hearth-stone would make a *cool* bed. See! I'll pick a spray of red roses and put it on the mantel. *That* should be the kind of fire he would want in summer. (*She picks a spray of red roses.*)

SNOW-WHITE (*Admiring roses*): A very beautiful fire, too. (*She walks to left window.*) And I shall put a white blanket over him—a summer blanket. (*She picks several sprays of white roses and puts them on* BEAR. *He stirs a little in his sleep.*)

ROSE-RED: Oh, dear, you're wakening him!

SNOW-WHITE (*Backing away on tiptoe*): I didn't mean to.

BEAR (*Growling in his sleep*): Gr-r-r! Gr-r-r! (*Gnashes his teeth and snarls; the girls back away farther.*) I'll find you! I'll get you! (*He waves his paws about.*) I say, I'll get you, you miserable little dwarf! (*He starts up, blinks his eyes, then goes back to sleep.*)

ROSE-RED (*Whispering*): Did you hear that?

SNOW-WHITE: Yes. How very odd! Do you suppose he's talking about that horrid little man with the long beard?

ROSE-RED: The one who left his big bundle here last winter? Is it still in the closet where Mother put it?

SNOW-WHITE (*Opening closet door and pointing to bundle*): Yes, it's still here. Do you suppose there is treasure in it?

ROSE-RED: If there is, I wonder why he hasn't come back

for it. (MOTHER *enters, panting and disheveled. Her dress is torn and her hair is flying about. She carries a bunch of flowers, which are limp and broken.*)

SNOW-WHITE (*Rushing to her*): Why, Mother!

ROSE-RED: Whatever is the matter? (*They help her to a chair.*)

MOTHER (*Sinking limply into chair*): It's that horrid little man, the one who was here last winter.

ROSE-RED: The dwarf?

MOTHER (*Trying to catch her breath*): Yes.

SNOW-WHITE: We were just talking about him.

ROSE-RED: Did he come for his bundle?

MOTHER: Yes, but when I told him that a bear was living in the house, he ran away.

ROSE-RED: He must be awfully afraid of bears.

MOTHER: Most people are.

SNOW-WHITE: They just aren't used to making pets of wild animals the way we are.

MOTHER: He wanted *me* to come back and fetch the bundle for him. I said no, because I remembered something I heard the Town Crier say when I was in the village.

SNOW-WHITE *and* ROSE-RED: What was that?

MOTHER: He said a bag of jewels had been stolen from the King's treasury last autumn. And when I thought about it, I remembered that the dwarf's bag looked just like the one the Crier described. We had better report this to the King at once.

SNOW-WHITE: Of course. But not until we have bathed your bruises and scratches.

ROSE-RED (*Going to table and pouring water from a pitcher into a basin*): Did that dreadful creature attack you?

SNOW-WHITE: Because you wouldn't fetch his bag? (*She takes a roll of bandages from her apron pocket and the two girls attend to MOTHER.*)

MOTHER: Yes. He acted like a mad man. He bit and kicked and scratched me. It was all I could do to tear away from him.

BEAR (*Waking up suddenly*): What? Where? Who? Who was scratched and bitten?

SNOW-WHITE: Our mother. Just look at her!

ROSE-RED: That terrible little dwarf did it!

BEAR (*Leaping up angrily and running to door*): The dwarf? Where is he? I'll catch him if I have to chase him around the world! (*He rushes out, growling and roaring.*)

SNOW-WHITE: My! I never knew he could be so fierce!

ROSE-RED: Or so angry.

MOTHER: Or so fast on his feet. I think he knows something about that dwarf that he's never told.

SNOW-WHITE: He does. He was talking about him in his sleep. (*A bell rings offstage.*)

TOWN CRIER (*Offstage*): Hear ye! Hear ye! Make way for His Majesty the King!

ROSE-RED (*At door*): Did you hear that?

SNOW-WHITE (*At window*): Yes! The King is coming!

MOTHER: What? Here, to our little cottage? What can he want with us?

TOWN CRIER (*Entering*): Make way for the King! (*The KING enters, followed by ATTENDANTS carrying pillows and a golden cloth, and MINSTREL, who carries a small harp. The girls and MOTHER draw back and curtsy deeply.*)

MOTHER (*Approaching KING and curtsying again*): This is a great honor, Your Majesty. What can my daughters and I do for you?

KING (*Wearily*): First, a chair, please. It has been a weary walk through the forest, for my coach could not get through the thick undergrowth.

MOTHER: I have nothing to offer but wooden stools, and

this one chair, left by a merchant for his own use when he comes to bargain for my daughters' handiwork. But I'm sure the merchant would be honored to have our King use it. (*To daughters*) Fetch the merchant's chair for the King. (*They quickly bring the chair to the* KING. *Two* ATTENDANTS *arrange pillows on the chair, and a third* ATTENDANT *throws the cloth over them. They help the* KING *to be seated.*)

SNOW-WHITE (*In quiet awe*): What a beautiful throne!

ROSE-RED (*Clapping her hands in delight*): Perfectly elegant!

MOTHER: Ah! That is more fitting for our king than a wooden stool.

KING (*Smiling*): If I were ten years younger, madam, I should perfer one of your wooden stools, for I know what hospitality goes with it; but my servants spoil me, and since I am an old, broken man, I am very glad to ease my joints. But, come, everyone, gather 'round me that I may tell you what this visit is all about.

ROSE-RED (*To* SNOW-WHITE): Doesn't the minstrel remind you of someone we know?

SNOW-WHITE (*To* ROSE-RED): Yes, he does. But I can't think who.

ROSE-RED: Could it be the merchant?

SNOW-WHITE: Of course! There's a strong resemblance!

ROSE-RED: Do you suppose he *is* the merchant?

KING: Fetch your mother a stool, young ladies, then come and sit at my feet where I can look into your lovely faces.

ROSE-RED (*Curtsying*): Yes, Your Majesty.

SNOW-WHITE (*Curtsying*): But we are not ladies, Your Majesty. We are only poor peasants.

KING (*Smiling*): Every girl, no matter what her birth, grows into a true lady when her heart is loving and her mind pure. (*They bring a stool.*)

MOTHER (*Happily*): What a beautiful thing to say! (*She seats herself on the stool, and the girls sit at the* KING's *feet. The* ATTENDANTS *stand grouped about the throne. The* KING *signals to the* MINSTREL, *who steps forward.*)

KING: I am going to let the minstrel tell you my sad story, as I haven't the heart to tell it myself.

MINSTREL (*Bowing to* KING): At your service, my good sovereign. (*He begins to strum and recites or sings the following ballad, to the tune of "Auld Lang Syne."*)

There was a prince, a gallant prince,
    A goodly prince to see.
He was the only son, my dears,
    Of this, His Majesty. (*He bows toward* KING.)
He was the only son, my dears,
    And on an evil day
A wicked band of dwarfs came by
    And stole the prince away.

ATTENDANTS (*Singing*):
A wicked band of dwarfs came by
    And stole the prince away.

MINSTREL:
The king then sent, both far and wide,
    His spies and fighting men
To catch that band and force them to
    Return the prince again.
But nowhere on the mountain top,
    Or in the hollow glen,
Could anybody find a trace
    Of those wicked little men.

ATTENDANTS:
Oh, nobody could find a trace
    Of those wicked little men.
(*Everyone sits silent for a moment.*)

SNOW-WHITE: How terrible!

KING: If I could only get my hands on that Dwarf King!

MINSTREL: And I!

ATTENDANTS (*Ad lib*): And I! And I! (*They shake their fists.*)

MOTHER: But when did this all happen? We were told the prince had journeyed to a far country for a visit, last fall.

KING: Ah, yes! (*He sighs deeply.*) Perhaps I was wrong to keep it from my people. But I was afraid the dwarfs would harm the prince if I spread the news. So I simply paid the ransom they asked for. But they never released my son. That Dwarf King is full of wicked magic.

MOTHER (*Aghast*): They demanded a ransom?

SNOW-WHITE: Was it a bag of jewels?

KING (*Startled*): Yes. How did *you* know?

MOTHER: A miserable little man came here for shelter this past winter, in the first snowstorm.

ROSE-RED: And he had a great bag on his shoulders.

MOTHER: It looked like the bag I heard the Crier describe when I went to town this morning.

ROSE-RED: He left it here because our pet bear scared him away.

SNOW-WHITE: The bag is still in the closet. I will get it for you. (*She starts toward closet as the* DWARF *enters.*)

DWARF: No, you will *not* get it. Stay where you are, all of you. (*He lifts his hands and chants.*)
Stand where you are! Stand where you are!
I'll freeze your feet so you can't go far.
(*The* ATTENDANTS *start toward him, but stiffen suddenly like statues before they can reach him. The* KING, MOTHER, *and girls stiffen in their places.*)
I'll numb your hands and I'll stiffen each head
Till your bones, hard as stones, make you heavy as lead.
You will be as useless as though you were dead.
Ha, ha, ha! Ha, ha, ha!
Now for the jewels! My black magic always works!

(*He runs to the closet and drags out the bag. There is a loud growling sound, offstage.*) Oh, no! What was that? (*The growling is repeated, much louder. In a panic,* DWARF *runs to door and looks out.*) I hear him coming. I can see him crashing through the woods! He is almost upon me! (*He drops bag and rushes about the room.*) Where can I hide? (*He runs to closet, but the* BEAR *enters with a roar and starts to chase the* DWARF *around the room, in and out among the others, who continue to stand as stiff as statues.*)

BEAR (*Growling*): I'll catch you yet!

DWARF (*As he runs*): Help, help! Save me, someone!

BEAR: No one can save you now! (*He trips and falls. The* DWARF *leaps for the bag of jewels and dashes toward the door with it. The* BEAR *scrambles to his feet, runs to* DWARF.) Oh, no! You can't run away from me! (*He catches the* DWARF, *just at the door, and holds him in a bear hug.*)

DWARF (*Kicking wildly*): Let me go! Let me go!

BEAR: I'll let you go when I've cut off your beard. (*He takes the scissors from* SNOW-WHITE'S *apron pocket, while the* DWARF *struggles and howls.*)

DWARF: No! No! Don't cut off my beard! Anything but that! I'll give back the jewels! I'll take the spell off your friends.

BEAR: No, you won't. I'll break the spell myself. I'm on to your tricks at last. Hold still! (*He holds the* DWARF *firmly with one of his paws, and with the other he snips off the beard up to the chin. The* DWARF *sinks to the floor limply. Then he crawls out the door whimpering. The* BEAR *turns to the others.*) And now, my friends, you can move again. (*He waves the* DWARF'S *beard above his head.*) The magic power of the evil dwarf was in his beard. The power of the evil dwarf is broken. Awake!

ALL (*Smiling and stretching, ad lib*): The spell is broken! Hurrah! At last! (*Etc. They move their arms and legs about, talking among themselves.* SNOW-WHITE *and* ROSE-RED *run to the* BEAR *and throw their arms around him.*)

ROSE-RED: Oh, you wonderful, wonderful friend!

SNOW-WHITE: How can we ever thank you? You have saved us from the wicked dwarf.

BEAR (*Laughing*): You have thanked me already. I'm sure I'm the first bear to receive a bear hug from human beings. (*All laugh.*)

MOTHER (*Going up to him and hugging him*): Then I shall give you another hug to set a record. (*All laugh again.*)

MINSTREL (*Stepping up to* BEAR *and bowing before him*): Sir Bruin, you have saved our lives. We thank you for the King as well as for ourselves. (ATTENDANTS *bow to* BEAR.)

BEAR (*Returning bows with smile*): I am glad to have served the King's servants, and there is nothing I would not do to serve the King.

KING (*Rising suddenly*): I prefer to thank Sir Bruin myself. (*He goes to* BEAR.) Would you do me one more favor please? (*He looks straight into the* BEAR's *eyes.*) Would you let me hear your voice again?

BEAR: Ah! So you recognize it! You are right, dear Father! (*He removes his bearskin and stands before them as the handsome* PRINCE.)

KING (*Throwing his arms around him*): My son! My son! I have found you at last! (*He wipes tears from his eyes.*)

PRINCE: Dear, dear Father! I have learned much since that night the dwarfs tied me up in my sleep and carried me off. I have learned a lot about overcoming evil; but luck was with me—or more likely it was your prayers that helped me to overcome my enemy. For when the wicked dwarf-king tried to weave a spell over me, I managed to confuse him, so that he said the wrong rhyme. He intended to change me into a small helpless animal, but instead he turned me into a bear by mistake. (*Laughing*) After that, he was afraid of me himself.

SNOW-WHITE (*Going to him and looking up into his face*): I was sure you were a prince in disguise. I could tell by looking into your eyes.

PRINCE: And I was sure you were a true princess, even if you were not born in a castle. And your family treated me *royally*. (*He bows to* MOTHER *and girls, and ushers them over to the* KING.) Now, Father, shall we take these three loyal subjects to the castle with us?

KING: Of course! Of course! They shall stay with us always.

PRINCE: And may I have your permission to make Snow-White my bride?

KING: You have not only my permission, but my blessing as well. There never will be another bride as beautiful except, of course, her twin. We shall marry Rose-Red to your charming cousin, the minstrel. I understand they are well acquainted already (MINSTREL *steps forward and takes* ROSE-RED's *hand.*)

ROSE-RED (*Smiling shyly*): Then you *are* the merchant! I did not think you noticed me on your visits.

MINSTREL: I have always admired you, my lady.

ROSE-RED: And I, you.

MOTHER: Was ever a mother more fortunate? (*She takes the* KING's *arm and they circle the room, the* PRINCE *and* SNOW-WHITE *following,* ROSE-RED *and the* MINSTREL *next,* ATTENDANTS *last. Music, such as a gavotte, begins offstage, and the couples dance a few steps, and all exit in a stately procession, as the curtain falls.*)

THE END

The City Mouse and the Country Mouse

Characters

COUNTRY MOUSE
CITY MOUSE
CAT
TWO SERVANTS

SETTING: *The home of the* COUNTRY MOUSE.

AT RISE: *The* COUNTRY MOUSE, *in a gingham apron, is sweeping her floor. On her plain little table is spread a simple meal.*

COUNTRY MOUSE (*In sing-song as she sweeps*):

It's good to have a little home along the meadow's edge.

A meadow mouse enjoys a house among the grass and sedge.

It's good to smell the clover bloom a-drifting through the door

When I am airing out my room and sweeping up the floor . . .

(*Her attention is caught by something outside, and she goes to the window, finishing her song as she goes.*)

A country home is very nice

For men, they say, as well as mice . . .

But who's that coming up the lane

This play may easily be adapted for presentation with hand puppets.

All dressed in feathers fine?
As sure as I am Mary Jane
It's Cousin Emmeline!
She's wearing bracelets by the dozen.
She's certainly my richest cousin.
  (*She runs to the door and opens it*)
Come in, come in, dear Emmeline,
You're welcome at this house of mine.
It's very plain, as you can see,
But warm with hospitality . . .
  (CITY MOUSE *enters. She carries a lorgnette and looks
  about critically through it.*)
CITY MOUSE:
  So this is where you live, my dear?
  A rather lonely place, I fear.
COUNTRY MOUSE:
  Oh, no, indeed! I like it here.
  (*She ushers the* CITY MOUSE *to a chair near the win-
  dow.*)
  Sit down and see my lovely view.
  Those mole hills that are always blue
  With distance . . . and that forest, too,
  Of rush and reed . . .
CITY MOUSE:
                    You do not need
  To point things out. It's quite a view,
  But what on earth is there to do
  In such a quiet place as this?
  You really don't know what you miss
  By never having seen the city . . .
COUNTRY MOUSE:
  But surely it is not as pretty
  As this meadow-marsh of mine . . .
  (*Her tone is offended*)
  Come, draw your chair up here and dine

With me. I was about to eat
When you came walking up the street . . .
CITY MOUSE (*Turning up her nose*):
No, thank you. I'm not fond of wheat.
COUNTRY MOUSE (*Holding up a wheat stalk*):
But wheat's a very wholesome grain.
This stalk is sweet, and fresh with rain.
(*She starts toward the door*)
I'll get you some spring water, too,
In acorn cups . . . or, sparkling dew . . .
CITY MOUSE (*Catching hold of her apron pulls her back*):
I'm sure that's very kind of you
But I'm not hungry . . .
COUNTRY MOUSE (*With a sudden burst of anger*):
                        That's not true!
You think my food is much too plain.
I'd like to have you please explain
What city foods are good as grain . . .
CITY MOUSE:
My dear, I do not like to boast
But have you ever tasted roast?
A roast of beef, done to a turn?
And coffee spilling from an urn?
And cheese, and pie, and cake, and fruit?
COUNTRY MOUSE:
But *that's* a banquet cooked to suit
A king . . .
CITY MOUSE: It's just my daily fare.
Dear me! You needn't stand and stare.
I came to take you home to visit . . .
COUNTRY MOUSE (*Dreamily and half to herself*):
Your home must surely be exquisite
If I'm to judge it by your dress.
I've been a simpleton, I guess.

I realize, now, it is a pity
That I have never seen the city.
I have been silly to delight
In simple pleasures, day and night . . .

CITY MOUSE (*Jumping up and taking her by the arm*):
Then you'll come with me?

COUNTRY MOUSE (*Picking up her sunbonnet and moving
with her cousin toward the door*):
                              Yes, indeed,
I'll come and live the life you lead . . .
(*The two exit together as the curtain falls.*)

* * *

SCENE 2

SETTING: *The home of the City Mouse.*
AT RISE: CITY MOUSE *and* COUNTRY MOUSE *enter.*

CITY MOUSE:
Well, here we are! This is my house.
Don't you agree I'm a lucky mouse?

COUNTRY MOUSE (*Looking about her in awe*):
A grander place I never saw!
This carpet's softer to the paw
Than moss could be. And what a nest
This pillow makes when one would rest!
(*She sits down on a cushion and takes off her sun-
bonnet.*)

CITY MOUSE: Come see the food spread on the table. (*She
opens the covered dishes one by one*)
There's cheese . . . and cake . . . and pie . . . and
meat . . .
All that a mouse could wish to eat . . .

COUNTRY MOUSE (*Leaping up and looking over her
shoulder*):

It's like a banquet in a fable . . .
(*She seats herself at the table.*)
Oh what a feast! Do let's begin it.
(*There is a scratching and purring sound outside. The* CITY MOUSE *looks around nervously.*)

CITY MOUSE: Perhaps we'd better wait a minute . . .

COUNTRY MOUSE (*Unaware of danger*):
I think I'll start with this big platter. (*She looks up and sees the other's startled expression*)
You're looking nervous. What's the matter?

CITY MOUSE (*In a terrified whisper*): I thought I heard a purring sound . . .

COUNTRY MOUSE (*Even more frightened*): You mean that there's a cat around? (*Enter* CAT *with a leap.*)

CAT: Meow! Meow! Meow! (*She chases the mice around in a circle. They squeak and squeal. The* CITY MOUSE, *who is at a safer distance from the* CAT, *dodges into a hole or hiding place. The* COUNTRY MOUSE *keeps running and squeaking with the* CAT *gaining upon her.*)

COUNTRY MOUSE:
Help! Help! I know he's going to catch me.
His paw is lifted up to snatch me.
His eyes are fiery as a coal . . .

CITY MOUSE (*Peeking from her hiding place*): Quick! Jump inside this little hole!
(*The* COUNTRY MOUSE *does as she is told, and just in time, too, for the* CAT *pounces, but only succeeds in pulling off the* MOUSE's *apron. The two mice disappear and the* CAT *stands defeated outside the hole.*)

CAT (*Angrily*): Meow! Meow! (*He sits in front of the hole for a moment or two then gets up and walks off in disgust. There is a short silence, then the* CITY MOUSE *pokes her head out of the hole. She looks around cautiously. She tiptoes out of her hiding place and makes sure the coast is clear.*)

CITY MOUSE (*To* COUNTY MOUSE *in a stage whisper*):
  Come out, come out, dear Mary Jane,
  The cat is gone. We're safe again . . .
COUNTRY MOUSE (*Poking her head out of hole, just a little way*):
  Oh no! I am afraid to come.
  My heart is beating like a drum.
CITY MOUSE (*Going to table and starting to nibble at things*):
  Pooh! Don't be silly, come and eat!
  This cheese is tastier than wheat . . .
COUNTRY MOUSE:
  Still, one can never really say
  What cats will do. They're very sly.
CITY MOUSE (*Crossly*): Sit down and have a piece of pie. . . .
COUNTRY MOUSE (*Seating herself gingerly*):
  I've always heard that there was danger
  In the city . . .
CITY MOUSE:
                You're a stranger.
  Give yourself a few short days
  To get used to city ways.
COUNTRY MOUSE (*Half to herself*):
  My! That cat was bold and vicious.
CITY MOUSE (*Trying to divert her*):
  Don't you think this food's delicious?
COUNTRY MOUSE (*Relaxing and nibbling a little*):
  Yes, I never thought I'd taste
  Chocolate creams and almond paste.
CITY MOUSE (*Eating rapidly*):
  Well, my dear, we must make haste . . .
  (*There is a sound of tramping feet offstage.*)
COUNTRY MOUSE (*Alarmed*):
  What was that? The cat again?

CITY MOUSE (*With a sigh*):

No. It's just the serving men . . . (*The sound comes nearer.*)

COUNTRY MOUSE:

But they mustn't find us here.

CITY MOUSE:

No, we'll have to hide, my dear. (*She takes her cousin's hand, and the two run quickly into the hole. Enter* SERVANTS. *They have large trays and begin at once to clear the table. The mice watch them from their hiding place.*)

1ST SERVANT (*Piling things on his tray*):

If we want our evening off,

We must clear this supper table

Just as fast as we are able.

2ND SERVANT (*Bending over to look more closely at the tablecloth*):

Quick, look here; and don't you scoff.

(*He points as he talks*)

Here some syrup has been dribbled.

There, some cake crumbs have been nibbled.

Surely there is not a doubt

That some mice have been about.

Yesterday you wouldn't own it.

1ST SERVANT (*Examining cloth*):

You are right. I should have known it.

We shall have to set a trap—

2ND SERVANT (*Nodding approval*):

One that has a snip and snap . . .

(*At the word "trap" the* MICE *withdraw their heads into the hole fearfully.*)

1ST SERVANT:

There'll be time enough tomorrow . . .

2ND SERVANT:

I'll find one that I can borrow . . .

1ST SERVANT:

Now we must wind up our labors

If we're calling on the neighbors . . .

2ND SERVANT (*As they go out*):

Yes, we'll finish up our labors

And go calling on our neighbors . . .

(SERVANTS *exit with trays. Again there is a short silence then the* COUNTRY MOUSE *comes warily out of the hole. She hurriedly puts on her sunbonnet and the apron, dropped by the* CAT. *The* CITY MOUSE *runs out after her.*)

CITY MOUSE:

But, my dear, you mustn't go.

You've scarcely seen my place, you know . . .

COUNTRY MOUSE (*Hurrying toward door*):

I've seen enough to understand

That there's no place, however grand,

As nice as my own little room

That overlooks the clover bloom.

I'd rather, far, be safe and poor,

Than rich, with danger at my door.

(*She goes out leaving the* CITY MOUSE *amazed, as the curtain falls.*)

THE END

The Hare and the Tortoise

Characters

HARE
FOX
TORTOISE

SETTING: *Stage is empty, except for post at left and bush right.*
AT RISE: HARE *runs in left.*

HARE (*Calling back over her shoulder*):
  Faster, faster, foolish fox,
  Jump the river, leap the rocks,
  Crash the briars, if you dare,
  But you'll never catch the hare . . .
  Ha, ha, ha!
  Ha, ha, ha!
  (*She sits down on a stump, laughing.*)
  Hear him pant! And see him puff!
  (*She peers offstage.*)
  I believe he's had enough
  Running for today. . . .
  (*She cups her paws and calls*)
  Hello!
  Why so tired? Why so slow?

This play may easily be adapted for presentation with hand puppets.

(Fox *enters limping.*)

Fox (*Flopping to the ground*):
    I'll admit I'm tired out.
    You're a swift one, without doubt.
    I can never hope to match you.
    Yet I always try to catch you . . .

HARE (*Rising and strutting about*):
    Is there anyone to match me?
    Even Reynard cannot catch me.
    Hounds and horses all may chase me,
    But there's no one who dares race me.

TORTOISE (*Entering*):
    I dare race you.

HARE (*Looking in every direction, amazed*):
    Who said that? No one's around . . .

TORTOISE:
    Here I am, close to the ground.

HARE:
    A tortoise!

FOX:
    Did you say that you would dare
    To go racing with the hare?

TORTOISE:
    Yes, I said that I would run . . .

HARE:
    But you said it just in fun?

TORTOISE:
    No, I meant it. I will race.
    When you choose the time and place.

Fox (*Tactfully*):
    But every tortoise has, you know,
    A name for being rather slow . . .

HARE (*Laughing scornfully*):
    Rather slow? Oh, do not bother
    To put in a word like "rather."

Fox:

> Even I can't catch this rabbit
> Though I have the chasing habit,
> Though I'm noted as a chaser,
> How can any slow poke race her?

Hare (*To* Tortoise):

> And you are the slowest poke! . . .

Fox:

> What you ask must be a joke . . .

Tortoise:

> What I ask is not in fun.
> I really do intend to run.

Hare:

> Very well, then, I will race you
> Though I don't like to disgrace you.
> When you find yourself the loser,
> Just remember you were chooser.

Fox:

> Would either one of you two grudge
> Me the job of being judge?

Hare:

> No, indeed. You'd better pace
> Off the course that we're to race.

Fox (*Indicating post, left*):

> Shall we use this little pole
> Both for starting-place and goal?

Tortoise (*Nodding*):

> Yes, that's just the proper pole
> For a starting-place, and goal . . .

Fox (*Pointing to bush at extreme right of stage*):

> Then you two can run and rush
> From this post up to that bush;
> Skirt the bush along its edge
> And come back around the hedge . . .

HARE:
  Yes, we two can run and rush
  From this post up to that bush.
TORTOISE:
  We can skirt the bush's edge
  And come back around the hedge . . .
Fox (*In a self-satisfied manner*):
  So the course is set for racing
  Without bothering with pacing.
HARE (*To the* TORTOISE):
  Have you had a change of heart?
TORTOISE:
  Not at all. When do we start?
Fox:
  Right away. I'll give the word.
HARE (*Aside*):
  All of this is so absurd!
  (HARE *and* TORTOISE *line up beside the* Fox, *at the post.*)
Fox (*Importantly*): Get ready. Get on your mark. Get
  set. Go! (*The two racers dart forward. But the* HARE
  is at the other end of the stage before the TORTOISE *has
  taken half a dozen steps. To* TORTOISE, *with a laugh*):
  It looks as though you're left behind.
  I'll sit down, if you don't mind . . .
  (*He takes a book out of his pocket*)
  While you're occupied with speeding
  I will have some time for reading.
  (*He buries his nose in the book while the* TORTOISE
  plods on and says nothing. HARE *moves to far side of
  bush, right, in view of the audience, but the* Fox *and*
  TORTOISE *cannot see her.*)
HARE:
  What's the use of all this running
  When I need a little sunning?

I can hop the course twice over
And still rest upon this clover
While the turtle's getting started.
(*She sits down and makes herself comfortable.*)
I am glad, now, that I darted
Far ahead—
Where the clover
Makes a bed,
Where the softest grass is growing,
Where mayhap
I can take
A little nap
Without their knowing.
(*She yawns, stretches and finally falls asleep.*)

Fox:

Here's a poem in this book
That is worth a second look.
(*He reads aloud as the* Tortoise *plods nearer and nearer to the bush.*)
The ears of the rabbit go "flippity-floppity."
The eyes of the rabbit go "pippity-poppity."
The feet of the rabbit go "hippity-hoppity."
Over the hill at the "tippity-toppity."
(*He chuckles and turns a page.*)
Here's one on the Tortoise:
A turtle's house is his own shell.
And why? It is not hard to tell;
For shell-less turtles could not roam.
They'd be too long in getting home . . .
(*He laughs heartily, then settles down to read in silence, as* Tortoise *reaches the bush.*)

Tortoise (*Skirting the bush and seeing the* Hare):

Why, who is this? . . . Oh, I declare!
It is my friend the bragging Hare!
Sleep well, my beauty, while I go

Around the bush on tippy-toe.
A footstep's safer when it's slow.
(*He disappears behind the hedge.*)
Fox (*Standing and stretching, then looking about*):
At last old Tortoise-shell is gone.
He's swallowed up by grass and lawn.
But what's delaying Mistress Bunny?
She's not here yet, and that is funny.
Oh, well, there's lots of time for her!
She's probably smoothing out her fur.
I'll read some more. I mustn't budge
From this goal post, since I'm the judge.
(*He again flips the pages of his book.*)
Here's something really very fitting,
After an article on "Sitting"
There's one on how to win a race
(*He drops the book.*)
Oh, dear! I've gone and lost my place.
(*He picks up the book and spends some time hunting
through it.*)
Ah, here it is! Page fifty-nine.
It's really only just a line.
(*He reads.*)
"The art of racing is a gift.
Victory, though it may shift,
Is not always to the swift . . ."
Tortoise (*In a loud voice, from behind hedge*):
"Victory, though it may shift,
Is not always to the swift . . ."
(*Enter* Tortoise. *He waddles forward toward the goal*)
Hare (*Awakening suddenly*):
What was that? The turtle's voice!
I must rush. I have no choice.
Look at him! Upon my soul!
He is almost at the goal.

(HARE *leaps the bush and runs behind the hedge, emerging at the far end, left, just as the* TORTOISE *touches the goal post.*)

Oh, this is a deep disgrace!

Fox (*Shaking hands with* TORTOISE *warmly*):

Slow and steady wins the race!

(*Curtain*)

THE END

The Lion and the Mouse

Characters

LION
MOUSE

TIME: *Any day, any month, any year.*
SETTING: *A woodsy place. A net is caught in the bushes.*
AT RISE: LION *enters left.*

LION (*Looking about*):
　Oh, for a nap in the jungle shade!
　Much too long on the plains I've stayed.
　Fine is my coat, but it's furry and hot,
　And I'd like to be where the sun is not.
　(*He finds a comfortable couch of grass.*)
　Here is a grassy bed for me
　With a vine overhead for a canopy.
　(*He settles himself comfortably, paws stretched out in front of him.*)
　Oh, let him tremble and let him weep
　Who dares disturb the lion in sleep!
　(*He yawns and closes his eyes. The* MOUSE *enters.*)
MOUSE (*Dancing about stage on tiptoe*):
　When a mousey starts a-dancing through the wildwood
　　on her toes,

This play may easily be adapted for presentation with hand puppets.

When a mousey goes a-prancing, in her childhood, no
one knows

That she passes through the grasses, for so quietly she
goes!

When a mousey starts a-dancing and a-prancing on her
toes.

(*As she dances, she circles nearer and nearer to the* LION
without seeing him.)

When a mousey starts a-leaping

She disturbs no one who's sleeping,

For she does the high jump nightly

And she practices it lightly,

Till she's really very sprightly

In her dancing and her leaping

And disturbs no one who's sleeping.

(*As she chants the last two lines she runs right across
the* LION's *paw.*)

LION (*Angrily*): What? What's that?

MOUSE (*Terrified*): Help! Help! (*She tries to run away,
but he holds her back with his paw.*)

LION (*Fiercely*):

Who dares disturb this kingly beast

Shall turn into a kingly feast . . .

MOUSE (*Pleadingly*):

No! Spare me, spare me, monarch royal!

I did not mean to be disloyal

Or disrespectful to your highness;

I'm truly noted for my shyness

And never would have been so bold

As to come near, had I been told

That you were sleeping in the jungle.

I really didn't mean to bungle.

I didn't see your outstretched paw . . .

LION: Then, it's surely time you saw it! (*He lifts paw
threateningly.*)

MOUSE (*Shrinking and trembling*):
>I pray you do not strike me.
>If you but knew me, you would like me.
>Please save my life, and when I'm braver,
>Some day I shall return the favor.

LION (*Now holding onto her with both paws*):
>Ha, ha! Ho, ho! My, what a joke!
>I never knew a mouse who spoke
>Of saving lions. That's absurd—
>The funniest thing I ever heard.
>(*He roars with laughter.*)

MOUSE (*Hurt*):
>My promise does not call for mirth.
>Strange things may happen on this earth.
>My mother taught me from my birth
>That even mice may be of worth . . .

LION:
>Well, I shall lift my giant paws
>And free you. But it's not because
>I think you'll ever be of use
>To one like me. . . . I've no excuse
>For letting such a silly go,
>Except that you're so small, you know,
>And I am much too tenderhearted.
>(*He releases her.*)
>There! Run along. It's time we parted.

MOUSE:
>Oh, thank you, thank you, gracious king!
>Your kindness is a noble thing
>As sure as there is sun and shade
>Within this wood, you'll be repaid.
>(MOUSE *rushes off.*)

LION (*Yawning and stretching*):
>I guess I'd better move along.
>(*He gets up.*)

The thrush begins its evensong,
The sunlight wanes. The shadows throng.
It will be time for hunting soon,
I hope there'll be a hunter's moon.
(*He starts to exit, right, but gets caught in the net.*)
Oh, what is this? I'm in a tangle.
(*He rolls over and gets more tangled.*)
I'm going to choke. I'm going to strangle.
I must be caught within a net,
A dreadful trap that men have set.
(*He roars as he struggles.*)
The more I pull, the tighter yet
These knotted strings and meshes get.
(Mouse *enters cautiously.*)

MOUSE:

Oh, did I hear the lion roaring
As though in pain? Or was he snoring?

LION (*Moaning*):

Take care, take care, and don't come near,
You foolish mouse! There's danger here.
I'm caught within a trapper's net
And there's not been a lion yet
Who could outwit the trapper man . . .

MOUSE:

Well, then, perhaps a mousey can.
(*She runs forward and examines the net.*)
Ah, well and good, it's made of rope . . .

LION:

And how can that fact give me hope?

MOUSE:

Because a rope will break with gnawing,
And my sharp teeth are made for sawing.
Now stop your struggling and your pawing . . .
(*She settles herself to gnaw the rope.*)

LION:

Could it be that a little mouse
Can free me from this prison-house
Of rope and string and knotted cord
Without a scissors or a sword?
(*He sighs.*)
Oh, no, there are too many ropes
For you to gnaw, I have no hopes . . .
In all this time you've gnawed but one.
The men will come before you're done.

MOUSE (*Holding up the severed rope proudly*):

One rope's enough, when it's a drawstring.
(*She pulls it out.*)
Let's see you do a little paw spring.
(*She unwraps the whole net easily now.*)

LION (*Leaping to freedom*):

See! I am free, quite free at last.
The rope no longer holds me fast;
And I no longer shall despise
Another creature for his size.

LION *and* MOUSE (*Joining hands and dancing offstage together*):

Oh, do not judge your friends in haste!
A kindness never goes to waste.
(*Curtain*)

THE END

The Storyteller's House

(A reading for Two Choruses, *reading alternately, and then in unison for last stanza.)*

1st Chorus:

In a clearing of the wildwood
   Where the pheasant and the grouse
Live together (fur and feather)
   With the rabbit and the mouse—
In a clearing of the wildwood
   Stands the Storyteller's house.

2nd Chorus:

It's a shabby little dwelling
   With an old and creaking stair,
With broken, crooked windows
   That perhaps one day were square.
The smoke curls from its chimney
   Like a lock of straying hair.

1st Chorus:

It's a shabby little dwelling
   But it has a friendly look,
And the people who live in it,
   From the mistress to the cook,
Sleep beneath a strange enchantment
   In the pages of a book.

2ND CHORUS:

    They're the queerest, quaintest people
        Who've been living there for ages:
    Salty seamen, weathered rustics,
        Knights and yeomen, fools and sages.
    You have only to address them
        To release them from their pages.

ALL:

    Oh, let us find the clearing
        Where the pheasant and the grouse
    Live together (fur and feather)
        With the rabbit and the mouse!
    Let us waken all the dwellers
        Of the Storyteller's house.

Between Book Covers

Here are the things that every child sees:
Dragonflies, pixies, bumbling bees,
Springtime and windtime, snow drops and stars,
Freight trains and airplanes, buses and cars;
Castles and brownies, smokestacks and sails—
The world is just bursting with wonderful tales,
Things you'll remember at think-about time
When a little night breeze sings a go-to-sleep rhyme.
Things you'll remember from breakfast to tea
That is, if you've once found the wonderful key
To the storybook house with its magical spells
Where the teller of tales in the quietude dwells.
Come see what enchanting rhyme-stories she tells!
COME! OPEN THE BOOK . . .

Books

I love my books
　They are the homes
Of queens and fairies,
　Knights and gnomes.
Each time I read I make a call
On some quaint person large or small
　Who welcomes me with hearty hand
　And leads me through his wonderland.

Each book is like
　A city street
Along whose winding
　Way I meet
New friends and old who laugh and sing
And take me off adventuring.

The Beaded Moccasins

Characters

RUTH
JONATHAN } *Pilgrim children*
INDIAN BOY
INDIANS
PILGRIMS

BEFORE RISE: *A group of* INDIANS *and* PILGRIMS *may enter before the curtain and sing Thanksgiving songs.*

* * *

TIME: *Just before the first Thanksgiving.*
SETTING: *A glade in the forest at the edge of a marshland.*
AT RISE: RUTH *and* JONATHAN, *two Pilgrim children, are busy preparing for the great feast day.* JONATHAN *is gathering sticks and tying them into bundles at left.* RUTH *is picking berries along the edge of the bog, right.*

JONATHAN:
Oh, what a feast it's going to be!
I'm proud that I am living
In such a place as Plymouth Town

To join the glad Thanksgiving.

RUTH:

Yes, what a feast it's going to be!
For grain has grown abundantly
And fruit has ripened on the tree.
With such a harvest there must be
A day of glad Thanksgiving.

JONATHAN:

Our mother has laid down her spindle
And tends the gaily bubbling kettle.
My twigs will be used to kindle
Fires beneath the caldron's metal.

(*He piles up his bundles of twigs.*)

RUTH (*Showing her pail of berries*):

And all these berries I will toss
Into the pot to boil for sauce.
They'll let us stir the pot, I hope.
I've stirred it often making soap.

JONATHAN (*Contemptuously*):

Making soap! A silly pastime!
Let me tell you for the last time
Work that girls do makes me smile.
It's boys who do the things worthwhile.
I won't stay home and use a ladle,
That's for babies in the cradle.
I go with Father hunting turkey
On mornings when it's raw and murky.
I spot the gobbler's head of flame
And help to carry home the game.

(*He swaggers about.*)

RUTH (*Hurt*):

But making soap's worthwhile, we've seen;
How else would all of us keep clean?

(*She takes a cake of soap from her apron pocket.*)

See! Here's a piece I made myself.

It's smooth as any on the shelf
That Mother made.

JONATHAN:

That may be true;
But I'll leave soap making to you.
I've more important things to do.

RUTH (*Sitting down on log*):

Oh, dear! You always make me feel
That girls are not of any use.
I'm sick of hearing such a thing.
I'm sick of teasing and abuse.

JONATHAN:

Don't tell me you're afraid of teasing!

RUTH (*Sobbing*):

You might try harder to be pleasing . . .

JONATHAN (*Sitting beside her*):

Oh, very well, I'll start in trying,
But it is I who should be crying . . .

RUTH (*Wiping her eyes on her apron and looking at him in surprise*):

And what have you to cry about?

JONATHAN:

Oh, nothing. You can't help me out.

RUTH (*Insistently*):

But what's the trouble you are facing?

JONATHAN (*Sadly*):

I cannot join the games or racing.
On feast day when the feast is done
And games and racing have begun
I cannot race. I cannot run.

RUTH:

But why? You are more swift and light
Than any Pilgrim boy your height.

JONATHAN (*Looking down at his feet*):

It's these old shoes, so thin and worn!

They've even lost their buckles;
(*He examines soles of the shoes.*)
And in the soles are lots of holes
As big around as knuckles . . .

RUTH:

But Father ordered you some shoes.
As nice a pair as you could choose.

JONATHAN:

They'll not be made by feasting day.
The shoemaker was called away
And won't be back in time, they say.

RUTH:

Oh, dear! Oh, dear! That's dreadful news!
If only you could wear my shoes!
But mine are not at all your size . . .

JONATHAN:

I wanted so to win the prize!
(*They both look dejected. A sudden swishing sound and
a loud "kerplunk" are heard offstage, right, then a
groan.*)

RUTH *and* JONATHAN (*Together, starting to their feet*):

What was that?
(*They rush to the edge of the bog, right, and look offstage*)

RUTH (*Shading her eyes with her hand*):

Can you see anything?

JONATHAN:

An Indian's stuck in that deep bog!

RUTH:

He must have tumbled from that log.

JONATHAN:

Quick! There's no time to call our folks.
Let's get him out before he chokes.
(*They rush offstage right. Shouting and commotion are
heard from offstage. Then, RUTH and JONATHAN re-*

enter, leading INDIAN BOY *between them. He is covered with mud.*)

INDIAN BOY: Ugh, ugh! Glug, glug!

(*They prop him against a tree. He coughs and sputters and tries to wipe the mud from his face.*)

JONATHAN (*Encouragingly*):

You'll be all right in just a minute.

That bog has too much mire in it.

INDIAN BOY:

Me catch 'em frog.

Me slip on log. Me fall in bog.

(RUTH *takes off her apron and uses it to wipe* INDIAN BOY'*s hands and face.*)

RUTH:

Oh, dear! This mud's such sticky stuff

A wiping won't be half enough . . .

INDIAN BOY (*Looking at his dirty hands in despair*):

No come off. White man scoff,

No can go to white man's feast . . .

RUTH (*Reassuringly*):

I will get you clean. At least

I have some soap to try

To wash you with—then you can dry.

(*To* JONATHAN, *as she empties berries from pail, and hands pail to him.*)

If you'll get water from the stream,

We'll make this soap a foamy cream.

JONATHAN (*Taking pail, and starting off*):

I'll bring you water you can use.

(*Wistfully*)

It's easier than finding shoes.

(*He goes offstage, left.*)

INDIAN BOY (*To* RUTH):

What him say about his shoes?

RUTH:

They're too old for games and racing,
Much too worn for tag and chasing.
So on feast day half his fun
Will be spoiled. He cannot run.

INDIAN BOY:

Me no fun. Redskins shun . . .
White men scoff till mud come off.

RUTH:

You'll not have to wait, I say,
Till this mud all wears away.
I will wash it off today.
(JONATHAN *re-enters, carrying pail.*)
See! My brother brings the pail.

JONATHAN:

Soap and water never fail . . .
(*He and* RUTH *begin scrubbing the* INDIAN BOY *with soap and water, using their kerchiefs for washcloths. As they work they sing to the tune of "Here We Go Round the Mulberry Bush."*)

JONATHAN AND RUTH (*Singing*):

Now we get ready for Thanksgiving Day
Thanksgiving Day,
Thanksgiving Day,
Now we get ready for Thanksgiving Day
Both with a scrubbing and rubbing.

INDIAN BOY (*Beating tom-tom at his waist*):

And with a rub-a-dub-dubbing.

JONATHAN (*Singing*):

Now, we get ready for feasting and play
Feasting and play,
Feasting and play,
Now we get ready for feasting and play,
All with a rub-a-dub-dubbing.

INDIAN BOY (*Beating tom-tom*):

All with a rub-a-dub-dubbing.

RUTH:

Now you're clean again and neat

From your head down to your feet.

INDIAN BOY (*Proudly, as he looks at clean hands, etc.*):

White man magic makes 'em clean,

Strangest magic ever seen.

(*He dances about happily, beating tom-tom.*)

Water, water not enough,

White man make a magic stuff . . .

RUTH:

"Soap" it's called. I'll give it to you.

(*She hands him the cake of soap.*)

INDIAN BOY (*Delighted*):

Magic, magic all for Redskin!

(*He puts the soap into his pouch.*)

For the pale face, strings of wampum . . .

(*He takes a string of shells from his own neck and puts it around* RUTH's.)

For the white brave, shoes of doeskin . . .

(*He takes off his moccasins and hands them to* JONA-THAN, *who takes them, hesitating.*)

I have others. White boy take them.

JONATHAN (*Putting on moccasins*):

Now I'll race and now I'll run,

Now I'll join in all the fun.

I will never blame, I hope,

Anyone for making soap.

(*He takes* RUTH *by the hand and whirls her around.* INDIAN BOY *dances about.*)

RUTH:

In the race you're bound to win

When you wear a moccasin.

INDIAN BOY (*Looking offstage, right, as drums sound*):

Redskins coming! Tom-toms drumming.

RUTH (*Looking offstage, left*):
All the fathers and the mothers,
All the Pilgrim sisters, brothers,
Come unto this place of meeting.
Come to give the Redskins greeting,
For they hear the tom-toms beating.
(PILGRIMS *enter from right,* INDIANS *from left.* INDIANS *circle around children with the characteristic Indian dance step.* PILGRIMS *march solemnly around* INDIANS, *singing Thanksgiving song, as the curtain falls.*)

THE END

Fire-Face and the Indians

Characters

PATIENCE ⎱ *two little Pilgrim girls*
PRUDENCE ⎰
INDIANS

TIME: *Early Colonial days.*
SETTING: *The kitchen of a log cabin.*
AT RISE: PATIENCE *holds a large ladle, with which she is stirring the great iron kettle that hangs in the fireplace up center.* PRUDENCE *is looking out the window at right of the fireplace. Her sampler lies on a chair near by.*

PRUDENCE:
   Oh, Patience, it is almost dusk!
   The dry corn rattles in the husk.
   Is it the dry corn on the stalk,
   Or is it whispered talk—
   Indian talk?
PATIENCE (*Pausing to glance out the window*):
   Indian talk? It's no such thing!
   No Redskin has been seen since spring.
PRUDENCE (*Not seeming to hear*):
   The dry leaves running, dry and thin,

This play may easily be adapted for presentation with hand puppets.

Run lightly as a moccasin.
The red leaves rising high together,
Bob through the corn fields like a feather.
I really can't tell whether
It is a leaf or feather.

PATIENCE:

It's my belief
It's just a leaf.
I wish you wouldn't worry so.
No Indians have been seen, you know . . .

PRUDENCE:

Since spring. I know.
It's twice that you have told me so.

PATIENCE:

They've been off hunting for a season.

PRUDENCE:

But isn't that the very reason
They may be coming back again
To winter near the white men?
They're tired of hunting and they'd rather
Rob an honest Pilgrim Father.

PATIENCE (*Going to window and looking out over* PRU-
DENCE's *shoulder*):

There's nothing in the fields but snow,
And nobody could come or go
Without a footprint or a track.
Our parents, too, will soon be back.

PRUDENCE:

They said they would be home by night,
Before we needed candlelight.

PATIENCE:

Then they'll be coming any minute.
Oh, dear! My pot still has soap in it.
I'll have to climb up on a stool
And pour it into crocks to cool.

You, too, had better finish working;
Our mother must not find us shirking.

PRUDENCE:

But I'm so tired of sampler stitches!
My thread all tangles up and twitches
As though it were bewitched by witches.

PATIENCE (*Going to chair and picking up sampler*):

Yet surely you are nearly through;
The last time that I saw it, you
Had only just a bit to do.
Oh, my! For shame!
There's just your name.

PRUDENCE:

Yes, I suppose I'd really better
Finish up the last, last letter.

PATIENCE (*Encouragingly*):

And if you finish very soon,
Before the rising of the moon,
Before blue shadows turn to black,
I'll show you how to make a jack.

PRUDENCE (*Clapping her hands in delight*):

A jack-o'-lantern? Oh, what fun!
I'll hurry up and soon be done.
(*Both girls work quickly, one sewing, the other ladling
the hot soap into crocks to cool. After a little while,
PRUDENCE looks up from her sewing.*)
Tell me, Patience, just how is it
You learned so much on one short visit
To Granny's house down Salem way?
I want to visit there some day.

PATIENCE:

Well, Granny's full of tales and rhymes
Of England in the olden times,
Because she lived there once, you know!
It must have been long, long ago.

PRUDENCE:
  And did she say she'd really seen
  A witch or two on Halloween?
PATIENCE:
  No. That she did not truly say.
  She said she kept witches away
  By carrying jacks, all candlelighted;
  Of them the witches are affrighted.
  She even said there was a scare
  In Salem town of witches there.
PRUDENCE:
  Well, witches aren't the thing I fear,
  And Salem town is far from here.
  It's Indians that I'm afraid of.
PATIENCE:
  But every Pilgrim must be made of
  Courage. That's what Father preaches.
PRUDENCE (*Sighing*):
  It's hard to be all that he teaches.
  If we were only Pilgrim boys!
  (*The face of an* INDIAN *suddenly appears at the window.
  The audience sees it, but the children do not. It disap-
  pears, as* PRUDENCE *looks around.*)
  Hark! Did you hear that stealthy noise?
  A noise of someone tippy-toeing?
PATIENCE:
  It's just an early night wind blowing.
  (*She puts down the ladle and takes off her apron.*)
  There! I am finished with my soap.
  Our mother will be pleased, I hope.
PRUDENCE:
  And I am through with sampler-making.
  My fingers and my eyes are aching.
PATIENCE:
  Well, we can make our lanterns now.

PRUDENCE (*Eagerly*):
  Yes, show me how. Quick! Show me how.
PATIENCE:
  I'll get the pumpkins from their places
  And we will carve them into faces.
  (*She brings out two hollowed-out pumpkins and two table knives from the cupboard, and the girls sit on the floor down center, each holding a pumpkin and a knife.* NOTE: *The pumpkins may be already carved, and the faces kept hidden until the girls finish working on them. Each pumpkin also contains a pencil flashlight which is switched on when the girls "light" them.*)
  Just yesterday I scooped them hollow.
  See! I will start, and you must follow.
  (*She begins to carve.*)
  I'll make an eye.
PRUDENCE (*Carving*):
  I'll make another.
PATIENCE:
  I'll carve a nose;
  You carve its brother.
PRUDENCE:
  And while we're carving, will you say
  The rhyme you taught me yesterday,
  The one with jack-o'-lanterns in it?
PATIENCE:
  You finish it, and I'll begin it:
  (*Reciting in sing-song*)
  "If a goblin comes a-hobblin'
  Down the street, street, street,
  And he's not the kind of goblin
  You would meet, meet, meet,
  Make a frightful jack-o'-lantern
  Of a pumpkin or a gourd,

For a goblin is more frightened
Of a lantern than a sword."

PRUDENCE (*Reciting*):

"If the witches from their ditches
Should hop out, out, out,
Do not be so scared you turn
Yourself about, 'bout, 'bout.
Light your jack-o'-lantern candle,
Hold the lantern by the handle,
And you'll put the naughty witches
All to rout, rout, rout.
And you'll put the naughty witches
All to rout."

PATIENCE (*Putting her carved pumpkin down on the floor
and getting to her feet*):

There, mine is done.
And such a fierce one!
(*She looks at it proudly.*)

PRUDENCE (*Holding hers at arm's length*):

Won't Father laugh and Mother smile
To see these lighted in a while?

PATIENCE:

I wish they'd come. I cannot wait.
(*She walks over to the window and looks out.*)
It's getting very dark and late.
(*She turns toward* PRUDENCE, *suddenly frightened.*)
Prudence, Prudence! Come and see
A sight that truly frightens me!

PRUDENCE (*Running to window and looking out*):

Footprints on the thin white snow!
They were not there a while ago.
(*The two girls look at one another in dismay.*)

PATIENCE *and* PRUDENCE (*Together*):

Indians!

PATIENCE:

    Oh, you were right! There was a scout
    Hid in the cornfield. He's found out
    Our father is not home today . . .
    The Redskins know that he's away!

PRUDENCE:

    Oh, Patience! Redskins! And we two
    Are all alone! What shall we do?

PATIENCE:

    I'll get the musket, since I'm bigger
    And know just how to pull the trigger.
    You get the ax and quickly bring it.
    Stand there beside the door and swing it.
    (They go to the corner where the musket and ax are,
    and try to lift them, but they can only drag them along
    the floor.)
    Oh, dear! I cannot lift this gun,
    And Father has the smaller one.

PRUDENCE:

    And I can never swing this ax.

PATIENCE *and* PRUDENCE *(Together)*:

    The both of us will break our backs.

PRUDENCE *(Dragging the ax back to its corner)*:

    We'd better hide these things away.

PATIENCE *(Hiding the musket)*:

    We can't do anything but pray.

PRUDENCE:

    If it were only witches coming,
    Instead of Redskins with their drumming,
    Then we could scare them with a jack
    So they would nevermore come back.

PATIENCE *(Interrupting quickly)*:

    Why, Prudence! That's the very thing!
    Come here. Let's do some whispering.

(*They whisper together. Then they pretend to take a lighted stick from the fire and "light" the jack-o'-lanterns. When the jack-o'-lanterns are lighted, the girls crouch down on either side of the window, each one holding a pumpkin. There is a sound outside.*)

PRUDENCE:

They're coming, now. I'm sure I hear them.

PATIENCE:

We must be brave. We must not fear them.

(*Three or four* INDIANS *appear suddenly at the window.*)

Now!

(*She raises her lantern above the sill, so that the face of the jack-o'-lantern faces the* INDIANS. *At the same time, she makes a loud, ghostly wail.*)

Owwwwwww!

INDIANS (*Drawing back*):

E—ow!

Fire-face! Fire-face!

PRUDENCE (*Lifting her jack-o'-lantern to face* INDIANS):

Owwwwwww!

INDIANS:

Two fire-faces! E—ow! E—ow! E—ow!

(*The* INDIANS *run away screaming, and the little girls peep out the window after them. Then they throw their arms around each other.*)

PATIENCE:

Safe! We are safe! They've gone away.

PRUDENCE (*Half-laughing, half-crying*):

They won't be back again today!

PATIENCE (*Pointing out the window in the opposite direction from the fleeing* INDIANS):

And see! Our father's drawing near,

And Mother, too. They'll soon be here.

PRUDENCE:
   Just wait until they hear about
   How we put Indians to rout!
   (*They go to door left, open it, waiting as the curtain falls.*)

THE END

A Thanksgiving Pageant

Characters

SPIRIT OF THE HARVEST
FARM LASS
FARM LAD
HUNTSMAN
FISHERMAN
BOY
GIRL

NOTE: *If a larger cast is desired, there may be several Farm Lasses and Lads, Huntsmen and Fishermen, and Boys and Girls. A leader should be chosen to speak for each group.*

SETTING: *The stage is decorated with autumn leaves, corn shocks, fruit, flowers, pumpkins, etc.*

AT RISE: *The* SPIRIT OF THE HARVEST *is standing in the center at the back, between two tables. The characters enter, two at a time—one from the left, one from the right. They join hands, down center, and walk slowly toward the* SPIRIT OF THE HARVEST, *offering her their gifts. She accepts the gifts and places them on the tables. The characters then take places, one on each side of the* SPIRIT OF THE HARVEST, *to make room for the next pair that enters.* FARM LASS *enters, carrying a small basket of apples.* FARM BOY *enters, carrying an ear of corn.*

SPIRIT OF THE HARVEST:

What do you bring to the harvest feast,
    O farmer lad, O farmer lass?
What do you bring to the harvest feast,
    When the harvest moon is waning?

FARM LAD:

I bring an ear of the golden corn
    Of the ripened corn, of the rustling corn.

FARM LASS:

I bring a basket of apples red
    To match the moon that's waning.

(*The* HUNTSMAN *and* FISHERMAN *enter. The* HUNTSMAN *carries a bow and arrow, and a bag supposedly containing game. The* FISHERMAN *carries a spear or net and a fish.*)

SPIRIT OF THE HARVEST:

What do you bring to the bounteous board,
    O huntsman brave, O fisherman fair?
What do you bring to the bounteous board
    To add to the glad Thanksgiving?

HUNTSMAN:

I bring a bag of the feathered game—
    A mallard duck, a turkey wild.

FISHERMAN:

I bring a fish from the foaming stream
    To add to the glad Thanksgiving.

(GIRL *and* BOY *enter next. She carries some autumn leaves. He carries a stalk of cattail.*)

SPIRIT OF THE HARVEST:

What do you bring from the meadow and marsh,
    O wandering girl, O wandering boy?
What do you bring from the fiery woods
    To deck the festive table?

GIRL:

I bring an armful of autumn leaves

Of maple-gold, of sumac-red—

BOY:

I bring a stalk of the cattail brown
To deck the festive table.

ALL (*Together*):

Praise to the sun and the rain, who freed
The yearning plant from the close, dark seed;
Who stretched to a stalk the tiny shoot,
Who coaxed the flower into the fruit—
Who filled the pod and gilded the grain
And brought us to harvest time again.

THE END

If I Were a Pilgrim Child

(The first three CHILDREN *may be dressed as Pilgrims. The last three wear modern clothes and may hold objects they mention—cranberries, turkey on a platter, etc.)*

1ST CHILD:

    If I were a Pilgrim child,
        Dressed in white or gray,
    I should catch my turkey wild
        For Thanksgiving Day.

2ND CHILD:

    I should pick my cranberries
        Fresh from out a bog,
    And make a table of a stump
        And sit upon a log.

3RD CHILD:

    An Indian would be my guest
        And wear a crimson feather,
    And we should clasp our hands and say
        Thanksgiving grace together.

4TH CHILD:

    But we were born in modern times
        And shall not have this joy.

Our cranberries will be delivered
   By the grocery boy.

5TH CHILD:
   My turkey will be served upon
     A shining silver platter.
   It will not taste as wild game tastes
     Though it will be much fatter.

6TH CHILD:
   And, oh, of all the guests that come,
     Not one of them will wear
   Moccasins upon his feet
     Or feathers in his hair.

Thanksgiving Magic

1ST CHILD:
Thanksgiving Day I like to see
Our cook perform her witchery.
She turns a pumpkin into pie
As easily as you or I
Can wave a hand or wink an eye.

2ND CHILD:
She takes leftover bread and muffin
And changes them to turkey stuffin'.
She changes cranberries to sauce
And meats to stews and stews to broths.

3RD CHILD:
And when she mixes gingerbread,
It turns into a man instead
With frosting collar 'round his throat
And raisin buttons down his coat.

4TH CHILD:
Oh, some like magic made by wands,
    And some read magic out of books,
And some like fairy spells and charms
    But I like magic made by cooks!

In Pilgrim Days

In Pilgrim Days the little girls wore gowns of homespun
gray
So long they almost trailed the ground when they went out
to play.

They wore white kerchiefs round their necks and caps to
catch their curls.
They dressed as grown-up women dressed, though they
were only girls.

In Pilgrim Days the little boys wore black hats, widely
brimmed,
And flapping capes and buckled shoes. Their tight gray
coats were trimmed

With cuffs and collars stiff and neat. It must have been a
bother,
When one of them went out to play, to be dressed up like
Father.

Oh, Pilgrim Days are past and gone and will not come
again,
And children dress like children now, and not like grown-
up men.

Talking Turkey

(This may be done in pantomime with a READER *and two boys taking the parts of the* INDIAN *and the* PILGRIM, *dressed appropriately.)*

Charles Sawyer was a Pilgrim lad
   Who, feeling very perky
One misty day, set out to hunt
   The wild New England turkey.
He scurried through the brush and bog
And hid himself behind a log;
And there he made a scratchy-squawk
   That sounded much like turkey talk.

An Indian, with colored feather,
That very morning wondered whether
He, too, could catch some gobbler game
And through the selfsame woods he came.
On hands and knees, instead of walking,
He crept, and also made a squawking
Till he and Charlie—calling, talking
Back and forth with gibberish word—
Each thought the other was a bird;
And, as they sought each other's place
Of hiding, they came face to face.
Then shots that might have followed after
Were changed to sudden peals of laughter.

The Indian, though just a grunter,
Told Charlie he was quite a hunter;
And Charlie, signing with his hand,
Soon made the red man understand
He much admired his decoying.
So off they went, those two, enjoying
Their little joke; and when a jerky
Wattled head peered through the murky
Morning at them, each cried, "Turkey!"
The quiet bowshot and the louder
Gunshot with its smell of powder
Brought the bird down in a minute
An arrow and a bullet in it.

Then such a feast the hunters had
Beside the fire! Lad and lad
Forgetting they were enemies
Among the wood anemones.
The fun soon led to friendly living
And to the Pilgrims' first Thanksgiving.

The Shoemaker and the Elves

Characters

SHOEMAKER
SHOEMAKER'S WIFE
GENTLEMAN
TWO ELVES

TIME: *A winter evening of long ago.*
SETTING: *The Shoemaker's shop.*
AT RISE: *The* SHOEMAKER *is sitting at his bench, working on leather for a shoe.* SHOEMAKER'S WIFE *enters, bringing two crusts of bread on a plate.*

WIFE (*Passing bread to* SHOEMAKER):
　　Shoemaker, Shoemaker, what shall we do?
　　We've nothing to eat but a bread crust or two.
　　The pantry is empty, and so is our purse.
　　We soon will be starving, and what could be worse?
SHOEMAKER (*Sighing as he takes one of the crusts*):
　　Yes, most folks are feasting. It's hard to believe
　　We only have bread crusts on Christmas Eve.
　　We've nothing at all we can market or use,
　　But just enough leather for one pair of shoes.

WIFE:

We're poorer than church mice who live in a pew.

O Shoemaker, Shoemaker, what shall we do?

SHOEMAKER (*Rising*):

I've done what I can. I've cut out the leather;

And early tomorrow we'll get up together.

We'll pound with the hammer; we'll sew with the thread.

We'll have the shoes done when folks get out of bed.

Then maybe some neighbor will come in to try them.

WIFE:

What good will that do us if no one will *buy* them?

And who will come shopping St. Nicholas Day?

At Christmastime people think only of play.

SHOEMAKER (*Moving toward door right, his* WIFE *following*):

We'll pray for God's help as we go now to rest.

WIFE:

But what of tomorrow?

SHOEMAKER:

We'll hope for the best.

(*They both go out right, eating their crusts. The room gets darker and there is a sound of music offstage—light, elfin music.* ELVES *enter left, skipping and running. They prance about for a few moments, climbing on the empty shelves, peeking over and under everything. At last, they leap up on the* SHOEMAKER's *bench and begin to sew and pound the pieces of cut-out leather into a pair of shoes.*)

ELVES (*As they work*):

Fly, magic thimblekin;

Fly, magic thread.

Work while the Shoemaker

Sleeps in his bed.

Work for an honest man;

Be spry and nimble,

Little white needlekin,
  Little gold thimble.
Fly, fly, fly!
Pound, little hammer head,
  Start on your pounding.
Make the toe pointing and
  Make the heel rounding.
Tap while the Shoemaker's
  Shutting his eyes.
Tap till the old man
  Starts to arise.
How he will smile when he
  Sees the surprise!
Tap, tap, tap!

1ST ELF (*Setting the shoe he has finished on the bench*):
There! That is done.
My, it was fun!

2ND ELF (*Puts shoe down*):
We finished fast. It's not too late
To do a dance to celebrate.
A good deed done on Christmas Eve
Should call for dancing, I believe.

1ST ELF (*Sadly, coming forward to address the audience*):
Yes, dancing's just what I would choose.
But we can't dance in ragged shoes.
For, though the floor is clean and neat,
It would put splinters in our feet.
And though we make shoes for the shelf
Of honest shoemakers, an elf
Must never sew things for himself.
On Christmas Eve that would be selfish,
And, anyway, it is not elfish.

2ND ELF (*To audience*):
In summertime we use oak leaves

For little coats with flapping sleeves.
We put the acorns on for caps,
And find some moccasins, perhaps,
Among the yellow orchid flowers;
But, in the winter, snows and showers
Soon wear to rags these clothes of ours.
(*They both turn away from the audience.*)

ELVES (*Together, as they exit*):
We hate to go out in the cold
In clothes that are so thin and old.
(*The music changes from gay to sad at the end of the elf scene. After the ELVES are gone, it changes to "Silent Night." Church bells chime in the distance. The stage gradually gets lighter. SHOEMAKER and WIFE enter. They carry a burnt-out candle, and are shivering with cold. They go over to the table and start to sit down by it. Suddenly they see the finished shoes. They look at each other in amazement.*)

WIFE (*Taking up one shoe*):
What's this? A shoe already made?
Is this some joke that you have played?

SHOEMAKER (*Taking up the other shoe and looking at it closely*):
No, no. I'm as surprised as you.
I never made so fine a shoe.

WIFE:
Someone has worked here in the night.

SHOEMAKER (*Puzzled*):
There was not even candlelight.

WIFE:
Elves work by moonlight when they choose—
These must be magic fairy shoes!
(*She looks around the room.*)
If fairies have been in this place,

They surely must have left some trace.
(*When she comes to the shelves, she lets out a little cry of surprise.*)
Come here and look upon this shelf.
Here is the footprint of an . . .
(*There is a sudden loud knocking at the door.*)

SHOEMAKER (*Going to the door and opening it*):
Come in, come in, good gentleman.
We're glad to help you if we can.
(*A very richly dressed* GENTLEMAN *enters.*)

WIFE (*Curtsying*):
Good morning, sir. Why do you choose
To come in here?

GENTLEMAN (*Bowing*)
I want some shoes.
For on my way to church alone,
I cut my boot upon a stone;
And so I want a brand-new pair.

SHOEMAKER (*Holding out the shoes the* ELVES *made*):
Are these the kind you like to wear?

GENTLEMAN (*Taking them and looking them over*):
Upon my word! What a surprise!
They are my style. They are my size.
I'm in a hurry. But before
I go, I want to order more.
(*He gets out his purse.*)
Here, take this gold and make another
Pair; and for my wife and brother
I will order some tomorrow.

WIFE (*Aside, to* SHOEMAKER, *while the* GENTLEMAN *counts out his money*):
This is the end of all our sorrow.

SHOEMAKER (*Wrapping up shoes and handing them to the* GENTLEMAN *in exchange for the gold*):

Oh, thank you, sir! I'll gladly do
Those other cobbling jobs for you.

GENTLEMAN (*As he exits with his package*):
Good. By tomorrow I'll be ready.

WIFE (*Sinking into a chair*):
Dear me! I'm feeling rather heady!

SHOEMAKER:
We shall be rich. Oh, I must know
Who came last night and helped us so!

WIFE:
It was a pair of little elves.
I found their footprints on those shelves.

SHOEMAKER:
If we could only thank them—bless them.

WIFE:
The best thing we can do is *dress* them.
Those footprints showed a ragged shoe,
And little toes all sticking through.
(*She gets up and takes her husband over to the empty
shelves to point out the footprints.*)
See! Aren't they tiny things, and cute?
I'm going to make each elf a suit.

SHOEMAKER (*Going over to the table and picking up scraps
of leather*):
And from these little scraps of leather
I'll make them shoes for any weather.
(*He takes his tape measure and measures one of the foot-
prints.*)

WIFE (*Suddenly fearful*):
But what if they should not come back?

SHOEMAKER:
All we can do is sew and tack,
And hope and pray they will come back.
(SHOEMAKER *and* WIFE, *carrying materials for dressmak-*

*ing and shoemaking, go out. There is a short pause, then
the ELVES tiptoe in. They are covered with snow. They
look cold and unhappy.*)

1ST ELF (*Blowing on his hands*):

My fingers are all blue with cold.

2ND ELF (*Drawing his tattered coat about him*):

My rags have grown so thin and old
I cannot make them keep me warm.

1ST ELF:

Mine almost blew off in the storm.

2ND ELF:

I'm sure the Shoemaker won't care
If we come in out of the air,
To wait until the wind stops blowing.

1ST ELF:

To wait until the snow stops snowing.
(*They sit down back to back on the floor near the work-
bench. They hug their knees and rock back and forth,
saying a lullaby in singsong.*)
Snuggle down, my little brother,
    Slumber where you are.
Out of doors the rocking treetops
    Cradle every star.
Out of doors the snow's white blanket
    Covers up the moon.
Go to sleep, my little brother
    To the night wind's tune.

ELVES:

Snuggle down, for you must know
Wool is warmer, far, than snow.

2ND ELF:

Hush you, now, my little brother,
    All things go to sleep:
Both the oxen in the stable
    And the folded sheep.

And the tired horses neither
  Stamp their feet nor neigh,
For the bells no longer jingle
  On their master's sleigh.

ELVES:

Snuggle down, for houses all
Are warmer than a barn and stall.

(*They grow sleepier and sleepier as they sing. Their voices fade. They fall asleep at the end of the song. Soft music sounds offstage. It continues for some time, then fades away.* SHOEMAKER *and* WIFE, *carrying finished clothes and shoes, enter.*)

WIFE:

My fingers never were so nimble.

SHOEMAKER:

I seemed to have a magic thimble.

(*They hold up their work for each other to see. Then they move toward the workbench, but start back in surprise as they see the* ELVES.)

SHOEMAKER *and* WIFE (*In a whisper*):

The elves
Themselves!

WIFE:

Just see their tattered coats and shoes!

SHOEMAKER:

We've made them something they can use.

WIFE:

Come quick! We have no time to lose.
We'll tiptoe softly up behind them
And put these clothes where they can find them.

(*They lay the clothes out on the workbench. Just as they are about to tiptoe offstage, the* SHOEMAKER *sneezes loudly. The* ELVES *jump and open their eyes. The* SHOEMAKER *and his* WIFE *hide quickly behind a screen or curtain. They peek out now and then.*)

1st Elf (*Waking up*):

What *was* that noise? What *was* that sound?

2nd Elf (*Looking about*):

I don't see anyone around.

1st Elf:

But what are those things over there?

(*He points to the new clothes on the table.*)

2nd Elf:

They look like clothes for elves to wear.

(*They jump up, clapping their hands in delight. They rush to the bench and begin to put on the little coats, hats, and shoes.*)

1st Elf:

These must be made for us. They're very
Small and only fit a fairy.

2nd Elf:

I'd almost wager with my life
They're from the old man and his wife.

1st Elf (*Waving his arms as though weaving a spell*):

Good luck to them! I'll make some magic
To keep their lives from being tragic.

2nd Elf (*Waving his arms*):

Good luck to them! I'll weave a charm:
"May kindness keep this cottage warm."

(*They look at each other, admiring the new clothes.*)

Elves (*Together, proudly*):

A hand for a sleeve and a foot for a shoe,
And two little elves are as good as new.

(*They clasp each other's hands and dance about the room. The* Shoemaker *and his* Wife *look out from behind the screen. They smile happily and wave after the* Elves *as they dance off into the night. Curtain falls.*)

THE END

Piccola

Characters

SNOW, *a young girl*
WIND, *a young boy*
FISHERMAN
WIFE OF FISHERMAN
PICCOLA, *their daughter*

TIME: *Christmas Eve.*
SETTING: *In front of a fisherman's hut in Brittany.*
BEFORE RISE: SNOW *enters from right, wearing a glitter-ing, white dress and carrying a small, artificial bird in her hand.*

SNOW (*Stroking the bird's feathers*): Poor little fellow! Did the naughty wind scare him? Such a bad, bad wind to chase a little birdie on a cold winter night. There, there! Snow will warm him. Mustn't make any noise, or—
WIND (*Offstage right*): Come here, you stupid bird! Come and feel my whip. (*Crack of whip is heard offstage.*)
SNOW: Sh-h-h! Here he comes! (*She cups her free hand over the bird.*)
WIND (*Running in and lashing his whip*): Come here, you bunch of foolish feathers! Don't you know I am your master? (*He stops suddenly as he sees* SNOW.)

237

WIND (*To* SNOW): Hello, Queen Snow. Out for a dance tonight?

SNOW (*Haughtily*): Not with you.

WIND: Why not? You know you like to dance with me. (*He moves toward her.*) Come on, just one little waltz.

SNOW (*Backing away*): Not tonight.

WIND: But I'll drive everyone else indoors—all the people into their houses, all the wild things into their holes. Then we'll have the whole wide world to ourselves— just to dance in.

SNOW: You are cruel and selfish! You do nothing but chase poor, harmless creatures.

WIND (*With bravado*): But I am master of the winter night. Don't forget that. Everyone must know I'm master. (*He cracks his whip, and the sound of a bird peeping is heard.* WIND *stops suddenly and listens.*) What was that? Sounded like a bird. Must be the one I was chasing.

SNOW: Nonsense! (*She holds the bird closer to her, and moves a step away from* WIND.)

WIND (*Sternly*): What's that you have in your hands?

SNOW (*Coquettishly*): Don't you wish you knew?

WIND: Tell me, or I'll— (*He raises his whip.*)

SNOW (*Laughing*): Perhaps it's a nice cold snowball for you to eat.

WIND (*Brightening*): Is it really?

SNOW: I said, "Perhaps." Now, open your mouth and shut your eyes . . .

WIND (*Obeying*): I like snowballs better than ice-cream cones.

SNOW (*Backing toward left on tiptoe*): . . . and I'll give you something (*She disappears off left, but her voice is still heard.*) . . . to make you wise.

WIND: Well, hurry up about it. (*He opens his eyes.*) I'll be blown! The little minx! She's tricked me! Snow! Snow! Where are you? (WIND *runs out left, after her.*)

* * *

SCENE 1

SETTING: *The main room of the Fisherman's hut in Brittany.*

AT RISE: *A dim fire is burning in the fireplace.* FISHERMAN *and his* WIFE *sit at either side of the hearth, mending a long fishnet stretched between them.*

FISHERMAN: Isn't it time for Piccola to come in?

WIFE: I told her she might go down to the village.

FISHERMAN: And why did you let her do that?

WIFE: She needed a change, poor child—shut in with the snow so long.

FISHERMAN: But have you forgotten what night this is?

WIFE (*Throwing up her hands in despair*): Goodness! It's Christmas Eve! I meant to keep the little one from knowing.

FISHERMAN: She would never have guessed at home. All days are the same by the sea.

WIFE: But down in the village, the shops will be filled with chocolate and toys . . .

FISHERMAN: And Piccola will see them.

WIFE: If only we could buy her some little thing.

FISHERMAN (*Shaking his head*): There's not a sou in the house. If it weren't for the fish we'd starve.

WIFE (*Wistfully*): She's never had a toy.

FISHERMAN: Perhaps next year . . .

WIFE (*Bitterly*): Every year we say, "Perhaps next year . . ."

FISHERMAN: Hush! Here she comes! (PICCOLA *enters right, gay and smiling, breathless with excitement.*)

PICCOLA (*Crossing to them*): Oh, Mother! Oh, Father! What do you think? This is Christmas Eve!

WIFE (*Weakly*): Are you sure?

FISHERMAN: How do you know, Piccola?

PICCOLA: I heard the children talking about it in the village. And the shop windows are full of toys—dolls and boats and little wooden animals!

FISHERMAN (*Trying to be cheerful*): That's the fun of Christmas—looking in at the shop windows.

WIFE (*Cheerfully*): Yes, toys are pretty to *look* at. That's mostly what they're for.

PICCOLA: Oh, but they're meant to play with, too! St. Nicholas rides around the world in his jingling sleigh and leaves a toy in every wooden shoe. That's why the boys and girls put their shoes by the chimney. See! I'm going to put mine there. (*She takes off one of her wooden shoes.*)

WIFE: No, no, Piccola! St. Nicholas won't come to this house. It's too small, and too far from the village. He won't even see it.

FISHERMAN: You don't understand, little daughter. Christmas gifts are for the rich, not for the poor—

PICCOLA: That's not what the children said. They know all about it. Some of them have *seen* him. They say he goes to *every* house, rich and poor. (*She sets her shoe in the chimney corner.*)

WIFE (*To her husband*): It's no use. She can't understand.

FISHERMAN: Put your other shoe by the fire, too, Piccola. And warm them for tomorrow.

PICCOLA: No, I couldn't leave *both* shoes. St. Nicholas would think I'm greedy. I'll put the other under my bed.

FISHERMAN: What? Are you going to bed so soon?

PICCOLA: The sooner I go, the sooner the good saint will come. (*She runs to her mother and throws her arms about her.*) Good night, Mother dear.

WIFE (*Kissing her*): Good night, Piccola. (*She takes a candle from the mantel.*)

PICCOLA: Good night, Father (*She kisses him.*)

FISHERMAN (*Sadly*): Good night, little one.

PICCOLA (*Taking candle from her mother*): Oh, I'm so happy! I can hardly wait till tomorrow. (PICCOLA *goes out right, with her candle. The* FISHERMAN *and his* WIFE *look after her sadly. There is a long pause.*)

WIFE (*Going to the hearth and picking up the little wooden shoe*): What will she do when she finds it empty? Poor little shoe. (*She shakes her head sadly*) You will never go dancing so lightly again.

FISHERMAN: Come, come. We'd better go to bed ourselves. It'll save the coals.

WIFE (*Astonished*): We've forgotten to eat supper! (*She replaces the shoe.*)

FISHERMAN: No matter. There'll be all the more for tomorrow. (*He takes another candle from the mantel.*)

WIFE: Yes. We'll make a bigger fire tomorrow, and have a second bowl of soup. Perhaps it will help Piccola forget.

FISHERMAN (*Doubtfully, sighing*): Perhaps, yes, perhaps . . . (*The* FISHERMAN, *carrying candle, leads the way out, and his* WIFE *follows. Gradually, the stage grows darker. A storm howls outside. The fire flickers.* SNOW *tiptoes in, right, and shuts door softly behind her. She is breathless and nervous.*)

SNOW (*In a hoarse whisper*): Are you all right, little bird? (*She takes the bird from inside her dress and smoothes its ruffled feathers. The sound of the bird peeping is heard.*) There! Were you frightened? Poor little fellow! Snow will find a place to hide you from the wicked Wind. (*She walks around the room looking in all the corners.*) Not here, nor here, nor here. Did you ever see such a house! It's so bare there's not a hiding-place in it. If only they had something besides wooden stools. You can see right over and under everything. There isn't even a clock on the mantel.

WIND (*Offstage*): Who-oo-oo-oo.

SNOW (*Clasping the bird to her*): Oh, dear! He's after us again. What shall we do? (*She runs frantically about.*) If there were only a place to hide you! (*She trips over* PICCOLA's *wooden shoe.*) What's this? (*She picks up shoe.*) A shoe! A wooden shoe! Just the thing! Whoever heard of a bird in a shoe?

WIND (*Offstage*): Who-oo-oo-oo! (SNOW *hastily tucks the bird into the wooden shoe and puts the shoe back in the chimney corner.* WIND *bursts noisily through the door at right.*)

WIND (*Seeing* SNOW): Oh-ho! So here you are!

SNOW (*Coldly*): Yes—here I am.

WIND: Thought you'd given me the slip, eh? Where's that bird?

SNOW: What bird?

WIND: I know you're hiding a bird. That's what you had in your hands. And you tried to make me think it was a snowball. Pooh! Give me that bird!

SNOW: Well, search me. (*She holds out her hands.*)

WIND (*Pushing her aside*): No! You've hidden him some-where in this room. (WIND *rushes about, looking under the stools and the table. He starts to explore the chimney corner, and* SNOW *cries out.*)

SNOW (*Trying to divert his attention*): Look, Wind! (*She runs to the window and rattles the latch.*) See how these windows rattle!

WIND: What of it?

SNOW: Think what wonderful castanets they would make!

WIND (*Excitedly*): You mean you will dance with me?

SNOW: That's just what I mean! (WIND *rushes over to* SNOW, *grabs her arms and they whirl about gaily, at times dangerously close to wooden shoe, as they dance with increasing animation, as curtain falls.*)

*　　*　　*

SCENE 2

TIME: *Christmas morning.*

SETTING: *The same as Scene 1.*

AT RISE: *The sun is streaming in through window. There are mounds of snow (cotton batting) around the room and the stools are turned over. The fire has gone out. The* FISHERMAN *and his* WIFE *enter right.*

WIFE (*Rubbing her hands*): Oh, what a cold, bitter world!

FISHERMAN (*With an effort at cheerfulness*): Things will be better when the fire is lighted. The wind must have blown it out.

WIFE (*Crossing to the window*): See how the snow has come in at the cracks.

FISHERMAN: We'll soon melt that. (*He lights the fire; the* WIFE *puts on the kettle, and then picks up a broom from corner of the room, and starts sweeping snow.*)

WIFE: I thought the wind would pull the house down last night.

FISHERMAN: Ah, but look how the sun comes in at the window! The day's making up for the night.

WIFE (*Mournfully*): But there'll be nothing in Piccola's shoe.

FISHERMAN (*Sighing*): No—nothing.

PICCOLA (*Offstage*): Merry Christmas! Merry Christmas!

WIFE (*In despair*): She's coming.

FISHERMAN: Poor child! (PICCOLA *enters, right.*)

PICCOLA (*Running to the window*): Oh, what a beautiful day! St. Nicholas has sent us the sun.

FISHERMAN (*Hopefully*): The sun is gift enough for one day.

PICCOLA: But he's left something in my shoe, too. (PICCOLA *runs to the wooden shoe. The* WIFE *covers her face with her hands. The* FISHERMAN *turns away sadly.* PICCOLA *takes the bird from shoe.*) Oh, see! See what good St. Nicholas has left me!

WIFE (*Looking up, startled*): What is it?

FISHERMAN (*Coming forward*): It's a bird!

WIFE: A bird!

PICCOLA (*Carefully holding the bird and smoothing its feathers*): It's much nicer than a wooden toy.

WIFE (*Aside, to her husband*): It must have flown down the chimney in the storm.

FISHERMAN: No—it seems as though it had been sent, especially for Piccola.

PICCOLA: Oh, how happy I am! (*She sets the bird on the mantel.*) Listen! He's going to sing! (*The bird bursts into song—a record may be played offstage for the bird's song, or a mechanical "singing bird" may be used. They all listen in happy amazement, as the curtain falls.*)

THE END

Christmas Pie

Characters

QUEEN OF HEARTS
KING OF HEARTS
PAGE
SEVEN COOKS
BOY (JACK HORNER)

TIME: *Christmastime, in the days of Mother Goose.*
SETTING: *The kitchen of the King of Hearts' palace.*
AT RISE: *The* QUEEN OF HEARTS, *wearing an apron over her court dress, is standing behind a table at left, facing the audience. She is cutting pastry and shaping it into tart shells which she then places on the tray of unfilled shells on the table. As she works, she sings the nursery rhyme about "The Queen of Hearts, she made some tarts," etc. The* KING OF HEARTS *enters, right, looks around, then sees* QUEEN.

KING:
  Oh, there you are, my Queen of Hearts!
  What are you doing?
QUEEN (*Proudly*):
  Making tarts.
  (*He goes to table and watches her cut the pastry.*)

245

KING:

Making tarts? For whom, I pray?

QUEEN:

For you, my king, a full-sized tray.
(*She holds up tray.*)

KING (*With irritation*):

But this is not a summer's day;
And tarts are best made out of berries
In summertime, or ripened cherries . . .

QUEEN (*Hurt*):

They're nice made out of jellies, too.

KING:

No. Jams or jellies will not do.
When snowflakes fall and Christmas comes
It's time for pies and sugarplums . . .

QUEEN (*Offended*):

But you have always thought it smart
That I, a queen, could make a tart.

KING:

Of course, my dear, but you must bake
Some other pastries for my sake.
Too much of one thing's apt to make
Even a monarch's tummy ache.
(*He puts his hand on his stomach.*)

I'm sure my royal bride is wise
Enough to bake me a surprise
Something in a pan this size . . .
(*He picks up a big pan.*)
One of those deep-dish Christmas pies!
(PAGE *enters breathlessly, and bows.*)

PAGE:

Your Majesty, a coach-and-four
Has just drawn up outside the door . . .

KING:

    Dear me! Our guests must be arriving.

    (*He turns to* QUEEN.)

    I'll leave you to your own contriving.

    No matter, dear, what size the crowd,

    I know you'll do your husband proud.

    (*He hurries out right, throwing her a kiss as he goes off, followed by* PAGE.)

QUEEN (*Calling after* KING *in bewilderment*):

    But, sir, I never made a pie.

    I don't know even how to try.

    (*She runs a few steps after him, then stops, sighing.*)

    He's gone! He's gone! My reputation

    Is now at stake before the nation.

    (*She wrings her hands.*)

    Alackaday, and dearie me,

    I must find a recipe!

    (*She claps her hands commandingly, and* PAGE *enters.*)

PAGE (*Bowing*): What is your wish, Your Majesty?

QUEEN:

    Send in to me the seven cooks.

    And see they bring their seven books.

PAGE (*Bowing again*):

    I'll call them from their scullery nooks.

    (PAGE *exits.* QUEEN *paces up and down nervously. The tramp of marching feet is heard off right, and then* SEVEN COOKS *enter, each carrying a cookbook. The* HEAD COOK, *who is first in line, wears a chef's hat decorated with a star. They march around the room and line up before* QUEEN, *singing "Pease porridge hot, pease porridge cold," etc.*)

QUEEN (*Interrupting them, clapping her hands*):

    That will do. Please don't discourage

    A pastry cook with thoughts of porridge.

(*They stop and stand at attention.*)
I sent for you in hopes that I
Could get some pointers on a pie,
A Christmas pie that's deep and wide.
Now tell me what should go inside.
(COOKS *scratch their heads, looking puzzled.*)

HEAD COOK:

If it's a pie, why, then it must
Have both a top and lower crust.

QUEEN (*Impatiently*):

Of course! That's how one must begin it;
But what on earth does one put in it?

2ND COOK:

We never heard until this minute
Of such a pie. But we can bake
A Christmas pudding, or a cake.

QUEEN:

No! No! The King must have a festive
Deep-dish pie that is digestive;
At any rate, those are his orders.

3RD COOK (*Looking frightened*):

And he's the star of all star-boarders.
His anger's something to be dreaded.
Let's hope we will not be beheaded!
(COOKS *burst into tears, sobbing in unison.*)

QUEEN:

Be still, be still, you coward cooks!
Take off those melancholy looks.
At least you can refer to books.

4TH COOK (*Brightening*):

At least we can refer to books.
(*They open cookbooks simultaneously and thumb through them.*)
Let's see, where is the list of pies?

QUEEN (*Looking over the shoulder of the* HEAD COOK):

It's in the "P's" beyond the "I's".

COOKS (*Reading in chorus*):

Apple, apricot, cheese, cherry,

Coconut, date-nut, huckleberry,

Lemon meringue, plum and pear . . .

QUEEN (*Interrupting*):

Goodness gracious! It isn't there!

(COOKS *shake their heads sadly and close their books,
except the* HEAD COOK *who keeps studying his.*)

5TH COOK:

Never a sign from "A" to "Z"

Of a Christmas pie and its recipe.

HEAD COOK (*Excitedly*):

On this page way up in the corner

There is a story of Jack Horner.

(*He clears his throat and reads.*)

"Little Jack Horner sat in the corner,

Eating a Christmas pie."

QUEEN (*In sudden delight*): *A Christmas pie!*

HEAD COOK (*Continuing*):

"He put in his thumb, and he pulled out a plum . . ."

QUEEN (*Ecstatically*): A *plum!*

HEAD COOK:

And said, "What a good boy am I!"

QUEEN:

Oh, wonderful! Read on, good sir.

Find out how I must mix and stir

The batter up. . . .

HEAD COOK:

I wish there were

More written here. But, oh, I doubt it.

(*He turns page.*)

No. Nothing more is writ about it.

QUEEN (*Looking in book*):

I fear you're right. There's nothing more.

We're not much farther than before.

HEAD COOK:

Except we know pies have plums in them.

6TH COOK:

And small boys sometimes stick their thumbs in them.

QUEEN:

If only we could find Jack Horner!

HEAD COOK (*Referring to book*):

He has no address but "The Corner."

OTHER COOKS:

It's turning out just as we dreaded.

Oh, dear! Oh, dear! We'll be beheaded. (*They sob again.*)

QUEEN:

No, no! Go off and stir your cakes.

I'll answer for my own mistakes.

7TH COOK:

It's good of you to take the blame.

The Queen of Hearts has earned her name.

(**COOKS** *bow and march off in the same way they entered.*)

QUEEN:

How can I keep my reputation

Of proudest cook in all the nation?

(*She sighs.*)

How can I do what seven cooks

Can't do with help of seven books?

(*She drops into a chair and begins to sob. There is a knock at the door, left.* **QUEEN** *dries her eyes hastily, rises, and goes to the door.*)

Who's there? Who's knocking at the door?

BOY (*Calling from offstage*):

A hungry child and nothing more.

QUEEN (*Opening door*):

A hungry child! Come in, come in.

At Christmastime it is a sin
For children to face cold and danger.
Come in, come in, my little stranger.
(BOY *enters, wearing a shabby cloak and hood.*)
BOY:

Oh, thank you, ma'am! Your hearth's warm stones
Will soon thaw out my icy bones.
QUEEN:

Sit down upon the corner seat.
I'll get you something hot to eat.
(*He sits down, and she begins to scurry about, opening cupboards, taking out dried and fresh fruits, all except the plums which are on the top shelf of one cupboard.*)
I've failed to meet my husband's wish.
I cannot make his favorite dish,
But I can fill a potluck pan
That will warm up a little man.
(*She takes up her rolling pin*)
I'll roll the tart dough into one
Big crusty crust.
BOY (*Running to help her*):
That will be fun.
QUEEN:

I'll line the biggest pan with crust.
BOY:

I'll sprinkle it with flour dust.
QUEEN (*Beginning to fill pie*):
A bit of apple will be nice
And dried-out plums and powdered spice.
BOY:

Yes! Dried-out plums!
They're on that shelf.
(*He points to plums on top shelf.*)
QUEEN (*Climbing on chair*):
I'll get them down all by myself.

(While her back is turned to the audience, BOY waves his hands over the pie as though casting a spell.)

BOY:

Mutter, mutter, bread and butter.

He who cooks must learn to putter.

(He goes over to chimney corner and seats himself, as QUEEN takes plums from shelf and climbs down.)

QUEEN:

Did you say something, little chap?

BOY *(Ignoring the question)*:

I think I'll take a little nap.

QUEEN:

Yes, take a very little one

Until this dish is baked and done.

(She begins singing a Christmas song to him. By the time she has finished singing, the pie is ready for the oven and the BOY is asleep.)

QUEEN *(Putting the pan in the oven)*:

There goes my foolish potluck dish. . . .

(KING enters.)

KING *(Seeing pie)*:

Ah, love, have you fulfilled my wish?

QUEEN *(Suddenly losing her gaiety)*:

How I did look! How I did try

To find a recipe for pie!

But not a one, sir, could I find,

That would have made the Christmas kind.

KING *(Angrily)*:

Neither dine nor sup shall I

Until you make my Christmas pie.

BOY *(Leaping suddenly to his feet and facing the KING)*:

Oh, what a wife! Oh, what a cook!

She made a pie without a book!

She made it, sir, not just for you

But for a hungry stranger, too.

KING (*Surprised*):

And who are you, there, in the corner?

(BOY *throws off his shabby cloak and hood and is seen dressed in fancy clothes.*)

BOY:

I am a boy they call Jack Horner.

QUEEN (*Amazed*): *Jack Horner!*

JACK:

Come one, come all, from nook and corner.

Come see the magic of Jack Horner.

(*He beckons left and right, and the* PAGE *and* COOKS, *enter. They watch spellbound as he waves his hands over the oven.*)

Mutter, mutter, bread and butter.

He who cooks must learn to putter.

He who cooks must dare to try

His own recipe for . . . *pie!*

(*At the word "pie," he opens the oven door, and a beautiful brown Christmas pie is revealed. It is decorated with holly.*)

ALL (*Delighted*): OOOOOOOH!

JACK:

There is a pie to make you jolly.

It is complete, sir, to the holly.

HEAD COOK:

Here is a pie to make us jolly.

It's even trimmed with Christmas holly.

KING (*Thoughtfully, to* QUEEN):

Now you've done this wondrous feat,

I shall no longer live to eat,

But eat to live, and live to give.

(*Turns to address others*)

My wife is smarter far than I.

She knows the joy of sharing pie.

(*He smiles at* QUEEN.)

She knows that Christmastime should be
A time of love and charity.
(*He pats* JACK HORNER *on head.*)
ALL:
She knows that Christmastime should be
A time of love and charity.
KING (*To* PAGE):
Call in the poor from west to east
And have them join our Christmas feast.
QUEEN (*Smiling radiantly and taking off her apron*):
Yes, call the poor from west to east,
And have them join our Christmas feast.
(PAGE *bows and goes out. The others form a procession and circle the room singing a Christmas carol:* JACK *first, carrying the pie;* KING *and* QUEEN *next, and* COOKS *last. They all march out, right, as the curtain falls.*)

THE END

What Will the Toys Say?

Characters

BROTHER
SISTER
JACK-IN-THE-BOX
RAG DOLL
WOODEN SOLDIERS
CAPTAIN OF WOODEN SOLDIERS
PATTIE PAPER DOLL
OTHER PAPER DOLLS
ELF KING

TIME: *Christmas Eve.*
BEFORE RISE: BROTHER *and* SISTER *enter, dressed in night clothes and carrying lighted electric candles.*

SISTER (*To* BROTHER):
   What will the toys say, one to another,
   Under the Christmas tree tonight,
   While they are waiting for someone to play with them,
   While they are waiting for morning's first light?
BROTHER (*To* SISTER):
   Will they tell secrets, one to another,
   Tell of the toy shops where they were made?
   And of store windows where they were displayed?
   Will each tell the other the whole of his history?

BROTHER *and* SISTER (*Together*):
   What will the toys say? That is a mystery!
   (BROTHER *and* SISTER *exit on opposite sides. The curtain opens.*)

* * *

SETTING: *A typical modern living room, with fireplace and Christmas tree and other Christmas decorations. A large fancy box stands near Christmas tree.*

AT RISE: CAPTAIN OF WOODEN SOLDIERS *stands stiffly to one side, as* RAG DOLL, PATTIE PAPER DOLL *and* OTHER PAPER DOLLS *sit or lie sleeping near tree. Sleigh bells sound offstage, and a jolly voice is heard in the distance calling "Merry Christmas to all, and to all a good night!" This is repeated three times, and each time it sounds fainter and farther away. A clock chimes twelve. After a moment, the toys begin to stir, stiffly at first. They yawn, stretch, and look at each other.*

CAPTAIN: Well, well, here we all are just where Santa Claus left us! Let's have a party and get acquainted!

RAG DOLL (*With flopping gestures*): Yes, let's! Since we're going to live in this house together we should introduce ourselves.

PATTIE PAPER DOLL: We'd better get to know each other right away.

OTHER PAPER DOLLS (*Together*): We love parties!

CAPTAIN: Very well, let me introduce myself. (*He bows.*) I'm a military man, as you see. But I can't tell you my history. That's a military secret.

1ST PAPER DOLL: Anyway, you'll protect us, won't you?

2ND PAPER DOLL: From rats and mice?

CAPTAIN: Of course! I'll call in my whole company of soldiers if necessary. (*A sudden, loud knocking is heard from box.*)

ALL (*Startled*): What was that?

CAPTAIN: It sounded as though it were coming from that box. (*All tiptoe over to the box and listen intently. There is another sudden knock and* PAPER DOLLS *fall back. Even the* CAPTAIN *moves back a step or two.*)

PATTIE PAPER DOLL: Oh, I hope it's not a mouse!

2ND PAPER DOLL: Mice love to nibble paper. (PAPER DOLLS *quiver and hide their faces.*)

RAG DOLL: I hope it's not a rat. That would be worse. They nest in cotton, and I'm all *stuffed* with cotton.

CAPTAIN (*Pulling himself together*): Don't worry, ladies, I'll call in the army. (*He takes a small toy bugle from his belt and blows on it.* WOODEN SOLDIERS *enter on the run. They look somewhat frightened and flurried. They line up before* CAPTAIN.)

Attention, everybody,

A Captain takes command.

It's time to reconnoiter

And take your swords in hand.

(WOODEN SOLDIERS *draw swords.*)

The enemy is in that box,

We'll pry the cover—break the locks—

Charge!

(WOODEN SOLDIERS *rush at the box and poke and pry the cover with their swords. There is a loud rumble and crash, with drums and cymbals if possible. The cover of the box flies open and up pops* JACK-IN-THE-BOX.)

JACK-IN-THE-BOX (*Smiling and waving his arms*): Boo! (*Everyone falls back, even the* SOLDIERS, *and some of the* PAPER DOLLS *sit down on the floor again.*)

CAPTAIN: Why, it's only Jack-in-the-Box! What do you mean by scaring the ladies like that?

JACK: I didn't mean to scare anybody. It was just a joke.

RAG DOLL (*Approaching him with a warm, wide smile*): Why! You're a clown! How nice! A clown will add a lot of fun to our party.

PATTIE PAPER DOLL: Yes, we'll take turns dancing with you.

OTHER PAPER DOLLS (*Crowding around him, ad lib*): I'm first! . . . No, I am . . . I am! I am! (*Etc.*)

JACK (*Waving them back politely*): I'm afraid I can't dance. I heard you talking about a party and—and—I wanted to come to it, but I forgot I can't dance. (*He wilts and hangs his head.*)

RAG DOLL: I've never heard of a clown that couldn't dance.

PAPER DOLLS (*Ad lib*): Neither have I . . . nor I . . . nor I . . . (*Etc.*)

CAPTAIN (*Stepping up and patting* JACK *on the back*): Tell us about it, old fellow. Maybe we can help you.

JACK (*Clearing his throat nervously*):
I once was an elf who lived by myself
On a mossy rock shelf in a glen, glen, glen.
I was not very pleasing. I spent my time teasing
And throwing small stones at old men, men, men.
But the Elf King, one day, saw my pranks and my play
As I hid in a crack of the rocks, rocks, rocks,
And he said, "You're a knave, and until you behave,
You had better be shut in a box, box, box."

ALL (*Astonished*): So that's why he lives in a box!

JACK (*Looking ashamed*):
Yes, that's why I'm here in a box that is drear
With a tight little cover that locks, locks, locks.
(*He crouches down and pulls the cover back over him so that it clicks. He is heard sobbing inside.*)

ALL (*Ad lib*): Poor thing! Let him out! Let's help him . . . (*They rush to the box and open it.*)

JACK (*Popping up*): Oh, thank you, thank you! I was afraid you might not want me around when you heard my story.

ALL (*Ad lib*): Nonsense! Of course we want you. (*Etc.*)

RAG DOLL: Anyone can see you're a reformed man.

PATTIE PAPER DOLL: You were very brave about telling the truth. I couldn't be that brave, but I'd like to be helpful. (*She reaches out her hand to him.*) Here, give me your hand. Maybe I could help you step out of the box. (*She pulls him with all her might, then lets her arm fall at her side.*) Oh, ouch! I've torn my arm!

JACK: Oh, dear! Oh, *dear!* I never should have let you try such a thing. I forgot I was *glued* in.

PATTIE PAPER DOLL (*Trying not to cry*): It wasn't your fault. I just forgot how tearable I am, and crumply, too.

JACK (*With sudden inspiration*): I know just the thing to mend and smooth you out! (*He reaches down into his box and brings out a big roll of sticky mending tape.*) Come closer, Pattie. (*She steps up to him, and he pastes the tape all up and down her arm. Then he spins her around for the others to see.*)

3RD PAPER DOLL (*Examining tape*): What a neat job!

PATTIE PAPER DOLL (*Admiringly*): You're a regular doctor!

JACK: If I ever get out of this box, I'm going to study to be a doctor. It's much better to mend people than to bruise them. (*There is a sudden flash of light and the ringing of a tinkling bell, and the* ELF KING *enters right. He skips lightly over to* JACK, *touches him with his wand and skips quickly offstage left.*)

ALL (*Rubbing their eyes and looking bewildered, ad lib*): What was that? Did you see that light? What could it be? (*Etc.*)

RAG DOLL: I saw a light!

PATTIE PAPER DOLL: So did I!

OTHER PAPER DOLLS (*In rapid succession*): And I! And I! And I!

1ST WOODEN SOLDIER: I saw an elf!

OTHER WOODEN SOLDIERS: And I! And I! And I!

JACK (*Pulling himself to full height and stretching ex-*

citedly): I'm free! I can move! See! I can climb out of the box!

PATTIE PAPER DOLL: *It's magic!*

JACK: The Elf King's magic!

ALL: *Christmas magic!*

JACK: Now we can have our party. Choose partners for the grand march. (*They all pair off.*)

(*The* WOODEN SOLDIERS *begin to play—or pretend to play—"The Parade of the Wooden Soldiers" or similar lively marching song. A record may be played offstage.*)

CAPTAIN:

Attention, everybody,

A soldier takes command.

It's time you all went marching

To a military band.

I've never seen a battle

Or heard a cannon roar,

But I can take you marching

As you never marched before!

(*They all get in line and march merrily around the stage, as the curtain falls. Sound of cock crow is heard in distance if possible.*)

* * *

BROTHER (*Entering in front of curtain from right*): Merry Christmas!

SISTER (*Entering in front of curtain from left*): Merry Christmas!

BROTHER (*Turning toward audience*):

It's morning! It's Christmas!

Oh, joy of all joys!

We can take down our stockings

And look at our toys!

SISTER (*Facing audience*):

It's morning! It's Christmas!

Oh, won't it be jolly
To sit by the hearthstone
And cuddle a dolly?

BROTHER *and* SISTER (*Together, to audience*):
We hope that you'll all have as much fun as we,
When you look at your presents and sit by your tree.
(*The curtains open and reveal the Christmas tree, with
all the toys in their original stiff positions.* BROTHER
and SISTER *utter a cry of delight and rush toward toys
as curtains close.*)

THE END

The Pudding-Bag String

Characters

KING
CHIEF COOK
TWO ASSISTANT COOKS
CAT
QUEEN
THREE ADVISERS
LORDS
LADIES

SETTING: *The palace kitchen, on the day before Christmas.*
AT RISE: *The* KING *is sitting in the chimney corner, watching the* CHIEF COOK, *who is mixing a Christmas pudding at the table. An* ASSISTANT COOK *stands on each side of* CHIEF COOK. *The* KING'S *crown is pushed back carelessly off his forehead, and his robe lies over the arm of a chair, and his sword leans against it.*

KING:
  Oh, what a pudding this will be!
  The biggest made on land or sea,
  Enough to feed my whole country—
  Oh, what a pudding this will be!
COOKS (*Together, as they bow stiffly*): Yes, yes, indeed, Your Majesty!

CHIEF COOK (*Examining mixture*):
>The finest flour ever ground,
>Rich suet, measured by the pound,
>Enormous cherries, red and round,
>And best of all, great pudding plums
>As big as any giant's thumbs.

KING:
>Where is the bag—the bag and string—
>So we can steam this luscious thing?

1ST ASSISTANT (*Running to cupboard and taking out a huge bag*):
>Here is the bag.

2ND ASSISTANT (*Running to cupboard and holding up string*):
>And here's the string!

CHIEF COOK (*Running to cupboard and taking out pot*):
>And here's the pot to steam the thing.
>(*All march proudly to table.*)

KING:
>Be specially careful of the string;
>It's such a very precious thing.
>I bought it, once, upon my travels.
>Let's hope it never breaks or ravels,
>For there is not in all the land
>Another string, another strand—
>(*A loud growl is heard from offstage, and all look toward door, up center, which is slightly ajar.*)

ALL (*Startled*):
>What's that?

CHIEF COOK (*In a whisper*):
>The Cat!

1ST ASSISTANT:
>The dreadful wild Cat!

2ND ASSISTANT:
>From the jungle!

KING:

　Quick! Lock the door, and do not bungle.

CHIEF COOK (*Frightened*):

　I'd do it, but my hands are sticky.

1ST ASSISTANT (*Nervously*):

　I'd do it, but the lock is tricky.

2ND ASSISTANT:

　I'd d-d-do it, b-b-but

　The d-d-door won't sh-sh-shut.

　(*The* CAT *enters through rear door.*)

KING: Too late! The monster's come upon us. (*He hides behind his chair. The* CHIEF COOK, *followed by his* AS-SISTANTS, *hurriedly crouches behind chairs.*)

1ST ASSISTANT: She'll gobble us all up. (*The* CAT *walks around room, sniffing contemptuously at* KING *and* COOKS. *She then picks up pudding-bag string and goes out with it.* ASSISTANT COOKS *rush to door and bolt it.* KING *and* CHIEF COOK *come out from behind chairs.*)

CHIEF COOK:

　There! She's gone. They've locked her out.

　They're very brave and strong, no doubt.

KING (*Straightening his crown, with dignity*):

　But why did you permit, I pray,

　A cat to take our string away.

　(*The* COOKS *look at one another and say nothing.*)

　Do you forget there's not a strand

　Of string remains in all the land?

　Like Tommy Tucker we must sing

　For supper, since we have no string.

2ND ASSISTANT (*Wringing hands*):

　"Sing, sing? What shall we sing?

　The Cat's run away with the pudding-bag string."

1ST ASSISTANT:

　"Do, do? What shall we do?

　The Cat has bitten it quite in two!"

KING (*Beginning to wail*):
　Our holiday, our Christmas feast,
　Is ruined by that dreadful beast.
　Won't someone go and get it back,
　The sack-string that ties up the sack?

CHIEF COOK:
　We'd like to, but alas, alack!
　We do not know the trail or track.

KING:
　If you were just a little wiser—
　(*With sudden inspiration*)
　I know! I'll call in my adviser.
　(*To* SECOND ASSISTANT)
　Go bring my wise men, one, two, three.

2ND ASSISTANT:
　I go at once, Your Majesty.
　(*Exits left, as* QUEEN *enters from right and looks about, frowning.*)

QUEEN:
　What's all this rumpus, all this noise?
　You look like guilty little boys.

KING (*Tragically*):
　The Cat's run away with the pudding-bag string!

QUEEN (*Bursts into laughter*):
　Is that such a serious thing?
　I'll go and get it right away—
　(*She picks up a bottle of milk from table and hurries to rear door.*)

KING:
　No! Do not go outside, I pray.

QUEEN:
　I won't be long, I won't be late;
　A Christmas pudding must not wait.
　(*She exits, closing door after her. The* KING *starts to follow her, but the* CHIEF COOK *holds him back.*)

CHIEF COOK:

> No, no, good King, stay where you are.
> The Queen will not go very far.
> She's always joking, night and day.
> Besides, the Cat is far away—
> By now.

1ST ASSISTANT:

> And you must plan to stay
> And hear what all the wise men say.

(THREE ADVISERS enter with 2ND ASSISTANT COOK. 1ST ADVISER carries a crystal ball, 2ND ADVISER, a huge book, 3RD ADVISER, a globe of the world. ADVISERS march around room.)

1ST ADVISER *(Marching)*:

> If all the world were bread and cheese
> And all the water ink,
> What would we poor mortals do
> But scratch our heads and think?
> If all the world were cheese and bread—

KING *(Clapping his hands commandingly so that THREE ADVISERS stop suddenly and bow before him)*:

> O do not talk of ink,
> Or anything but pudding string;
> Yes, scratch your heads and think
> Where I can find my pudding string.

1ST ADVISER *(Holding up his crystal ball and gazing into it)*:

> I look into my crystal ball
> But do not see your string at all.

3RD ADVISER *(Twirling globe)*:

> I'm scanning every inch of sphere,
> No pudding string is labeled here.

2ND ADVISER *(Studying book)*:

> I'm reading all the solemn pages,
> Written by the wisest sages

But no one tells where string is bought
Or how a wild cat can be caught.

KING (*Distressed, disgusted*):

Oh, dear, oh, dear, I sometimes wonder
Why I hire these men who blunder!
How can I waste time in talking
When my Queen perhaps is walking
Into danger? Where's my sword and robe?
I'll chase that Cat around the globe.

(*He snatches up his sword and robe and starts toward
the door. As he reaches door, the* QUEEN *bursts in, carrying the pudding-bag string. Following her is the* CAT,
who is purring and quite tame.)

ALL (*Drawing back*):

The Queen! The Cat!

QUEEN (*Laughing*):

What's wrong with that?
Don't tremble so. Don't be afraid,
For cats, I'm very sure, were made
To be our pets. A little child
Could see this Cat's no longer wild.

KING:

How did you tame her, lovely Queen?

QUEEN:

I've known a hundred cats, I ween,
For in the land from which I came
All cats are pets, all cats are tame.
I took this one a bit of milk
And let her rub against my silk.
She wanted love. I stroked her fur,
And now just listen to her purr!

ADVISERS (*Together, in chorus*):

She wanted love. Let's stroke her fur.
We'll make a palace pet of her.

(*All crowd around* CAT, *stroking and petting her.*)

QUEEN (*Holding the string*):
  And here's the string to tie the bag.
  Come, steam the pudding—do not lag!
  Our feast will turn out as we wish
  And we shall give the Cat a dish.
ALL (*Crowding around table to help with the pudding*):
  A Merry Christmas it will be
  For all who live in this country!
  (LORDS *and* LADIES *of the court enter left and right, singing Christmas carols. All others join in singing as the curtain falls.*)

THE END

Ye Olden Festival of Christmas

Characters

KING
LORD MAYOR
CRIER
MINSTREL
TWO PAGES
VILLAGE MAID
MANSERVANT
MAIDSERVANT
LADIES OF THE COURT
LORDS
TWO WOODSMEN
TWO BOYS
CHILDREN
HUNTSMAN
JESTER
TWO GUARDSMEN
VILLAGERS
PEASANTS

TIME: *Medieval times.*

BEFORE RISE: CRIER *enters before the curtain, ringing bell. He walks to front of stage, as* LORD MAYOR, VILLAGERS, PAGES, PEASANTS, *and* VILLAGE MAID *enter from right and left and gather behind* CRIER *as he speaks.*

MINSTREL, *carrying a harp concealed under his cape, enters right and stands at one side, unnoticed by crowd.*

CRIER:

I am the crier who cries for the King.
Hark to the wonderful tidings I bring.
All loyal subjects from west unto east
Are bidden to come to the holiday feast.
All loyal subjects from island or isthmus
Are bidden to come to the castle for Christmas.

VILLAGERS (*Ad lib*):

Yea! Yea! Hurray! Long live the king! (*etc.*)

CRIER:

Our King's been crusading in lands of the south
But sends you his greeting by word of the mouth
He bids all his people from west unto east
To come to the castle and join in a feast.

1ST VILLAGER:

Yea! Yea!
We have something to say.

2ND VILLAGER:

Come, Mayor, and name it!
Oh, gladly proclaim it!

MAYOR (*To* CRIER):

Our King, he is kindly; and kind is his offer.
Each year he has opened his castle and coffer
To give us good gifts; but today we shall proffer
Gifts of our own—good gifts for the King.

3RD VILLAGER:

We'll come to the feast, but the feast we will bring.
(*Crowd bursts into laughter.*)

CRIER:

I'll spread the good news with a loud jingle-ling.
(*Rings his bell*)

4TH VILLAGER (*Protesting*):
  You must not tell the King!
CRIER:
  I shall not tell the King!
  (*Everyone goes out except* VILLAGE MAID, PEASANTS,
  PAGES, *and* MINSTREL, *who stands apart, right.*)
1ST PEASANT (*Boastfully*):
  I'll give a gift that will glitter and shine.
  Even the King will declare it is fine!
2ND PEASANT (*Thumping his chest*):
  Nobody's gift will be better than mine.
VILLAGE MAID:
  Mine will be tied with a silvery string.
1ST PAGE (*To* MINSTREL):
  What will the vagabond give to the King?
2ND PAGE:
  Chase the boy off. He has nothing to bring.
  His coat is all ragged,
  His cap is all torn.
VILLAGE MAID:
  Nay, he can't help being poor and forlorn.
  (*She exits, followed by all but* MINSTREL, *who lingers
  behind briefly, then looks toward audience, throws back
  his cape and reveals his harp. He strums it once wist-
  fully, then drops his cape over it again and exits.*)

*　*　*

SETTING: *Throne room of the castle.*
AT RISE: *Room is empty, then loud knocking is heard.*
  MANSERVANT *and* MAIDSERVANT *enter, right. Knocking
  grows louder.*

MANSERVANT (*Crossing to door*):
  It must be the King! Oh, it must be the master!

MAIDSERVANT (*Looking offstage*):

His horsemen are coming, but he has come faster.

MANSERVANT:

I'll open the door, and I'll draw up his chair.

(*Glances around room wryly*)

But I don't like this room, looking empty and bare.

MAIDSERVANT:

To think it is Christmas, and not anywhere
Are there trimmings or greens. Of course it is bare!
His Honor, the Mayor, gave very strict orders—
No holly, no ivy, no banners, no borders!

MANSERVANT:

Yes, I heard him declare that he wanted it bare.
He hasn't much sense, for all his gray hair.

(*Knocking is heard again*)

MAIDSERVANT:

You'd better go quickly. The King's waiting there.

(MANSERVANT *exits left, hastily, and* MAIDSERVANT *looks around room again.*)

Empty and bare! Empty and bare!
He hasn't much sense, for all his gray hair.
Who would believe that the yuletide is here?

(*She wrings her hands.*)

It's all very queer! It's all very queer!

(*She goes to window and looks out as* KING *and* MANSERVANT *enter.*)

KING (*To* MANSERVANT):

My man, it is good to be back in my home.

(*He takes off shield, helmet, and sword and hands them to* MANSERVANT.)

I trust that I shall not be called on to roam
Out in the world for another long year.

(*Sees* MAIDSERVANT *at window.*)

You wait for my guardsmen? Oh, they'll soon be here.
I rushed on ahead, for I thought to prepare—

(*He stops suddenly as he looks around the bare room.*)
How is it the throne room is empty and bare?

MAIDSERVANT (*Curtsying*):
We really don't know, Sire.

MANSERVANT:
We don't know, I swear.
(*Puts away sword, shield, and helmet*)

MAIDSERVANT:
We followed our orders. We followed with care.

MANSERVANT:
There's something we can't understand in the air.

KING:
There's not even food on the table to eat!
(MAIDSERVANT *nods sadly.*)
It's all very strange. My messenger fleet,
Perhaps did not get here or did not repeat
My order correctly.

MANSERVANT (*To himself, aside*):
We'll find out directly.

KING:
I ordered some ivy, I ordered some holly.
I wanted the room to be festive and jolly.
(*He points to table and fireplace.*)
No feast on the table. No faggots to light!
Have people forgotten it's Christmas tonight?

MAIDSERVANT (*Sighing*):
They must have forgotten it's Christmas tonight!

KING:
I ordered a banquet. I called for a feast.
Invited my subjects from west unto east.

MAIDSERVANT (*Pointing offstage excitedly*):
They're coming, Your Highness, the greatest and least!

KING (*Distracted*):
But how shall I greet them? Oh, it will be cruel
To tell them there will be no gifts for the yule!

(*Enter* LORD MAYOR *and* CRIER, *right. They approach* KING *and bow.*)

MAYOR:

You could not be mean, Sire.

CRIER:

You could not be cruel.

MAYOR:

Because it's the time for rejoicing and giving,
Because it's the season for new joy in living,
Because our King's goodness has won him renown,
We bring him the gifts of the country and town.

CRIER:

So long you have given us good gifts and new,
This year we should like to bring Christmas to you!

KING (*Astonished*):

Bring Christmas to me? I'm puzzled, I own.

MAYOR:

You shall see what you see. Come, sit on your throne.
(*With great ceremony, the* LORD MAYOR *leads* KING *to throne.*)
Now, Crier, it's your turn; so ring loud your bell.

CRIER (*Ringing bell and crying aloud*):

Come, ladies, fair ladies, and in your gay manner
Present to the King your tapestry banner.
(LADIES OF THE COURT *enter. They are dressed in white and carry a tapestry.* TWO LADIES *take tapestry and approach throne and bow to* KING.)

1ST LADY (*Pointing to tapestry*):

In picture and symbol a record we've made
Of all that we've heard of your wondrous crusade.

KING (*Examining tapestry carefully*):

Skilled with your needles, you've carefully wrought
The sights that I saw and the battles I fought.
I'm grateful, fair ladies, for all of your labors.
I'll hang up this banner to warn warlike neighbors.

Needles are sometimes as forceful as sabers.

(KING *takes tapestry;* LADIES *curtsy, then mingle with crowd around stage.*)

CRIER (*Ringing bell and calling loudly*):

Now come in, ye woodsmen! Come out of the storm
And bring us the yule log to make the place warm!

(TWO WOODSMEN *enter, dragging a yule log. They are accompanied by* TWO BOYS *carrying bundles of sticks.*)

1ST WOODSMAN (*Bowing before* KING, *as* BOYS *kneel*):

We bring a great tree trunk—a log for your fuel.
This is our gift for the tide of the yule.

KING (*Happily*):

This is a heart-warming gift that you bring.
Light up the fire. We'll hear the flames sing!

(WOODSMEN *light the fire and then take their places with* BOYS *in crowd.*)

CRIER (*Ringing bell and calling*):

Where are the leaves and the berries and greens?
Bring them to cover this barest of scenes.

(CHILDREN *enter, carrying wreaths and sprays. They cross to* KING, *then kneel and hold up their greens.*)

CHILDREN (*Together*):

Here are the wreaths to hang up in a row—
The holly, the ivy, the white mistletoe.

KING:

Oh, drape them around and hang them about.
The green of the holly will keep winter out!

(*The* CHILDREN *start to decorate the hall assisted by others, while the* CRIER *speaks again.*)

CRIER (*Ringing bell*):

And now bring the feast for the King and his pleasure—
Viands and sweetmeats and fruits without measure.

(*Several* VILLAGERS *and* PEASANTS *enter, carrying large platters and trays piled high with food—fruits, meats, breads, pastries, etc. One is a* HUNTSMAN *who carries a*

*large covered platter, decorated with holly. They all
walk around room, toward throne, displaying the platters, then go to table right and arrange platters and
trays.* TWO GUARDSMEN *enter and go to stand beside
throne.*)

HUNTSMAN (*As he holds platter before* KING):
I bring a platter of savory meat—
Wild game that's fit for a monarch to eat.

KING:
It will be good both to dine and to sup
With a plate of choice viands and a brimming-full cup.
But better than this, it is pleasant to be
Among merry friends and in good company.
(HUNTSMAN *walks left, followed by several others, who
pass throne without speaking.* VILLAGE MAID, *carrying
basket of fruit, approaches throne and bows.*)

VILLAGE MAID:
We bring the fruit of the vine and the tree.
We bring the seeds of the nut and the pod.

KING (*Reverently stretching out his hands over the food*):
Blessed forever the harvest shall be,
Blessed forever the bounty of God.
(JESTER *enters, carrying large plum pudding. He ap-
proaches throne.*)

JESTER:
I bring you a pudding all puffed up with plums.

KING (*Laughing*):
Be careful you don't poke them out with your thumbs!
(*He rises.*)
Thank you, kind friends, for your generous attitude.
There is no gift that is sweeter than gratitude.

MINSTREL (*Coming forward and kneeling before* KING):
There's one more gift that heaven has sent.
I bring it to you in an instrument.

1st GUARDSMAN (*Aside, to* KING):
    He's naught but a beggar. There's not any treasure
    That he could present to a king for his pleasure.
KING:
    There's no one so poor in this land where we live
    That he hasn't at least a small something to give.
MINSTREL (*Throwing back his cape and holding up his harp*):
    Behold! The gift I bear the King
    Is a grateful heart and a song to sing!
ALL (*Ad lib*):
    Music! A song! Play a tune for Christmas! (*Etc.*)
KING (*Rapturously*):
    It's the gift of sweet song! Oh, do let us hear it.
    There's no gift so great as a gift of the spirit.
1st VILLAGER: Oh, lead us in song!
2nd VILLAGER: Please play your harp for us!
MAYOR:
    You sing all the stanzas
    We'll join in the chorus.
    (MINSTREL *begins to play and sing any familiar Christmas carol, and they all join in the chorus.* LORD MAYOR *leads* KING *to food table, as singing continues and curtain falls.*)

THE END

The Snowman Who Played Santa

Characters

JOHNNY
SNOWMAN
JACKDAW
SQUIRREL

TIME: *Late afternoon on Christmas Day.*
SETTING: *A snowy backyard.*
AT RISE: JOHNNY *is putting the finishing touches on the* SNOWMAN, *who stands motionless at center. Then he steps back to view his work.*

JOHNNY:
There, Mr. Snowman, you're all made!
But you don't look much like Santa, I'm 'fraid.
You haven't his twinkle, you haven't his smile,
And I just couldn't dress you in Santa Claus style.
(*He picks up snow shovel and starts offstage, right. He looks a little sad.*)
Oh, I did so hope and half believe
That Santa would come on Christmas Eve!
And he didn't come with his pack and sleigh
And now it's the end of Christmas Day!
And he'll never get here to bring me toys

This play may easily be adapted for presentation with hand puppets.

As he does the city girls and boys,
For I live too far from the beaten track
And he can't wade over this snow with his pack.
(JOHNNY *turns and waves to* SNOWMAN.)
Good night, Mr. Snowman! I wish there were laws
To change you tonight into Santa Claus.
(*He goes out, right.*)

SNOWMAN (*Bursting into sobs*):
Boo-hoo-hoo! Boo-hoo-hoo!
My nose isn't red and my eyes aren't blue,
And I can't help Johnny at all, because
I'm just not a bit like Santa Claus!
(JACKDAW *enters from left.*)

JACKDAW:
Did I hear a sigh? Or was it a shout?
(*Sees* SNOWMAN)
What in the world are you crying about?

SNOWMAN:
Poor little Johnny! He didn't get toys
On Chrismas Eve, like most of the boys.
His cottage is too far out of the way
For Santa to find with his reindeer sleigh.
Oh, I'd like to do something for John! You see,
He went to the trouble of making me!

JACKDAW:
Yes, Johnny's a dear. When winter comes,
He always remembers to toss me crumbs.
I think it's dreadful he shouldn't have toys.
(SNOWMAN *and* JACKDAW *burst into tears.*)

SNOWMAN:
Boo-hoo! Boo-hoo! Oh, what shall we do?
The day will be gone in an hour or two.

SQUIRREL (*Entering left*):
Did I hear a sigh? Or was it a shout?
(*He sees the others.*)

What in the world are you crying about?

JACKDAW:

We're crying because of the snowy drifts
That keep old Santa from bringing John's gifts.

SQUIRREL:

But why should you be so blue about it?
Let's think of something to do about it!

SNOWMAN:

I'd like to pretend I'm Santa Claus
But I can't dress up because . . . because . . .

SQUIRREL:

Because you haven't a thing to wear.
Do you see that washing over there?
(*Points offstage.*)
I'll get you the red coat off the line
And the hat with the fur that looks like mine.

SNOWMAN:

But where shall I look for a toy or trinket?

JACKDAW (*With sudden inspiration*):

My nest is the place, though you never would think it!
(JACKDAW *and* SQUIRREL *run out left, greatly excited.*)

SNOWMAN:

Dear me! I cannot understand
Just what it is those two have planned!
How can they quickly cheer the boy
Both with a Santa and a toy?
(JOHNNY *is heard from offstage singing a carol.* SNOW-
MAN *listens sadly.* SQUIRREL *and* JACKDAW *enter, laden
with bags and bundles, which they begin to open im-
mediately.*)

SQUIRREL (*To* JACKDAW):

Just a minute! You'd better pause
And help me dress up Santa Claus.

JACKDAW:

Oh, very well! With beak and claws

I'll help you dress up Santa Claus.

SNOWMAN:

These clothes are very, very fine,
Though only borrowed from a line!
(*He looks pleased and proud.*)

SQUIRREL (*Opening a bag*):

Here are some nuts I'm glad I stored
Last autumn, underneath a board.
(*He fills* SNOWMAN'S *pockets with nuts.*)

JACKDAW (*Opening another bag*):

And here are different kinds of toys,
Enough to please a dozen boys.

SQUIRREL (*To* SNOWMAN):

The Jackdaw, though you don't suspect her,
Is one bird who's a great collector.
She gathers things from east and west
To see them sparkle in her nest.

JACKDAW:

Yes, here's a jackknife and a key,
And marbles, one and two, and three . . . and . . .
(*There is a noise offstage, right, of door closing.*)

SNOWMAN:

Quick! Johnny's coming! Don't you hear him?
(SQUIRREL *and* JACKDAW *finish their work in a hurry and
withdraw, each to a distant corner of the stage.*)

SQUIRREL *and* JACKDAW (*Together*):

Let's hope our strange surprise will cheer him.
(JOHNNY *enters, stops stock-still when he sees* SNOWMAN.
He rubs his eyes in wonder.)

JOHNNY:

I must be dreaming! When off I ran,
I thought you were only a poor snowman!
But now I see you're Santa Claus—
The nicest saint that ever was!
(*He takes toys, nuts, etc. from* SNOWMAN'S *pockets.*)

You've brought me nuts! You've brought me toys!
(*Turns to audience.*)
Oh, I'm the happiest of boys!
(SQUIRREL *and* JACKDAW *chuckle.* SNOWMAN *smiles broadly, as the curtain falls.*)

THE END

The Child Who Was Made of Snow

Characters

OLD MAN
WIFE
SNOW MAIDEN
CHILDREN

SCENE 1

TIME: *Christmas Eve long ago.*

SETTING: *The yard in front of the old couple's cottage.*

AT RISE: *The* OLD MAN *is pretending to chop a log at right, and his* WIFE *is at left gathering sticks and twigs.*

OLD MAN (*Singing to tune of "O Christmas Tree"*):
Swing high the ax, swing high and higher.
And hew a log to build a fire.

WIFE (*Singing*):
Go search for branches in the snow
To make the red flame leap and glow.

OLD MAN *and* WIFE (*Singing*):
For it is now the Holy Night,
The Baby Jesus seeks a light.
Oh, keep your hearthstone burning bright,
The Baby Jesus seeks a light.

OLD MAN (*Laying down ax*): How goes it, good wife? Are the sticks ready?

WIFE: Yes. I have found plenty.

OLD MAN: And I have hewn a giant log. It will make a great blaze, for once it was a mighty tree. Come, let us go inside and start the fire. (*He starts toward exit, right. Sleigh bells are heard in the distance, from off left.*)

WIFE: Hark! I hear sleigh bells! (OLD MAN *stops, then goes to left, and peers off into distance.*)

OLD MAN: Yes, I see a sleigh coming up the hill. (WIFE *joins him.*)

WIFE (*Looking off left*): It is filled with boys and girls.

OLD MAN: It is stopping now. The children are climbing out.

WIFE (*Excitedly*): Perhaps they are coming here!

OLD MAN: Most likely they are cutting across the fields to get home early. (*Sound of bells grows louder and singing is heard.*)

WIFE: Look! Here they come! (CHILDREN *enter left, singing a Christmas carol.* 1ST CHILD *carries a wreath,* 2ND CHILD *holds a candle, and* 3RD CHILD *has a spray of evergreens. When they finish singing, the* WIFE *smiles at them.*) Well, well, little ones. What a good time you are having!

1ST CHILD: Yes. We've had a wonderful ride.

2ND CHILD: Up and over the hills where the snow lies thickest.

3RD CHILD: And down into the hollows where the shadows are blue. We've been stopping at every house and singing carols.

OLD MAN: Where are you going now?

1ST CHILD (*Holding up wreath*): I'm going home to hang this wreath in the window.

2ND CHILD (*Holding up candle*): I'm going home to light a candle to put in the window.

3RD CHILD (*Waving spray of evergreens*): I'm going home to decorate the house.

WIFE: But what about the rest of you? Won't you come in and visit us? I've plenty of Christmas cakes.

CHILDREN: Oh, no! We can't come in!

1ST CHILD: We are all going home to sit around the fire and listen to Christmas stories.

2ND CHILD: My mother will tell me about the Three Wise Men who followed the star to the stable in Bethelehem.

WIFE (*Sadly*): Yes, yes. You must go to your homes and listen to your mothers tell you stories. Here, I will give each of you a stick from my bundle to light your Christmas fires. (*She divides her sticks among them as her husband looks on in astonishment. Then he helps her.*)

CHILDREN: Oh, thank you, thank you, good dame! Thank you, thank you, old man! (*Several* CHILDREN *throw their arms about the old couple and kiss them. Then all the* CHILDREN *exit left, some throwing kisses, others calling out, "Merry Christmas." Sleigh bells and the singing are again heard. The old couple stand looking off into the distance until the sounds die away.*)

OLD MAN: What are we going to do for sticks for our fire? You have given them all away.

WIFE (*Sadly*): What does it matter? The brightest fire in the world will not add cheer to our hearthstone.

OLD MAN (*Sighing*): Yes, I know. It is children's faces that bring cheer to a home. And we have no little ones. No little ones at all.

WIFE (*Beginning to cry*): No little ones at all. No children to make the Holy Night happy. (OLD MAN *gently puts his arm about her, trying to lead her toward the house. She shakes her head sadly.*) No, let us not go into the house. It is lonely there.

OLD MAN: But it will be more lonely out here with the night coming on. (*He picks up a handful of snow and lets it filter through his fingers. Suddenly he straightens up and smiles.*) I know! Let us make a child of snow!

WIFE (*Brightening*): Why, yes! We can make her just the way we want her to be, with long curls and dancing feet.

OLD MAN: And laughing lips. See! I will begin with this mound of snow. (*He walks over to mound and begins to mold it with his hands.*)

WIFE: And I will make a snowball for her head. Oh, we will make a lovely maiden! (*She picks up some snow and starts to roll it in her hands.*)

CURTAIN

* * *

SCENE 2

TIME: *Later the same evening.*

SETTING: *The same as Scene 1. The stage is in semidarkness, with a white light to represent moonlight.*

AT RISE: *The* OLD MAN *and his* WIFE *are putting the finishing touches on the* SNOW MAIDEN, *who is dressed in white. She is standing motionless on a mound of snow at center and does not move until the* OLD MAN *and his* WIFE *go into the house.*

OLD MAN: There! She is finished at last!

WIFE (*Stepping back to view the* SNOW MAIDEN): Yes, all finished. How beautiful she is!

OLD MAN: More beautiful than I ever thought a child could be.

WIFE (*Putting her arms around the statue*): She is ours! Ours! Our very own child! (*There is a moment's silence. Then* WIFE *draws back.*)

OLD MAN: What is the matter?

WIFE: She is so cold, so cold! She is nothing but snow and ice. She can never put her arms about me, or run, or laugh, or play.

OLD MAN (*Sadly*): No. She can never run, or laugh, or play.

WIFE (*Beginning to cry*): When morning comes, the sun will melt her. She will melt away to nothing.

OLD MAN (*Putting his arm about his* WIFE): It will do no good to cry. Let us go into our cottage. It is almost midnight, and the cold grows keener. You are shivering.

WIFE: I am shivering because my heart is turning to a lump of ice. (*They go off right. After a short silence, a clock offstage chimes the hour of midnight. Soft music is heard. Slowly the* SNOW MAIDEN *begins to come to life. She comes down from the mound. Then she dances lightly over the snow.*)

SNOW MAIDEN (*Chanting as she dances*):
Come out, come out into the night.
The white snow swirls and dances, light.
On hillocks where the moon has smiled,
In hollows where the wind blows wild,
The snow is dancing like a child.
(WIFE *enters from right. She is carrying a lantern, which she holds up as she looks about, bewildered.* OLD MAN *follows her.*)

OLD MAN: Why do you come out here into the cold again?

WIFE: I thought I heard someone singing.

OLD MAN. It's only the wind in the firs.

WIFE: But see! Isn't that someone dancing, whirling about in the wind?

SNOW MAIDEN (*Coming toward them*): Oh, there you are! Father! Mother! (*She runs up and embraces them.*)

WIFE: It's the Snow Maiden!

OLD MAN: She has come to life!

SNOW MAIDEN: I have come to live with you always.

OLD MAN: It is a miracle!

WIFE: A miracle of the Holy Night!

SNOW MAIDEN: No. Just the miracle of love! (*Soft Christmas music is heard from offstage as the curtain falls.*)

THE END

Santa's Send-Off

Characters

SANTA
MRS. SANTA
THREE ELVES

TIME: *Christmas Eve.*
SETTING: *Santa's house, at the North Pole.*
AT RISE: SANTA *is asleep on a couch, fully dressed in traditional costume.* MRS. SANTA *is shaking him, trying to wake him up, and the* ELVES *help her.*

MRS. SANTA (*Leaning over* SANTA *and shaking his arm vigorously*):
O Santa, dear Santa, be up and away!
I've packed the last cookies and toys in the sleigh.
I've put up a snack you may eat on your way—
O Santa, dear Santa, do hurry, I pray!
(SANTA *turns over in his sleep, but does not wake up.*)
1ST ELF:
The reindeer are stamping their dark dainty hoofs.
They simply can't wait to alight on the roofs.
(SANTA *snores.*)
2ND ELF:
The skies are a-prickle with sharp little stars;
The great northern lights are uplifting their bars.

3RD ELF:
  But storm clouds will lumber like shaggy white bears
  All growling with thunder and padding in pairs.
  (SANTA *grunts*.)
1ST ELF:
  Before all the skies in a snow-fog are swirled
  Be off on your journey to circle the world!
MRS. SANTA (*In a louder voice, as she continues to shake* SANTA's *arm*):
  The children are sleeping, they're dreaming of you.
  They've cleaned out the chimneys for you to come through.
  They've hung up their stockings or put out a shoe . . .
  (SANTA *stirs, then opens his eyes and begins to rub them. He sits up slowly and stretches.*)
2ND ELF (*Pleadingly*):
  O Santa, dear Santa, be up and away!
  Tonight is the eve, tomorrow the day
  When no one is lonely and everyone's gay.
  Because of your coming. . . . Be up and away!
  (MRS. SANTA *claps her hands, then helps pull* SANTA *to his feet.*)
SANTA (*As he gets up and looks around*):
  What? Up and away?
MRS. SANTA (*Pushing him toward door*):
  Yes, up and away!
ALL (*Except* SANTA):
  Tonight is the eve, tomorrow the day!
SANTA (*Agreeably, as he opens door*):
  I'm well on my way now, I'm well on my way! (*He laughs and exits, and they all laugh and wave to him as he leaves.*)

THE END

Father Christmas

(Two groups of children, one on each side of the stage, skip around in circles, reciting stanzas alternately, in singsong fashion. Bells are heard ringing offstage.)

1ST GROUP:
   Here comes Christmas
      With his jingling bells;
   Here comes Christmas
      Weaving wondrous spells;
   With the holly berry's glow,
      And the magic mistletoe.
   Here comes Christmas!
   (FATHER CHRISTMAS *enters, carrying sack.*)

2ND GROUP:
   Coming in without a knock,
      Making sturdy chimneys rock,
   Doors and hearts he shall unlock
      With a breath of laughter.
   And his merriment will shake
      Every room and rafter.
   Even Scrooges shall awake
      And go trooping after. . . .

(FATHER CHRISTMAS hands children stockings, which they hang at fireplace mantel which may be at rear of stage.)

Here comes Christmas!

(After hanging up stockings, children may follow FATHER CHRISTMAS offstage, in a procession, singing "Up on the Housetops" as they go off.)

The Snowman's Christmas

(There may be an unlighted Christmas tree, center, with
SNOWMAN *at one side, and with* NARRATOR *nearby. Birds*
may walk over to SNOWMAN *as they speak. There is a*
window on rear wall.)

NARRATOR:
> A snowman stood out in the lonely front yard,
> Where there used to be flowers and lawn,
> And he cried icy tears (which he'd not done for years)
> Because all of the house shades were drawn,
> And he could not look in through the windows to see
> The wonderful lights on the Christmas tree.

CROW:
> "But why don't you go in at the door?" asked the crow.
> "They'd let you sit down by the hearthstone, I know."

SNOWMAN:
> The snowman cried harder (so badly he felt),
> "If I ventured inside, I'd be certain to melt."

RED BIRD:
> "Then why don't you whistle to someone you know
> Indoors?" said the red bird, who stood by the crow.

292

SNOWMAN:

"I never could whistle or pucker up quick
These lips," said the snowman. "My mouth is a stick."

NARRATOR:

So the cardinal whistled a happy refrain,
And the crow with his beak tapped the dark window-
    pane.
(*Birds do so.*)
Then the curtains were raised with a laugh and a shout
(*Lights of tree go on.*)
(You can't bottle Christmas; it has to come out.)
And the snowman felt happy the rest of the night,
For he glittered and gleamed in the Christmas tree's
    light.

The Christmas Candle

(Each child may carry electric candle which he puts on as he speaks. Members of CHORUS *may put theirs on during last two lines.)*

1ST SOLO:
> I had a Christmas candle.
> > I lit it with a match.
>
> Outside my window, on the snow,
> > It made a golden patch.

CHORUS:
> And rabbits, running to and fro,
> Turned golden in the candle's glow.

2ND SOLO:
> I lit a Christmas candle—
> > Its small light flamed and flittered,
>
> And suddenly the empty dark
> > That rimmed my window, glittered

CHORUS:
> With icicles, all pale before . . .
> (Long, golden fingers at my door!)

3RD SOLO:
> The fingers beckoned, and the light

That dripped from them into the night
Guided opossum, coon and hare
To little feasts I had spread there
Beneath the candle's golden glare. . . .

CHORUS:

  Oh, Christmas candlelight can bring
  A golden touch to everything!

The Unhappy Fir Tree

(THREE SOLOS *and* THREE CHORUSES *speak alternately*.)

1ST CHORUS:
> A fairy walked in the forest.
> > She heard a fir tree whine,

1ST SOLO:
> "The other trees don't have to wear
> > Sharp needles such as mine.
>
> I wish that I had golden leaves
> > That glittered in the light."

2ND CHORUS:
> The fairy waved her wand and changed
> > The fir tree overnight.
>
> She changed her to a golden tree
> > That brighted all the air,
> But thieves came by and stole the gold
> > And left the fir tree bare.

2ND SOLO:
> "Boo hoo! I wish my leaves were glass,"
> > The little fir tree wept.

3RD CHORUS:
   The fairy waved her wand again
      And changed her as she slept.

   Her leaves of glass were pretty things
      That sparkled in the sun,
   But winds blew by and hail came down
      And broke them one by one.

3RD SOLO:
   "If I could just have leaves of green
      As oaks and maples do!"

1ST CHORUS:
   The fairy heard the fir tree say,
      And made her wish come true.

   But soon a hungry goat came by
      And gobbled up the green
   So that the fir tree stood once more
      All bare and brown and lean.

2ND SOLO:
   "And would you like your needles, now?"
      The fairy asked the tree.

1ST SOLO:
   "O yes," the little fir replied,
      "Please give them back to me;

   And thank you for your magic gifts,
      You merry woodland elf,
   You've taught me that it's best for me
      Always to be myself."

Come Out and Join the Caroling

(An introduction to a program of Christmas music which may be given by two boys and two girls. Carolers may stand behind them, ready to sing.)

1st Boy:

> Come out and join the caroling,
> Good friends and neighbors jolly!
> Across the candle-lighted snow.
> A troop of singers we shall go
> And stop beneath the mistletoe
> Or laughing wreaths of holly,
> To sing the songs of yesteryear,
> That old and young delight to hear.

1st Girl:

> The snow will hush our eager feet,
> And we shall fill the silent street
> > With burst of happy song,
> That those who sleep may dream more sweet
> > Because we pass along;
> That those who wake, true joy may take,
> > In this our festive throng.

2nd Boy:

> The hollow night will be our bowl,
> > The wind, our wassail stinging;

Good will flows forth from soul to soul
As underneath the stars we stroll
   Exultant in our singing.

2ND GIRL:
   But when the chimes in yonder tower
   Give warning of the midnight hour,
   The winding way we shall retrace
   And, with a good-night's parting grace,
   Shall leave the frosty skies behind,
   And each a hearty welcome find
   Within the Yule log's warm embrace.

1ST BOY AND 1ST GIRL (*Together*):
   Come out and join the caroling,
      Good friends and neighbors jolly!
   Come, let us wreathe the world with song
      More brilliant than the holly!

The Snow Maiden

(*This may be effectively performed with the Reader standing at one side, and three characters in costume perform-
ing the action in pantomine. The* SNOW MAIDEN *wears
a white sparkling ballet costume. She remains motionless until the appropriate line. The* MAN *and* WIFE *are
dressed as peasants. The stage may be divided to represent the inside and the outside of the hut, with a simple
winter backdrop.*)

One Christmas, long and long ago,
Two peasants made a child of snow—
Two peasants who lived all alone
And had no children of their own.
(MAN *and* WIFE *pretend to mold* MAIDEN *out
of snow.*)
All day they shaped the smiling face
And gave the little body grace
Until the child was good to see
As they would wish their own to be . . .
"But she is only snow," they said,
And sorrowfully they went to bed.
(MAN *and* WIFE *shake heads sadly and go right,
inside hut. They lie down on floor and go to
sleep.*)
Then in the night, when storms were rocking
Their humble hut, they heard a knocking

300

(*A knock is heard, and peasants go to door.*)
At the door, and went to see
What poor lost stranger it could be
Outside upon a night so wild
Calling like a frightened child.
(MAN *opens door, and The* SNOW MAIDEN
stands there, alive and radiant.)
"Look!" cried Peter to his wife,
"Our snow maiden has come to life!"
Yes, sure enough, for there she stood
As rosy now as flesh and blood.
(*Happily, they take her by the hand and lead
her inside hut.*)
The good wife wept, the old man cried
For joy to see her step inside
Their cottage poor, and fill with laughter
The barren room from floor to rafter;
(SNOW MAIDEN *and* MAN *and* WIFE *embrace.*)
And this strange child, who'd known no other
Parents, called them "Father!" . . . "Mother!"
And thanked them for the hearthstone warm
That saved her from a life of storm . . .
And so one Christmas long ago,
Love worked a miracle in snow.

Christmas Cheer

1ST GIRL:
  What shall you do for Christmas cheer?
  What shall you do for Christmas?

1ST BOY:
  I'll hang a wreath in the window here.
  That's what I'll do for Christmas cheer,
  That's what I'll do for Christmas.

2ND GIRL:
  What shall you do on Christmas night?
  What shall you do on Christmas?

2ND BOY:
  Three tall candles I will light
  To make the snow more gold than white—
  This I will do for Christmas.

3RD GIRL:
  What shall we sing by the Yule log's blaze?
  What shall we sing for Christmas?

ALL (*Together*):
  Let's sing a carol of joy and praise,
  Of Bethlehem in the olden days—
  Let's sing a carol for Christmas!
  (*All may join in singing a familiar Christmas carol, with
  the audience joining in.*)

On Christmas Eve

MOTHER:
  Did you hang the little stockings in a row
    By the chimney?
  Did you place a little candle, just so,
    In the doorway,
  Where its glow
  Makes a beacon on the snow
  That the traveler may know
  Where to go?

FATHER:
  Look! I see a lantern gleaming in the street
    Pausing, gliding—
  Do you hear the heavy tread of booted feet
    And the clumping
    Of a hoof
    On the roof?

MOTHER:
  Hark!
  A wind blows down the chimney
  Making dark
  The fire; a wind
  And something after—
  Do you hear an old man's laughter

And the clink
Of a toy
Caught in the chink
Of a brick?

FATHER:
Quick!
Did you see a little sleigh
Drive away?

Christmas Round the World

(A reading for four girls and three boys)

AMERICAN GIRL:
When Christmas comes it's time to make
Our wreath of hollyberry,
And wonder how the boys and girls
In other lands make merry.
Here in America I place
My stocking by the tree.
I know that Santa Claus will come
And fill it up for me.

DUTCH GIRL:
I do not hang a stocking up.
I use a wooden shoe.
And I call Santa Claus "St. Nick,"
As all Dutch children do.

DANISH BOY:
In Denmark, Father Christmas comes
Wiping his snow-boots on the mat.
He lights the candles on the tree
With a burning candle in his hat.

FINNISH GIRL:
On Finland's starry Christmas Eve

305

The house is washed and swept.
I sleep upon a bed of straw
As the Babe in the manger slept.

ENGLISH BOY:

In English homes the Yule log burns.
We hang the mistletoe once more,
And sing the carols in the streets
At every candle-lighted door.

SWEDISH GIRL:

The Swedish children do not feast
Or sing gay Christmas-carol words
Until they've trimmed a Christmas tree
Out in the storm, for hungry birds.

SPANISH BOY:

Around the Christmas crib we dance
And sing our Spanish airs.
The jingling tambourines are gay
But silent are our prayers.

Christmas Carillon

This day has drawn dark curtains tight
   Across its light.
A church lifts high its spire-finger
   In the night
As though to hush the noisy world.
   Above, unfurled,
White clouds lie soft as angels' wings,
   Spanning all things.
A star puts forth its golden ear
   That it may hear
What psalm the talking tower tells
   In voice of bells.

The Little Fir Tree

I met a little fir tree, once,
   Climbing up a hill
On the way to my house
   (The night was very still)
And I could hear it singing
   A piney little song
   As it went along.

It must have made a short cut
   Over field and stone
Because, although I passed it
   And hurried home alone,
There inside my doorway
   The little fir tree stood!
Its snowy cape had fallen off,
   So had its peakèd hood;

And, oh, it wore a lovely dress
   Of stars and ribbon-gold.
It stretched its arms as if to say:
   "Come in out of the cold."
   (I did as I was told.)

Nature's Christmas Card

Fly, snowflakes, fly!
The wind and I
Shall play with you
As you pass by.

The wind will swing and swirl you
And I shall catch and hurl you
In snowballs round and bright
Or build a snowman, white
And fat and round
Where you fall on the ground.

Fly, snowflakes, fly!
The wind and I
Shall make a Christmas card
Of this, my own front yard.

Once More . . .

Once more the Christmas candles burn,
  The living holly flaunts its berry,
Once more the carolers return,
  The world makes merry.

The Christmas Tree Angel

There was a little angel
  Lived on a Christmas tree
But she was not angelic
  As angels ought to be.
She kicked her little heels up
  And waved her arms in air
And wore her halo crooked
Upon her golden hair.
  (What's more, she didn't care.)
She had such silly manners
That of course it was quite plain
She wasn't made of *real* stuff
  But just of *cellophane*.

Getting Ready for Christmas

Who's getting ready for Christmas tonight?
"I," said the snow, "I have turned the world white."
"I," said the frost, "with my magical mixture
I've painted on everyone's window a picture."
"I," said the forester, bringing home fuel,
"I've gathered faggots and logs for the Yule."
"I," said the cook. "I have roasted a pheasant
And cooked a great boar's head to make the feast pleasant."
"I," said the minstrel, "I've made up a ballad
To sing to the king while he's eating his salad . . ."

Who's getting ready for holiday mirth?
Why! All happy children all over the earth!

PART TWO

The Seasons

The Earth Is Turning

The earth is turning—
  Spring is here!
  Summer comes singing!
  Autumn goes winging!
  Winter draws near
With hearthstones burning.
  Spring is here!
The earth is turning.

The Magic Weaver

Characters

ELVES
ELF KING
SPRING
ELFIN MAID
CRICKET
SPIDER
FAIRY QUEEN
FAIRIES

TIME: *A spring evening.*
SETTING: *Elfland.*
AT RISE: *The* ELVES *are singing. At left, the* CRICKET *is playing the fiddle. At right, the* SPIDER *huddles up in a ball, asleep. The* ELF KING *sits on a toadstool.*

ELVES (*Singing to the tune of "Merrily We Roll Along"*):
Merry is our Elfin Land, Elfin Land, Elfin Land,
Merry is our Elfin Land, in the month of May.
(*They rise and dance in a circle around* ELF KING.)
Let's go dancing hand in hand, hand in hand, hand in hand,

Let's go dancing hand in hand, in the month of May.
(*Bugles sound in the distance and the circle breaks up.
Two other* ELVES *enter, one from left and one from
right, carrying artificial trumpet-flower bugles. They
blow bugles, and the other* ELVES *gather round them.*)

1ST ELF (*Mounting a toadstool and intoning like a town
crier*):
The Fairy Queen is coming!
She's traveling this way.
She will arrive in Elfland
Before the break of day.

2ND ELF (*Also standing on a toadstool and intoning*):
The Fairy Queen is coming!
She comes from out the east.
Oh, roll a mossy carpet out
And spread a fairy feast.

ELF KING (*Clapping his hands in command.* ELVES *kneel
in a semicircle around him*): Did you hear that? The
Fairy Queen is coming! She has no doubt left Fairyland
already, which means she will soon be in Elfland. We
must get ready at once. (*He claps his hands again.*) Go
call Lady Spring and ask her to bring a mossy carpet.
(1ST *and* 2ND ELVES *start to go, but are halted by* SPRING,
who enters with a roll of carpeting under each arm.)

SPRING (*Curtsying to* ELF KING): Here I am. I heard the
bugle. I have brought not only a carpet of moss, but one
of violets, too. (*She unrolls them on the ground.*)

ELVES: Oh, oh, how beautiful! (*Several* ELVES *turn somer-
saults on the carpets, in their delight.*)

ELF KING (*Sharply*): No time for fun and frolic now!
Fetch the food.

ELVES (*Scrambling to their feet*): Yes, yes, Your Majesty.

ELF KING: The best nectar from the freshest flowers, and
honey from the hive.

ELVES: Yes, yes, Your Majesty. (*They bow, and several* ELVES *scamper off.*)

SPRING (*Taking things from her basket and bowing to* ELF KING): See, I have picked fresh twigs for forks and the greenest acorn cups.

ELF KING: Ah! Spring magic can do everything.

SPRING (*Sadly*): Not quite everything, I fear.

ELF KING (*Not listening*): And now we must set the toadstool table. Bring out the cloth of finest lace. (ELFIN MAID *enters, running.*)

ELFIN MAID: Here it is, Your Majesty. (*She curtsies and places the folded cloth in his hands.*)

ELF KING (*Proudly, as he unfolds it*): It is the loveliest lace ever made. See! (*He shakes it out and holds it up. There is a ragged tear right in the middle of it.*)

ELVES (*Aghast*): A hole!

ELF KING: What? A hole?

ELVES (*Excitedly*): How did it get there? What shall we do?

ELF KING (*With a groan*): We have no other cloth good enough. And whoever heard of a fairy feast without a tablecloth?

ELVES (*With a wail*): What shall we do? What shall we do?

ELF KING (*With sudden inspiration*): Lady Spring, where are you?

SPRING (*Stepping forward*): Here, Your Majesty.

ELF KING: Why are you not offering your May magic now, when we need it most?

SPRING (*Sadly*): Because my magic will not mend your tablecloth.

ELF KING: What? What do you mean? (*He drops the cloth to the ground.*)

SPRING (*Plucking a large leaf with a hole in it and holding it up*): See this leaf? I made it unfurl from the bud.

But someone else made this hole—a greedy insect, no doubt—and I cannot even patch it. My work is to make, not to mend.

ELF KING: Oh dear, oh dear, this is terrible! Is there no one who can mend this hole?

CRICKET: I'll try! I'll try! (*He puts down his violin, hops over to the cloth, spreads it out and kneels on it. Then he begins to nibble around the edges of the hole.*)

ELF KING: But you're nibbling it! You're only making it bigger! (*Everyone looks alarmed.*)

CRICKET: Yum yum! There's *starch* in it. (*He chews greedily.*)

SPRING: You greedy creature!

1ST *and* 2ND ELVES: He can't sew at all. (CRICKET *continues to chew.*)

ELF KING: Pull him away! Take him by the legs!

ELVES: Pull him away! Take him by the legs! (*They grab the* CRICKET *and pull him back to his toadstool.*)

ELF KING (*Sternly*): Stick to your music hereafter.

ELVES (*Putting* CRICKET's *fiddle into his hands*): Stick to your music! (*Bugles sound in the distance.*)

ELF KING (*Rushing about frantically*): The Queen! The Queen! She's coming!

ELVES (*Talking in rapid succession*): We have no table-cloth . . . The hole seems bigger than ever . . . We're worse off than before . . . What shall we do? (*They wail and moan. The noise awakens* SPIDER.)

SPIDER (*Coming out of her ball with a yawn and a stretch*): My, my! What's the matter? Anyone would think the world was coming to an end.

ELF KING: It is—almost!

1ST ELF: The Fairy Queen is coming here to feast.

2ND ELF: And our best tablecloth has a hole in it!

ELF KING: And nobody can mend it!

ELVES: Nobody can mend it!

SPIDER: Nonsense! I can mend it!

ELF KING: You? How can you? You seem to be all thumbs.

SPRING: Looks are sometimes deceiving.

SPIDER: Where is the cloth?

SPRING (*Handing it to her*): It's here. Please hurry. I should have thought of you before.

ELF KING (*Still nervous*): Don't nibble it the way the cricket did.

SPIDER (*Laughing*): I don't nibble. I weave and sew.

ELF KING: But where is your needle?

SPRING: She doesn't need one. (*She chants.*)
A spider spins fine laces
For tabletop or shelf.
She does not thread a needle,
She simply threads herself.

ELF KING (*Suddenly curious*): Gather around, everyone, I'd like to see this. (SPIDER *twirls on her toes to unwind thread. All gather around her, so the audience can see only the* SPIDER'S *arms moving above her head.* SPIDER *hides the old cloth under her apron and brings out a new one.*)

ELVES (*Talking in rapid succession as they watch*): Of all things . . . Look at her. . . . She sews like lightning . . . She weaves like a whirlwind. (*Etc.*)

ALL: Oh! It's done! (ELVES *part, and the* SPIDER *holds up the new cloth for all to see.*)

ELF KING (*In awe*): A cobweb cloth! I never saw anything so beautiful in my life. (*Bugles sound again off-stage.*) The Queen! Set the table, quickly. She's almost here.

ELVES (*Setting to work at once and chanting as they work*):
With twigs for forks, with acorn cups, we set the elfin table.
Oh, Cricket, tune your violin, as soon as you are able.

Oh, Spring, put flowers in a vase upon the cobweb cloth
That is as full of rainbow tints as any winged moth.

There never was so fine a feast within the forest green
As this we spread in Elfin Land to greet the Fairy Queen.

(QUEEN *enters, with a retinue of* FAIRIES. *The* ELF KING *steps forward and greets the* FAIRY QUEEN *with a deep bow. There is a great deal of bowing, also, among* FAIRIES *and* ELVES. ELF KING *and* FAIRY QUEEN *circle around the toadstool table, and the others following two by two, making a gay processional. Music may be played in the background. The* ELF KING *and* FAIRY QUEEN *stop back of the table, and the circle breaks so that all face the audience in a semicircle.*)

ELF KING (*To* FAIRY QUEEN): See, Your Majesty, the fairy feast is spread.

FAIRY QUEEN: Oh, oh, oh! I never saw anything spread so charmingly, so daintily. And where did you ever get such a beautiful tablecloth? Why, it's as sheer as a cobweb.

ELF KING (*Indicating* SPIDER): You must thank Dame Spider for that.

FAIRY QUEEN (*Going over to* SPIDER): Ah, I always heard you were a fine needlewoman! Perhaps some day you will weave me a cloth like that.

SPIDER: I should love nothing better.

ALL: You are a wonderful spinner and weaver!

ELF KING: Let's all dance around her before we dine!

FAIRY QUEEN: Yes, yes, let's dance. (*All dance merrily to background music. Curtain falls.*)

THE END

School for Scamperers

Characters

LONG-EARS ⎤
BOB-TAIL ⎬ *three little rabbits*
WIGGLE-NOSE ⎦
MAMMY RABBIT, *their mother*
ROVER

TIME: *A spring day.*

SETTING: *A clearing in the woods. At right is a hollow log or stump, and at left is a bramblebush.*

AT RISE: LONG-EARS, BOB-TAIL, *and* WIGGLE-NOSE *hop onstage, single file, carrying carrots.*

LONG-EARS, BOB-TAIL, *and* WIGGLE-NOSE (*As they circle stage*):
We're three little rabbits. We hippity-hop it. (*They hop to front of stage.*)
We nibble. We dribble. We flippity-flop it. (*They nibble their carrots and flip and flop their ears.*)
We're three little rabbits with rabbity habits,
We're off for the hill, to top it and crop it.
We're looking for blossoms of sweet-smelling clover. (*Sound of barking is heard offstage.*)
Oh, dear! Did you hear that? It's horrid old Rover! (*They huddle together.*)

LONG-EARS (*Frightened*): Where's Mammy? (*They all look around.*)

BOB-TAIL: I don't know.

WIGGLE-NOSE: Oh, dear! Oh, dear! (MAMMY RABBIT *enters in a hurry.*)

MAMMY: Here I am, bunnies. Don't be afraid. Rover may *sound* near, but that's just an echo, I'm quite sure. It's fooled me before.

LONG-EARS: But what if it *isn't* an echo? (*He shivers.*) What if it's fooling you again?

BOB-TAIL: What if he's really coming? (*He trembles.*)

WIGGLE-NOSE: What would we do? (*She wails.*)

MAMMY: Dear me! Don't be so scared. All you have to do is remember what I taught you. You don't have a big bark like Rover, do you?

LONG-EARS, BOB-TAIL, *and* WIGGLE-NOSE (*In chorus*): No.

MAMMY: So you can't scare him, can you?

LONG-EARS (*Shaking his ears*): No.

BOB-TAIL (*Shaking his ears*): No.

WIGGLE-NOSE (*Shaking her ears*): No.

MAMMY: Then you must fool him. Rover is very noisy. So you must be very quiet.

LONG-EARS: Oh, I remember the lesson:
We must come and we must go
On paddy-waddy tippy-toe.

BOB-TAIL:
So nobody will ever know
We go and come, and come and go.

MAMMY: Good. But you must not only run as soft as a shadow—you must go as swift as a flying cloud.

LONG-EARS: *I* can do it! See? (*He runs around the stage at a great rate.*)

BOB-TAIL: So can I! (*He follows.*)

WIGGLE-NOSE: So can I! (*She follows.*)

MAMMY: That will do. That will do! (*They all stop and come over to her.*) I know you're all good runners. But suppose the wind was blowing the wrong way and you couldn't sniff which way Rover was coming. Then what would you do?

LONG-EARS: I'd hide in a hollow log.

BOB-TAIL: I'd jump into a bramblebush.

MAMMY (*After a small silence*): And what would *you* do, Wiggle-Nose?

WIGGLE-NOSE: I—I'd climb a tree.

LONG-EARS (*Laughing*): Sounds just like a girl!

BOB-TAIL (*Scornfully*): Don't you know rabbits can't climb trees?

WIGGLE-NOSE: I—I'd follow Mammy's tail that's like a white light in the forest bobbing up and down, always ahead of me.

MAMMY: Well, that was the *first* lesson, of course. It was very safe when you were a baby, but now that you're getting big, you can't depend on me. You have to learn how to protect yourself.

WIGGLE-NOSE: I know! I remember the last lesson. I'm supposed to *freeze.*

MAMMY: That's right. Can you remember the rhyme?

WIGGLE-NOSE: Yes. It goes like this:
Crouch and scarcely draw a breath,
Freezing up as still as death,
Never twitching nose or ear
When a barking dog comes near.

LONG-EARS *and* BOB-TAIL: *She* would freeze just out of fear! (*They laugh.*)

MAMMY: Freezing is the hardest lesson you've had so far.

LONG-EARS (*Cockily*): Not for *me*. Just watch *me* do it. (*He freezes all but one ear, which twitches.*)

MAMMY: No, no, no! You're twitching an ear. Any little move like that would show Rover where you are.

BOB-TAIL: Watch me. *I* can do it. (*He freezes all except one paw, which trembles.*)

MAMMY: Oh, dear, no! Your left paw is still shaking. Look at your sister. She hasn't moved a muscle. (*Barking is heard again.*) *That* doesn't sound like an echo.

LONG-EARS: It's Rover! He's coming this way! (*He hides in hollow log.*)

BOB-TAIL: Help! Help! (*He jumps into bramblebush.*)

WIGGLE-NOSE: What shall I do? (*She wails.*)

MAMMY (*Frantically*): Just stay *frozen.*

WIGGLE-NOSE: But what about *you?*

MAMMY: Don't worry about me. I'll get that dog all mixed up. Just watch! (*She weaves about the stage, making intricate paths around bushes, trees, logs, stumps, etc., finally dodging behind a tree.* ROVER *enters, running in circles and sniffing. Then he pauses, puzzled.*)

ROVER (*With a growl*): Now where in thunder did that rabbit go? I know I saw one. (*He looks about bewildered, and spies hollow log.*) Ah, I'll wager it went in there! (*He runs over to log and sniffs.*)

MAMMY (*Coming out quickly from behind tree*): No, it didn't. It's here! (*She stands in full view of* ROVER. *He turns and chases her. They gallop all over the stage till* MAMMY *again dodges out of sight behind tree.*)

ROVER (*Pausing, panting*): Those rabbits are such crazy creatures! They run in and out and round about till they make me dizzy. (*He sits, panting. Then he gets up with sudden inspiration.*) I know! That rabbit must have jumped into the bramblebush. (*He starts toward bush, but* MAMMY *leaps from behind tree and runs in front of bush.*)

MAMMY (*Tauntingly*): No, here I am—not behind the bush at all. Catch me if you can. (*She begins to weave about stage with* ROVER *trying to follow her, sniffing along her path. When he approaches* WIGGLE-NOSE,

MAMMY *darts across stage calling, "Here, here." * ROVER *dashes after her yelping and barking as she leads him off-stage.*)

LONG-EARS (*Coming out of hollow log*): My, my! Did you see Mammy mix up that dog?

BOB-TAIL (*Leaping out of bramblebush*): Did you see all those little scrambly paths she made? Just like a Chinese puzzle!

WIGGLE-NOSE (*Relaxing from her "freeze" and rushing over to look offstage*): Dear, oh, dear! Mammy took such terrible risks! Do you realize she saved all our lives?

LONG-EARS: But Rover couldn't have caught *me* in the log.

BOB-TAIL: Nor *me* in the bush.

WIGGLE-NOSE: He could have starved you or dug you out. Dogs sometimes do. They wait and wait, and dig and dig . . . until . . . (*Faint barking is heard again offstage.*)

LONG-EARS: My! Rover sounds far away!

BOB-TAIL: I can't hear him at all now.

WIGGLE-NOSE: You don't think he caught her, do you?

LONG-EARS *and* BOB-TAIL (*Together*): Caught her? (*They all suddenly wail.* MAMMY *enters.*)

MAMMY (*Breathless*): Here, here! What's all this weeping and wailing?

LONG-EARS, BOB-TAIL *and* WIGGLE-NOSE (*Running to her and hugging her*): Mammy, Mammy, Mammy! You're safe!

MAMMY (*Breathlessly*): Whew! That was a chase if there ever was one! Up hill, down dale, around and around. (*She laughs.*) When I got Rover all mixed up, I doubled back on my tracks, and here I am!

LONG-EARS *and* BOB-TAIL: Is he still running?

MAMMY: Yes. In the wrong direction. (*They laugh.*)

WIGGLE-NOSE (*Still serious and frightened*): Oh, I'm so

glad you're all right! (*She gives* MAMMY *an extra hug.*)

MAMMY (*Lightly and cheerfully*): Making puzzle-paths can be fun when dogs are as stupid as Rover.

LONG-EARS: Is that the next lesson? Making puzzle-paths?

BOB-TAIL: And mixing dogs up?

WIGGLE-NOSE: Oh, let's have the lesson now!

LONG-EARS *and* BOB-TAIL: Yes, yes, yes.

MAMMY: Well, I was going to give you that lesson to-morrow, but since you've all shown me how well you learned the other lessons—

LONG-EARS, BOB-TAIL, *and* WIGGLE-NOSE: Yippee!

MAMMY: Here goes. Just watch me, and do what I do. (*She recites, acting out her words while the little rabbits imitate her.*)

Make a puzzle of your track,
Running forward, doubling back,
Racing round a tree or stump
Or a hillock, or a hump,
Freezing up as still as death
While you pause to get your breath
Then go circling all about,
Out and in, and in and out. (LONG-EARS, BOB-TAIL, *and* WIGGLE-NOSE *follow* MAMMY *as she winds off-stage.*)

ALL RABBITS (*Offstage, dwindling in the distance*):
Make a puzzle of your track,
Running forward, doubling back.
(*Curtain*)

THE END

Waking the Daffodil

Characters

GIRL
SUN
RAIN
ROBIN
DAFFODIL

SETTING: *Outdoors on a spring day.*

AT RISE: DAFFODIL *is lying curled up asleep, center. She wears a gray shawl over her yellow and green costume, and is covered with a white sheet as she sleeps.* GIRL *enters, skipping rope.*

GIRL:

Hippity-hop, hippity-hop,
Up on the hill at the tippity-top!
Hoppity-skip, hoppity-skip,
Over the hill at the toppity-tip!
One, two, three—
(*She trips over the rope and sits down suddenly, rubbing her knee and elbow. She looks about her, and frowns.*)
Dear me! The day is dark and chill!
How bare it is upon this hill!
Won't someone wake the daffodil?

(GIRL *goes over and shakes* DAFFODIL, *who rolls over without opening her eyes.* SUN *enters, right.*)

SUN:

Oh, I will wake the daffodil!

I'll fold away this quilt of snow.

(SUN *removes sheet, but* DAFFODIL *just rolls over without opening her eyes.*)

GIRL:

She does not heed the sun or dawn.

She does not even stretch or yawn.

SUN:

And I supposed that anyone

Could be awakened by the sun.

Perhaps I have been over-proud.

I'll go right back behind a cloud.

(SUN *exits.*)

GIRL:

And now, with all the sunlight gone,

It's barer still, across this lawn.

Won't someone wake the daffodil?

RAIN (*Calling from offstage*):

I'm coming, little girl, I will!

(RAIN *enters, wearing a raincoat and carrying a cup of water. Kneeling next to* DAFFODIL, RAIN *splashes a little water on* DAFFODIL's *face.*)

I'll make the daffodil get up

By splashing raindrops from my cup.

DAFFODIL (*Yawning and stretching so that one of her arms comes out like a green sprout*):

Go 'way, go 'way, you make me fret,

You silly rain, do you forget

Folks stay inside when it is wet?

(*She draws shawl more tightly about her.*)

A blanket's made for crawling under,

In times of lightning and of thunder.

(She curls back into a ball, leaving one arm extended.)

RAIN *(Sighing)*:

I've only made her huddle down
More snuggly in her dressing gown.
Her eyes won't open up at all.
I used to think the raindrop's call
Would waken flowers large or small
And make them get up out of bed.
I'm so ashamed I'll hide my head
Inside a cloud as gray as lead.

(RAIN exits.)

GIRL:

Again it's dark, again it's chill
And bare as ever on this hill.
Won't someone wake the daffodil?

(ROBIN enters, hopping.)

ROBIN:

I'll try! I'll try! I'll flit and fly
And sing a song to wake her by.

(He goes over to DAFFODIL and tries to waken her.)

Get up, get up, you lazy bud!
It's no fun lying in the mud
When all the air is soft with spring
And there's a song in everything.

(DAFFODIL stirs and stretches.)

Oh, do not waste a single hour
Of happy springtime, foolish flower!

DAFFODIL *(Opening her eyes and looking around)*:

Who calls to me? Who sings a song?
I have been waiting all night long
To hear that voice . . . Oh, is it true
That winter's gone and skies are blue?

ROBIN:

Of course. It's true as true can be!
Get up. The children want to see

The golden flower you will be.

DAFFODIL (*Rubbing her eyes and getting slowly to her feet*):

I'll rub the sleep out of my eyes
And stand up straight to see the skies.
I do not want to miss a thing
If it is spring!

(*She throws off her shawl and reveals a bright green and yellow costume—green tights and leotard and yellow cape and bonnet.*)

GIRL (*Gleefully*):

Yes, it is spring!
And you are here, you darling flower!
You would not come for sun or shower.
It takes a robin's song to make
A golden daffodil awake.

(*SUN and RAIN re-enter. They are carrying a rainbow between them.*)

SUN and RAIN (*Holding the rainbow over DAFFODIL's head*):

O welcome to you, little flower!
You would not come for sun or shower.
It takes a robin's song to make
A golden daffodil awake.

(*Curtain.*)

THE END

Awake, Little Seed

(Two girls may represent Spring *and the* Wild Flower
Seed. Spring *may wear a wreath of flowers over a pastel-
colored dress; the* Wild Flower Seed *should wear a
light brown hooded cape over a green dress and flower
hat.)*

Spring *(Calling to* Wild Flower Seed *who is asleep, with
her cape drawn around her)*:
Awake, little seed, awake and stir
Out of the black earth's sepulcher.
Rise from the ground in a leafy tower.
All the world is in need of a flower.
Awake, awake, awake!

Wild Flower Seed *(Rubbing her eyes, sleepily)*:
Why do you call to me? Why do you waken me,
    You who come knocking with fingers of rain?
Out of a beautiful dream you have shaken me . . .
    Let me go back to my slumber again.
To sleep, sleep, sleep.

Spring:
Hark, little seed, to the voice that calls!
Burst through your roof top, tear down your walls.
Earth may be cozy, and quiet, and deep,

But there's something far better than dreaming and
   sleep.
Awake, awake, awake!

WILD FLOWER SEED:
   Spring, is it you who are knocking and calling?
      Help me to throw off this blanket of night!
   (She stands and throws off her hooded cape.)
   Toss me a rope of your sunshine to climb on
      That I may open my leaves to the light.
   (SPRING *holds out circle of gold paper representing the
   sun.*)

SPRING:
   Yes, open your leaves to the light.

A Wind Runs by at Morning

(A reading in verse for two boys and two girls.)

1ST GIRL:
A wind runs by at morning
    And calls me as he runs,
And draws across my eyelids
    Gold ribbon of the sun's.

1ST BOY:
"Get up," he cries, "it's playtime
    And morning time
    And Maytime!"
A wind runs by at morning
    And calls me as he runs.

2ND GIRL:
But who shall call the robin
    Asleep inside the shell?
His little house is sealed so tight
    How can he ever tell
That it is spring and playtime
    And morning time
    And Maytime?

2ND BOY:
And yet he seems to know it

333

And know it very well.
For now he has arisen
And broken through his prison

ALL (*Together*):
What voice awakes the robin
　Asleep inside the shell?

Conversation with an April Fool

GIRL:

    "Which is the way to the nearest town,
      To the nearest town at hand?"
    I asked of an odd little April Fool
    Who looked at himself in a woodland pool
      And scribbled a scroll in the sand.

APRIL FOOL:

    "Just follow the path of the April rain
      That mists and twists in the gale,
    Past where the pussy willow purrs
      And the dogwood wags its tail.
    There, at the edge of a dune of sand
    You'll come to the nearest town at hand. . . ."

GIRL:

    (But I was thinking of Farmerville
      And he of Fairyland.)
    "How long does it take to the nearest town,
      To a door where I may knock?"

APRIL FOOL:

    "As long as it takes for a frog to jump
      From this pool to that hanging rock—

A whiff and a puff, and a puff and a whiff
  By the dandelion's clock,
And the house that has a golden door
  Is the one at which to knock."

GIRL:

Oh, the fool was less of a fool than I,
  For the road and route he planned
Led not into dreary old Farmerville
  But straight into Fairyland.

A Puss and a Pixie

(*This may be done effectively with two* SOLOS *reciting alternately.*)

1ST SOLO:

There once was a pixie who had a pet cat,
All fluffy and gray and exceedingly fat.

2ND SOLO:

(She looked like a puff ball whenever she sat.)

1ST SOLO:

The two lived together inside a seed pod;
And when the wind blew their house gave a nod.

2ND SOLO:

(Now wasn't that odd?)

1ST SOLO:

They might have been living there even today
If Puss had not taken to prowling away.
She went out each night and deserted her master.
She slammed the front door till she cracked all the
    plaster.
When Pixie ran after, she only ran faster.
At last came an evening when Pussy was shocked.
She tried to go home but the front door was locked.
She couldn't get in though she hammered and knocked.

2ND SOLO:

(The pixie, of course, was asleep in the pod—
So tired he only could snoozle and nod—
Now wasn't that odd?)

1st SOLO:

Poor Puss went away with a lonely "meow"
And climbing a tree, she lay down on a bough.

2ND SOLO:

(She's sleeping there now.)

1st SOLO:

Attached to a twig she's as safe as can be;

2ND SOLO:

(That's how pussy willows first grew on a tree.)

The Lady Slipper

(This may be acted out in pantomime by one girl as it is recited by another.)

A fairy found a slipper
A-growing on a stem.
She said, "I think I'll wear it
If I find a pair of them—
A pair of golden slippers
That haven't any zippers,
That haven't bows or laces
To make them tight in places."

A fairy found a slipper
A-waving in the air
But though she looked all over,
Through grasses and through clover,
She couldn't find a pair.
She said: "I must be stopping
This hunting and this shopping,
I really can't go hopping
On one foot everywhere."

And so she ran off barefoot
And when she felt the dews
Between her toes, she said, "I s'pose
It's best to wear no shoes."

Spring Secrets

The March Wind tries to tell me things
In little secret whisperings
But, oh, instead he shouts aloud
Because, I s'pose, he's over-proud
And gets excited
And delighted
At all the secrets that he knows—
Like where the first spring violet grows
And where the pussy willows doze
And robins nest and pansies pose.

I'd like to learn these secret things
But all I hear are bellowings.
(The wind makes noises so absurd
I cannot understand a word.)
So I must search, like fay or elf,
Each forest nook and rocky shelf
To find spring secrets for myself.

I Met A Little April Fool

I met a little April Fool.
I'm sure he'd never been to school
Because the things he asked were silly,
Like, "May I pick a piccalilli?"
And, "What's more daffy than a dilly?"
He also begged me to explain
If dandelions wear a mane
With silky hairs that blow away
When they have turned from gold to gray.
He asked, "Do screech owls like to screech?"
And, "What does Jack-in-the-pulpit preach?"
And can a cutworm sail a cutter?"
Then, last of all, I heard him mutter:
"If I should look into a pool,
Oh, would I see an April Fool?"

When Pussy Willow Comes

When pussy willow comes in spring
She does a lot of slumbering.
She curls herself into a ball
And does not lift her head at all;
And though she's dressed in kitten fur
She does not ever mew or purr.

Our pussy's gone away by fall.
(We do not see her go at all.)
Perhaps by then she's grown too big
To sit upon a willow twig.
Perhaps she leaps into the street
And pads away on kitten feet.

April Puddle

The rain falls down upon the grass
And makes a silver looking glass,
So all the buds may bend and see
What kind of flowers they will be.

I Know a Hill

I know a hill where little gnomes
Are said to live in cavern homes
Far from the daylight, underground,
Month in, month out, and all year 'round.
And all they do, so I am told,
Is dig, and dig, and dig for gold.
What good is all the gold they mine
If they can never see it shine
Like dandelions in the sun?
I'm sure gnome children have no fun.
I'd rather live *outside* the hill
And pick a golden daffodil!

Kite Day

(Children may march around room carrying the different kinds of kites mentioned in poem.)

It's kite day, it's kite day!
　　The kites are all out sailing:
The red kite, the blue kite,
　　The kite with golden tailing:
The box kite, the fish kite,
　　The kite that's like a dragon,
The giant kite that's such a height
　　They load it on a wagon
When it comes down. Oh, all the town
　　Can see the kites out sailing:
The red kite, the blue kite,
　　The kite with the golden tailing!

Spring Cleaning

Make the skies clean,
    O winds of March!
With brooms of maple
    And oak and larch,
With trees for brooms
    That sweep and swash,
With clouds for sponges
    That squeeze and wash.
Make the skies clean
    For surely it's wrong
That the gray webs of winter
    Should hang there so long!

Umbrella Plants

"Umbrellas up!" the May Queen cried,
  "Here come the spattering showers!"
Then down the wooded countryside
The leaf-umbrellas opened wide
  To shelter white May flowers.

Maying

Oh, come let's go a-Maying!
   I want to see once more
Jack-in-the-pulpit kneeling
   Upon the forest floor;
And pussy willows napping
   Along the willow boughs;
And woodpeckers a-tapping
   To build themselves a house.

On every friendly doorknob
   Our baskets we will swing,
So those who can't go Maying
   Shall have a glimpse of spring.

Fairy Housecleaning

There once was a fairy who went out to shop.
She needed a scrub brush. She needed a mop.
She wanted some soapsuds for windows and screening . . .
This neat little fairy was planning spring cleaning.

With thimbles for buckets she flew to the sky
And scooped the white suds from a cloud passing by.
The scrub brush she bought was a sharp little burr
The burdock had saved through the winter for her.

A bright dandelion—as bright as a candle—
She chose for a mop with the stem for a handle.
But before she got home, within less than an hour,
Her house had been cleaned by a sudden spring shower . . .
For the home of this fairy was inside a flower.

Cat and Dog Fight

"Please grow for me a little cat,"
  I begged the pussy willow,
"And make him gray and sleek and fat
And very smooth for me to pat
  And puffy as a pillow."
"I will," said pussy willow.

"Please grow for me a little dog,"
  I asked the barren *dog*wood,
"And give him just a little bark
So he can grumble in the dark
  As bold as any *frog* would.
  "I will," agreed the *dog*wood.

But when the "cat" and "dog" were born
They scratched and fought from dark to dawn.
  (They didn't bark or make meows.
  They clawed each other with their boughs.)
And so we had to turn to *log*-wood
The pussy willow and the *dog*wood.

Where Does the Wind Sleep?

Where does the wind sleep when he stops blowing,
When he stops coming, and when he stops going
      Where does the winds sleep?

Nobody knows, but if you ask me
I think that he sleeps in a great hollow tree—
      That's where the wind sleeps.

The King's Holiday

Characters

KING
QUEEN
WISEMAN
PRIME MINISTER
LORD CHAMBERLAIN
GYPSY

TIME: *A summer day.*

SETTING: *The royal palace. At the right is the counting-house and at the left is the parlor. They are separated by attractive folding screens, with a opening in between for a door.*

AT RISE: *The KING is in his countinghouse, counting out his money; the QUEEN is in the parlor, eating bread and honey.*

KING (*Counting aloud as he piles coins all over the table*): One-million, nine hundred and ninety-nine thousand, nine hundred and . . . (*His hand slips and the coins*

*spill all over the floor. He cries out loudly and grabs
at the coins.*) Help, help! there goes my money.

QUEEN (*So startled she drops her slice of bread*): And there
goes my honey. (*She wails. They rush toward each other
and meet in the doorway.*)

KING *and* QUEEN (*Together*): What's the matter?

KING: I spilled my gold and I'll have to count it all over
again.

QUEEN: And you made me drop my bread and honey.

KING: Buttered side down?

QUEEN (*Pouting*): Honey side down!

KING: Oh, dear! I'm sorry.

QUEEN: It wouldn't matter, except that there's nothing
else to do around here but eat bread and honey.

KING: Or count out money. (WISEMAN *enters right.*)

WISEMAN: Good gracious me! What a clutter! It's the third
time this week you've spilled things all over.

KING *and* QUEEN (*Together*): Is it?

WISEMAN: It surely is. I think you both need something
for your nerves.

KING: I believe we do.

QUEEN: A little medicine, perhaps, but not too bitter. You
could give it to us in honey.

WISEMAN (*Shaking his head*): It isn't medicine you need.
It's a holiday.

KING: By Jove! I believe you're right. We both need a
change.

QUEEN: Yes. Sitting all day cooped up in a parlor isn't any
fun.

KING (*To* WISEMAN): What would you suggest we do?

WISEMAN: Why don't you ask your people?

KING (*Shocked*): What? A king ask his people what to do?
Why, I'm supposed to tell *them* what to do!

WISEMAN (*Shrugging*): Whatever you like. But I thought
you said you needed a change. (*He exits.*)

KING: Very well, we'll turn the tables. Here come the Prime Minister and the Lord Chamberlain. We'll ask them how we should spend our holiday. (PRIME MINISTER *and* LORD CHAMBERLAIN *enter right, in a hurry.*)

PRIME MINISTER (*Bowing profusely*): Your Majesty! We thought you were not up yet.

QUEEN: We *did* get up very early, but we started the day all wrong.

KING: Yes, we spilled everything all over. (*He gestures.*) Our nerves are on edge. The Wiseman tells me we need a holiday.

PRIME MINISTER *and* LORD CHAMBERLAIN (*Together*): Of course, Your Royal Highness, of course you need a holiday.

QUEEN: But we don't know what to do or where to go.

KING: Any suggestions?

PRIME MINISTER (*Bowing*): If I may be so bold, Sire, why don't you have a grand ball, with gay music and bright decorations, and a banquet to start the ball rolling?

QUEEN: Oh, yes, yes! A ball! How I love to dance! (*She goes waltzing about the room.*) One, two, three . . . one, two, three . . . one, two, three. Remember, Your Majesty, how you taught me to waltz when we first met?

PRIME MINISTER: You waltz as lightly as flying feathers.

LORD CHAMBERLAIN: Or whirling snowflakes.

KING (*In dismay*): But I couldn't do it now. I'm too fat. I'd be out of breath before the first dance was over.

QUEEN: Couldn't you just try?

KING: No, no, my dear. Waltzing would not make a holiday for me. It would be harder work than counting gold. As for a banquet—it would ruin my digestion.

LORD CHAMBERLAIN: But a ride through the city streets in the golden coach—how would that be, Your Majesty? You could go to call on your brother, the duke, and your aunt, the duchess, and have tea in the courtyard.

KING: Bravo! That's a splendid idea. Go order the horses to be hitched and the coach made ready. We'll take a nice ride.

PRIME MINISTER and LORD CHAMBERLAIN (*Together, bowing as they speak*): Yes, Your Majesty, at once. (PRIME MINISTER and LORD CHAMBERLAIN *exit in a hurry*.)

QUEEN: But I don't want to go riding in a stuffy old carriage. (*She sobs loudly*.)

KING: What? Not many people have a golden coach to ride in.

QUEEN: I can't help it. I don't want to go. We'll have to spend all our time along the way bowing to the people in the street.

KING: We could pull the coach curtains.

QUEEN: No, no, no! We wouldn't get any fresh air and sunshine then.

KING: Yes, we would, in the courtyard at my brother's.

QUEEN: Maybe a little, but your aunt would make us gloomy talking about her ills, and your brother would groan about taxes.

KING (*Sighing*): I'm afraid you are right.

QUEEN: If only we could be alone together, the way we were when we first met.

KING: When I got lost from my hunting party and saw you by the brookside?

QUEEN: Yes. It was much more fun being a peasant than a queen.

KING: Hush! You mustn't say that. No one must know you were a peasant.

QUEEN (*Angrily*): I suppose I have to keep on pretending I was a princess from a far country.

KING (*Musing and not listening*): It was wonderful picking daisies in the fields and wandering together over the hills. Why can't we do it today? Now?

QUEEN (*Sadly*): How can we, with a coachman and foot-man and a half a dozen bodyguards watching us?

KING (*Sighing*): Oh, dear! I forgot. They'd insist on tag-ging along. Why can't we be free, just for today? (*Sing-ing is heard off-stage.*)

QUEEN: Listen! (*She runs to left and looks offstage.*)

GYPSY (*Offstage, chanting to background music*):
Come over the hills with me, my King.
Come over the hills, my Queen.
There are wonderful things I'll show to you.
There are magical things to be seen.

KING (*Spellbound*): Who is it?

QUEEN: It's a gypsy. She's coming in at the back window and she has a great bag over her shoulder! (*She runs to* KING *in excitement.*) Oh, do let her finish her song!

KING (*Smiling*): Of course. I never heard a better one. (GYPSY *enters through window.*)

GYPSY: You like my song? (*She puts down her bag.*)

QUEEN: Yes, yes, do finish it!

GYPSY (*Chanting again and pretending to strum a guitar or lute*):
There are brooks that run over stones, my King,
There's a river that runs to the sea.
It has something to say, for it sings night and day—
Come down to the river with me.

QUEEN (*In great excitement*): Could we wade in the river?

KING: And ride on a raft?

GYPSY: Of course. (*She continues her song.*)
There's a lake with a shore and caves to explore
And secrets you never could guess
Till you wander afar and follow a star
Into the wilderness.

KING: I love to explore.

QUEEN: I love to find out secrets.

GYPSY: Then why do you both stay all shut up here in a stuffy palace?

QUEEN (*Sadly*): We never can get away by ourselves.

KING (*Hopelessly*): A king and queen must have body-guards, you know.

GYPSY: Well, at least gypsies are free.

QUEEN: If only we could be gypsies.

KING: Just for today!

GYPSY: Why shouldn't you be? I have all kinds of rags and tags in this pack. See? (*She dumps her bag upside down and out fall all sorts of brightly colored clothes.*) Dress up in these and I'll show you the road to adventure.

QUEEN (*Picking things out of the pile and putting them on with great glee*): Here is a bandanna for my head, and great earrings for my ears. And look at this apron. It has all the colors of a patchwork quilt.

KING (*Watching her*): They are very becoming to you.

QUEEN: And they're so loose and comfortable. (*She dances about gaily.*)

KING: I'd like to try a few rag tags, too. (*The* KING *dresses as they talk.*)

QUEEN (*To* GYPSY): Do you think we could do this once a week?

GYPSY: I don't see why not.

QUEEN: It's the most wonderful idea!

KING: But won't someone find out?

GYPSY: Not if you lock the door to the countinghouse and the parlor. (KING *locks doors and hands the keys to the* QUEEN.)

KING: Wonderful!

QUEEN: They'll think we're in here!

KING: We'll leave our crowns here, so no one will know who we are. (KING *and* QUEEN *take crowns off.*)

GYPSY: This may help, too. (*She takes two "Do Not Dis-*

turb" signs from pile and hangs one on either side of the screen.)

KING (*Locking arms with the* QUEEN *on one side and the* GYPSY *on the other*): Now we're off for the time of our lives!

KING, QUEEN *and* GYPSY (*To the tune of "I Saw Three Ships"*):

There were three gypsies dancing by, all dancing by, all dancing by.

There were three gypsies dancing by, one summer's day in the morning.

They all looked gay and they all looked spry. They danced and sang and I'll tell you why—

They loved the hills and the open sky on a summer's day in the morning.

(*They exit through the window, as the curtain falls.*)

THE END

Miss Muffet and the Spider

Characters

LITTLE MISS MUFFET
CHIPMUNK
BLUEJAY
SPIDER

TIME: *In the days of Mother Goose.*
SETTING: *Miss Muffet's yard.*
AT RISE: MISS MUFFET *is seated on a tuffet at the right of the stage. She is eating curds and whey.* CHIPMUNK, BLUEJAY, *and* SPIDER *enter from the left, unseen by* MISS MUFFET.

CHIPMUNK (*To* BLUEJAY):
  I am a chipmunk. Who are you?
BLUEJAY:
  I am a jay, all black and blue.
SPIDER:
  I am a sprawly, crawly spider.
CHIPMUNK (*To* BLUEJAY):
  She's so small that a leaf could hide her.
  (*He points at* SPIDER *and giggles.*)
BLUEJAY:
  She doesn't wear wings—

This play may easily be adapted for presentation with hand puppets.

CHIPMUNK:

And she's not very hairy.

BLUEJAY:

She's much too small to be bold or scary.

CHIPMUNK:

Oh, I can scare any child or pet.

BLUEJAY:

And I could scare anyone I met.

CHIPMUNK:

But she's as wee as an elf or fairy.

She never would, never could, make herself scary.

SPIDER (*To* CHIPMUNK *and* BLUEJAY):

It's true you are big, very big, beside me,

And I am so small that a leaf could hide me.

I can't grow wings and I'm not very hairy,

But, believe it or not, I can really be scary.

(CHIPMUNK *whispers to the* BLUEJAY.)

BLUEJAY (*To* SPIDER):

All right, we'll see if your boast is true.

We'll see who's the fiercest, we or you.

CHIPMUNK (*Nodding in the direction of* MISS MUFFET):

Right over there on a little grassy tuffet

Is a pretty little girl and her name is Miss Muffet.

She's eating her curds, and she's drinking her whey.

We'll soon see which of us can frighten her away.

BLUEJAY:

Let me try first. It will save you both from trying.

I'll scream at her and rush at her, hopping and flying.

(BLUEJAY *hops up to* MISS MUFFET. *He flaps his wings at her, then shrieks and squawks.*)

MISS MUFFET (*Looking up, shoos him aside with a wave of her hand*):

Go away! You silly jay!

I haven't time to run or play.

I have to eat my curds and whey.

(BLUEJAY *hops back to* CHIPMUNK *and* SPIDER. *He hangs his head sadly.*)

CHIPMUNK (*Laughing*):

Is that the way you do your scaring?

Watch me. I'm really much more daring.

(CHIPMUNK *goes up to* MISS MUFFET *and circles around her very fast. He makes scolding noises as he runs.*)

MISS MUFFET:

You silly little chippy-munk!

Run up the branch and tippy trunk

Of that big tree, away from me.

You're just a nuisance on the ground.

I will not have you run around

While I am sitting on my mound.

(*She claps her hands angrily.* CHIPMUNK *runs back to* BLUEJAY *and* SPIDER.)

BLUEJAY *and* CHIPMUNK (*Together*):

We cannot make her feel afraid.

She's not a scary sort of maid.

SPIDER:

It's *my* turn, then. I'll go and see

If she will be afraid of me.

BLUEJAY *and* CHIPMUNK (*Together*):

Ha, ha! Ho, ho! We'll watch you go.

You can't do what *we* can't, you know.

(SPIDER *crawls over to* MISS MUFFET *and stands before her, perfectly still, waiting for her to look up.*)

MISS MUFFET (*Suddenly seeing the* SPIDER *and jumping up*):

Help! Help! A spider!

(*She screams and runs off the stage.*)

BLUEJAY (*Coming up to* SPIDER *and shaking hands*):

You did it! You did it! You wonderful Spider.

CHIPMUNK:

You scared her the minute you sat down beside her.

SPIDER:

Yes, I may be small, but it isn't just size
That makes men and animals scary and wise.

THE END

The French Doll's Surprise

Characters

FRENCH DOLL
FAIRY
JACK-IN-THE-BOX

TIME: *Midnight on a summer night.*
SETTING: *A dimly lighted nursery or playroom. There are five small chairs in a row at center. A huge box stands right and a record player on a table left.*
AT RISE: *A pretty* FRENCH DOLL *sits on one of the chairs center. A clock is heard striking twelve, and as the last stroke dies away, a* FAIRY *enters right and stands briefly at the side, then runs center.*

FAIRY (*Bowing to audience*):
It's twelve by the clock, and without any noise
I come into the playroom to wake up the toys.
(*She runs lightly over to the chairs and pauses at each in turn as she speaks.*)
But where's the tin soldier whose smile was so jolly?
And where's the toy panda? And where's the rag dolly?
And where is the bear that will wind up and dance?
There's nobody here but the French Doll from France.

---

* This play may easily be adapted for presentation with hand puppets.

(*She bows to the* FRENCH DOLL *and waves her wand over her.*)

Wake up, lovely lady, why are you the only
Toy left in the playroom? You must be quite lonely.

FRENCH DOLL (*As she "wakes"*):

Of course I am lonely, and you would be, too,
If everyone had a vacation but you.
Boohoo! Boohoo! Boohoo!

FAIRY:

You mean the whole household has gone on a trip?

FRENCH DOLL (*Nodding sadly*):

They went to the seashore with suitcase and grip.

FAIRY (*Surprised*):

And left you behind? Why even the boys
Considered you one of the favorite toys!

FRENCH DOLL:

They said if they dressed me in sunsuit or slacks
The heat of the sunshine would melt all my wax.

FAIRY:

That's true. I'd forgotten that you're a wax dolly.
To sit in the sunshine would only be folly.
You'd turn to a grease spot in less than a day,
And surely you wouldn't like melting away!

FRENCH DOLL (*Sobbing*):

I'd rather be melting right down to the bone
Than sitting here friendless and living alone.

FAIRY (*Puzzled*):

It's strange that they didn't leave someone to stay with
     you,
Someone to talk to you, someone to play with you.

FRENCH DOLL (*Pointing to box*):

All that they left is that silly old box.
I s'pose it is full of new bonnets and frocks.
What good will they do me? There's no use in dressing
With no one to see me.

FAIRY:

But aren't you just guessing?
For nobody knows what secrets are hid
Inside of a box, till he opens the lid.

(*She goes over to the box and walks around it, looking at it closely. There is a knocking sound from within. The* FAIRY *jumps, but the* FRENCH DOLL *does not notice it. She is too busy crying. The* FAIRY *puts her ear to the box. She smiles and winks at the audience. To the* FRENCH DOLL.)

I think you are silly to do so much crying.
You might be quite happy if you would start trying.
I'll bid you "Goodbye" now. It's time I was flying.

(*She bows to* FRENCH DOLL *and runs lightly toward exit.*)

FRENCH DOLL (*Imploringly*):

Don't leave me alone. Oh, how can you do it?

FAIRY (*Smiling*):

You're not all alone, if only you knew it.

(FAIRY *goes out.*)

FRENCH DOLL (*Sitting up straight, surprised*):

Now, what in the world did she mean by that?
There isn't a dog and there isn't a cat,
Nor even a mouse to play with me—
No one in this house to stay with me.

(*She sighs.*)

Well, I might as well open the box, I guess,
I ought to be glad of a brand-new dress.

(*She turns up the light, goes to the box, and lifts the lid. There is a thunderous sound and a shout. Then out jumps* JACK-IN-THE-BOX, *dressed in a harlequin suit. The* FRENCH DOLL, *surprised, sits down on the floor with a thump.*)

Who are you?

JACK (*In sing-song, and dancing as he talks*):

I'm Jack-in-the-Box and I always shout

When they open the box and let me out.
How I like to stretch and frolic about!
(*He yawns and stretches.*)
It was nice of you to lift that lid,
It's the nicest thing that you ever did.
(*He bows to the* FRENCH DOLL.)

FRENCH DOLL:

But I would have done it long ago
If I'd known you were there and doubled up so.

JACK:

Well, never you mind! What game shall we play,
From midnight to morning, from darkness to day?

FRENCH DOLL (*Astonished and delighted*):

You mean that you've really come to stay?

JACK:

Of course, of course! I have come to dance
Every night with the little French Doll from France.
(*He turns on the phonograph and whirls her about, as
the curtain falls.*)

THE END

A Mermaid in a River

1ST GIRL:
  I saw a little mermaid
    Down where the streams meander . . .

2ND GIRL:
  (Was it a little mermaid,
    Or just a salamander?)

1ST GIRL:
  She sat a-sunning, sunning,
    Upon a river rock
  And water birds passed over
    All flying in a flock . . .

2ND GIRL:
  (One seemed to pause a moment
    As if to chat and talk.)

1ST GIRL:
  I heard the mermaid humming
    A song both old and wise . . .

2ND GIRL:
  (Was it the mermaid humming,
    Or just the dragonflies?)

1st Girl:

I waved to her and shouted,
"Come to the bank and play."
But mermaids shy at people . . .

2nd Girl:

(At least that's what they say.)

1st Girl:

She slid into the water
And slithered far away.

Vacation Dreams

BOYS:
  Oh, travel, travel, travel
    By a train or plane or car
  On a highway made of gravel
    Or a skyway near a star!

GIRLS:
  Oh, to see the many places
    We have picked out on the maps
  And to pack such bulky baggage
    We must hold some in our laps!

BOYS:
  Oh, to journey to the seashore
    And to play upon the sands
  Kicking up the golden glitter,
    Building castles with our hands . . .

GIRLS:
  Or to drift along a river
    In a rowboat or canoe
  Till we come upon a city
    With a skyline and a zoo!

BOYS:

> How we dream and dream of travel
>> From the dawning to the dark;

ALL:

> But most likely our vacation
>> Will be picnics in the park.

The Homemade Ship

1st Boy:

    I made a little sailing ship
      All on a summer day
    And sailed it in the meadow where
      I always like to play;
    For meadowlands and fields can be
    As green as any lake or sea,
    And all the little winds that pass
    Put waves and ripples in the grass.

2nd Boy:

    And so I made a sailing ship
      For sailing far and fast.
    The hull was just a packing box,
      A yardstick was the mast.
    The sail was just a worn-out shirt
      That flapped before the blast.

1st Boy:

    But, oh, I took such happy trips!
      My travel was unending,
    For anyone can travel when
      He's playing and pretending;

2ND BOY:

> And since the seashore's far away
>   And far off is the sand,
> I'll do my sailing here upon
>   A bit of meadowland.

Lazy Daisy

1ST BOY:
  As lazy
  As a daisy
    Is what I'd like to be
  When August breathes a hot, hot breath
    On field and hill and tree . . .
  (I'd like to grow upon a stalk
  And never have to work or walk.)

2ND BOY:
  As lazy
  As a daisy
    Who hears the latest news
  From caterpillars climbing up
    Her stem without their shoes.
  (They're full of flower gossip
    And say things to amuse.)

BOTH (*Together*):
  But when the August heat is gone
  And raindrops splash upon the lawn
  Then I would rather skip and scoot
  And not have any kind of root.

Listen Well

Listen well, oh, listen well
To the singing of the shell,
To the secrets it can tell
 Of the sea;
Of the place few men have seen
Deep beneath the seaweed's green,
Where the giant kelp trees lean
With the current; and the clean
Purple waters rush between
 Coral turrets of the castle
Of the mermaids and their queen.

Listen well, oh, listen well
To the singing of the shell;
For the shell's a pink-lined ear
That for eons and a year
Harkened carefully to hear
All the secrets of the sea
Just to tell to you and me
In a little whispered song.
Listen well and listen long
To the singing of the shell,
To the secrets it can tell
 Of the sea.

The Sand Castle

I built a golden castle
   In the sand upon the shore
And I hung a silver seashell
   For a trumpet by the door;
And my castle was so splendid
   That the wind, in passing by,
Walked on tiptoe, lest he crush it
   And the sea birds, sailing high,
Paused a moment, just to see it,
   For there had not been before
Such a stately golden castle
   In the sand upon the shore;
But the sea became an ogre
   Who rose and trampled o'er
Wall and rampart, moat and drawbridge
   Of my castle on the shore,
And I even heard him laughing
   With a kind of guttural sound
As he hastily retreated
   From that drab and shapeless mound.

Then I took my tiny trumpet
   And I thought me of a rune
That an ancient book had taught me,
   And I sang it to the tune

Of a witch song, for I realized
   Only magic could disarm
Such an ogre; and an hour
   Proved the power of my charm.
For the tide slipped down to nothing,
   And I heard a muffled roar
In the little silver seashell
   That had graced my castle door.
I had quite transformed that ogre
   By the magic of my spell,
And he roared, a midget captive,
   In the hollow of my shell.

O Little Singing Summer!

O little singing summer,
  I love to hear you come!
I love your cricket chorus,
  Your low bee-hum,
Your brook's gay grace note,
  Your birds' bright whistles,
The soft sound the breeze makes
  Blowing down from thistles.
O little singing summer,
  Come tell each living thing
In grasses, bush and treetop
  To sing, sing, sing!

The Secondhand Shop

Down in the grasses
Where the grasshoppers hop
And the katydids quarrel
And the flutter-moths flop—
Down in the grasses
Where the beetle goes "plop"
An old withered fairy
Keeps a secondhand shop.

She sells lost thimbles
For fairy milk pails
And burnt-out matches
For fence posts and rails.
She sells stray marbles
To bowl on the green
And bright scattered beads
For the crown of the queen.

Oh, don't feel upset
Over things that you lose
Like spin tops or whistles
Or dolls' buckled shoes
These may be the things that
The fairies can use.

For down in the grasses
Where the grasshoppers hop
A withered old fairy
Keeps a secondhand shop.

Fairy Washing

The fairies hung their washing out,
  Their linens and their laces,
And some of them were raggedy
  And very torn in places.

But busy old Dame Spider
  Brought out her silver thread
And darned each dainty tablecloth
  And mended every spread.

The fairies were so happy
  They said, "You dear old spinner!
We'll set the toadstool table now
  And you must stay for dinner."

The Garden Soda Fountain

I like to walk on summer days—
   (When thunder is not mumbling)
A-down the soft and sunny ways
   Where bumblebees are bumbling;

Where bumblebees and honeybees
   Pay not a cent of money
To sip at flower fountains where
   The flavor's always honey.

The Bug and Beetle Circus

I saw a silly circus
In a wildwood where I went,
A Bug and Beetle Circus
Beneath a burdock tent,
 (An open tent, I should explain,
Not much protection in a rain.)
A spider walked a tightrope there
And did not trip or fall.
She even kept her balance well
Without a parasol.
The very smallest insects
Were hanging by their knees
Or swinging upside down upon
A little twig trapeze.
The mumbling, bumbling June bug
Was always falling down.
He waved his hands and kicked his feet
Just like a circus clown.
The caterpillar moved about
Like any well-trained seal.
She did a kind of wriggly dance
Without a toe or heel.
Oh, everything was going fine
Until the rain came down!
Then all the actors ran and hid
So none of them would drown.

In Dry July

If all the ladders in the world
  Were tightly tied together
I'd climb up to the sky and see
  If I could change the weather.

I'd take the dipper made of stars
  And spill out all the rain
And then I'd hurry,
             hurry,
                  HURRY
  Back to earth again!

I Saw a Fairy

I saw a fairy take a spill
Sliding down a mushroom hill.
She gave a nervous little cough,
Her bluebell bonnet tumbled off.
She lost a golden lady slipper
Because it had no lace or zipper.
And now she's taking tiny stitches
To mend her muddy "Dutchman's breeches."

Swinging at Dusk

The swing goes up, the swing goes down,
It shows me all the lamp-lit town
Where roofs are dark but windows wink
With lights that look like stars, I think.

The swing goes down, the swing goes up,
It shows me all the sky's blue cup;
And there the dark cloud-houses are
Each lighted with a candle-star.

I Once Lived in a Lighthouse

I once lived in a lighthouse
 With windows long and high,
Where neither cars nor carriages
 But only ships went by.
I had no yard to play in,
No garden-place to stay in,
Just miles and miles of water
 Fenced in by far-off sky.
 (A lonely boy was I.)

I wove a net of moonlight,
 I braided moonbeams three.
I said, "I'll cast my silver mesh
 Into the purple sea."
I cast it in the shadow,
 I drew it in by sun;
And, oh, the wonder of my catch!
 It was a magic one!

I'd caught a little mermaid
 With curling, seaweed locks.
All day we swam together
 Among the lighthouse rocks.
And she became *a playmate*—
 A playmate all my own—
I wish that I could find her now
 That I am great and grown.

The Beach in July

In July we go away
To a sandy beach to play:
There the rumpled sea runs by
And bumps its waves against the sky.
There the sky looks like the ocean,
 (When its cloud-boats are in motion)
There the sea gulls float and fly
In July.

How I like to let the sand
Go slip-sliding through my hand
When it's glittering white and dry;
But when it is wet I make
Sandy pies and wedding cake.
Then I cook them in the sun
Till they're golden-brown and done;
And the crayfish, crawling by,
Look as though they'd like to try
Nibbles of my cake and pie . . .
In July.

Rainbow's End

Characters

GOBLIN
SPARROW
RABBIT
GIRL

SETTING: *A meadow. Colored ribbons representing rainbow hang down from tree.*
AT RISE: GOBLIN *enters left, carrying a pot of gold. He tiptoes to center and puts pot down.*

GOBLIN:
   I am the goblin who guards the gold
   Here at the rainbow's end,
   (*He gestures toward rainbow ribbons.*)
   More than anyone's pockets can hold,
   More than a man can spend.
   But no one as yet has discovered the spot
   Where I keep this gold in an earthen pot.
   (*He picks up the pot and puts it under the rainbow, then pounds his chest.*)
   If no one at all has eyes to see,

The treasure belongs to me . . . to me!

(*The sound of running steps is heard.* GOBLIN *puts a hand to his ear and looks off to see who is coming.*)

Well! A sparrow is coming now.

I'll hide the gold with a hawthorn bough.

(*He picks up some brushwood and puts it over the pot, then stands with his back to it.* SPARROW *enters.*)

SPARROW (*Halting suddenly and drawing back, startled*):

Dear me! There's a goblin . . . or is it a gnome?

GOBLIN:

A goblin, good lady. But what brings you from home?

What do you see that has captured your eye?

SPARROW (*Pointing to rainbow*):

The rainbow's end hanging out of the sky.

They say that it points to a treasure-filled pot.

Oh, can it be true?

GOBLIN:

    . . . Surely not! Surely not!

Why don't you look out there beyond

The hickory tree, near the lily pond? (*He gestures offstage.*)

SPARROW: No, no! It is nearer. I'm sure it must be.

I think I'll look right under *this* tree.

(*She rushes over to dig in the brushwood pile.*)

It's under the rainbow, likely as not.

I'll find what I came for. Oh, here is the pot!

(*She uncovers it.*)

GOBLIN (*In great distress*):

Oh, dear, oh dear! To think you found it!

Even though leaves and boughs surround it.

Now I must *give* it to you, my friend,

For that is the law at the rainbow's end.

SPARROW (*Taking handful of gold pieces out of pot and
studying them*):

But what are these pieces so hard and cold?

GOBLIN:

They're gold, you silly; they're pure, pure gold!

SPARROW:

But that kind of treasure is very absurd!
Who ever heard of gold helping a bird?
I wanted a birdhouse, all painted and new
With a little round door to go hip-hopping through.
(*Disgusted, she tosses coins back into pot.*)

GOBLIN:

You mean that you don't want the gold in this pot?

SPARROW:

Certainly not! Most certainly not!

GOBLIN (*Snatching up the pot and dancing about with it*):

Then this is for me, the gold, the gold!
Stacks of it, packs of it, riches untold!

SPARROW (*In disgust*):

You're welcome to keep it. But, oh, for a home!
Can you find me a birdhouse, you good little gnome?

GOBLIN:

I'm a goblin, not a gnome; and I'm not very good,
But I'll answer your question. Within that thick wood
(*He points offstage, right.*)
There's a pretty log cabin that stands in a glade
And beside it, a birdhouse that children have made.

SPARROW:

Oh, thank you, dear Goblin! How happy I'll be
With a nest in a birdhouse high up in a tree!
(*SPARROW exits.*)

GOBLIN (*Putting down pot of gold*):

Ha, ha, ha! Ho, ho, ho!
What that sparrow does not know!
The worth of gold . . .
(*He pauses, kneels near pot, and lets pieces of gold fall through his fingers. Then, speaking hesitatingly.*)
. . . so I've been told!

(*Sounds of running footsteps are again heard from off-stage.* GOBLIN *jumps to his feet, puts hand to his ear, then puts other hand to shade his eyes, as he peers off-stage.*)

I see a rabbit is coming now!

I'll hide the gold with a bigger bough.

(*He puts more brushwood over the pot, then jumps away.* RABBIT *enters. He does not notice* GOBLIN *but runs around the stage sniffing and poking in several places, but not near the pot of gold.*)

RABBIT:

It must be here—the treasure, the treasure!

Something good for a rabbit's pleasure.

GOBLIN (*Moving over and stretching out his hands to block* RABBIT'S *path*):

Look out, you silly! Oh, can't you see

There's never a bit of gold near me?

RABBIT:

Well, well! A goblin right on my track!

I think there's something behind your back.

GOBLIN (*Pointing to branches*):

There's nothing at all but a hawthorn bough.

RABBIT (*Peeking around* GOBLIN):

An earthen pot! I see it now!

(*He leaps forward, picks up the pot and peers inside.*)

GOBLIN (*Wringing his hands*):

Oh, dear, oh dear! To think you've found it!

Even though leaves and boughs surround it.

Now I must *give* you the treasure, my friend,

For that's the law at the rainbow's end.

RABBIT (*Taking a gold piece from the pot and trying to to nibble it*):

What *are* these pieces so hard and cold?

GOBLIN:

They're gold, you silly; they're pure, pure gold!

RABBIT:

What earthly good will they do a bunny?

GOBLIN:

You mean you don't want them? Don't be funny!

RABBIT:

Pieces of gold may be kept in a garret
But what I would like is a nice golden carrot.

GOBLIN: (*Dancing about*):

The treasure's still mine—the gold, the gold!
Stacks of it, packs of it, riches untold!

RABBIT:

You're welcome to keep it; but, begging your pardon,
Please point the way to a vegetable garden.

GOBLIN:

Yes, yes, to be sure. Right over that hill.
(*He points to opening at right.*)
Peas, parsley and carrots—just eat your fill.
(RABBIT *bows to* GOBLIN *and dances offstage, right.*
GOBLIN *kneels beside the pot and plays with the pieces
of money, laughing to himself.*)
Ha, ha, ha! Ho, ho, ho!
What that rabbit does not know!
Things couldn't be better if they'd been planned.
I still have a fortune right in my hand.
(*There is a sound of running steps offstage.* GOBLIN
*jumps and looks to see who is coming. He listens with
hand cupped to ear.*)
Hark! A child is coming now.
I'll hide the gold with a bigger bough.
(*He puts more branches over pot.* GIRL *runs in left. She
is barefoot. She stops short when she sees* GOBLIN.)

GIRL:

Hi, there, funny man! Ho, there, friend!
Can you tell me the way to the rainbow's end?

GOBLIN:
What do you want? Are you hunting for treasure?
GIRL:
Yes, I've heard there is gold without measure.
Rabbit and Sparrow both said to me
I'd find a rainbow caught in a tree. (*Points*)
There it is! There it is! Don't you see?
GOBLIN:
I see the rainbow in all its glory,
But as for the gold, *that's* just a story.
GIRL:
Only a make-believe? Only pretend?
No. I am sure you're mistaken, my friend.
(*She digs in the brush and sees the pot.*)
Here it is! At the rainbow's *end!*
GOBLIN (*Wringing his hands*):
Year in and year out I've guarded and hoarded.
Surely I should have been better rewarded.
But now I must give you the treasure, my friend,
For that is the law at the rainbow's end.
GIRL:
You've had no good of the money, you miser.
I shall go spending it; I shall be wiser.
I shall go carry it off to a store.
Slippers and bonnets I'll buy galore!
(*She strains to lift the pot.*)
Oh, I can't carry this clumsy old pot!
GOBLIN (*Grinning*):
You are not strong enough—certainly not!
GIRL:
Well, I can pack up these pieces of gold,
All that my pockets and apron will hold.
(*She kneels, stuffs her pockets full and gathers more in
her apron. Then she staggers to her feet. She takes a few
steps, then falls down with a thump.*)

GOBLIN:

Careful, there! Careful, there! Hope you're not hurt.
It's not very rocky here—only soft dirt.

GIRL (*Rubbing her arms*):

Those pieces of gold! They've bruised me like stones.

GOBLIN:

Cheer up! I am sure you have no broken bones.
(*He pulls her to her feet, and* GIRL *begins taking the gold pieces out of her pockets and throws them back into the pot.*)

GIRL:

Why should I bother with stony old gold?
It's bulky to carry and heavy to hold.
My feet want to dance and to jump and to leap;
But when I hold this . . .
(*She extends her hands with the last of the gold in them.*)
. . . why, I can't even creep!
(*She throws the coins into the pot in disgust.*)

GOBLIN:

But you have just told me that money's to use.
You said it would buy you a hat and some shoes . . .

GIRL:

So I did, so I did! But I've changed my mind.
Shoes are a nuisance and hats, too, I find.
I'd rather go barefoot through rippling grasses
And feel the wind rumple my hair when it passes.
So let the gold stay on that rocky old shelf!
If you think it's worth guarding, then guard it yourself.
I'll look for a playmate to share in my playing . . .
(GIRL *runs out.*)

GOBLIN (*Sighing and suddenly looking forlorn*):

Now everyone's left me! Why should I be staying?
(*He cups his hands to his mouth and calls offstage.*)
Wait, little girl, I'm following after!
I don't want the gold. I'd rather have laughter.

(He runs out, right. After a pause, the RABBIT *re-enters, left.)*

RABBIT:

The play is over, and all the gold
Is still in the pot. But I have been told
That if you find it, or you, or you,
(Pointing to different people in audience)
You may take it all and keep it, too.
You may hunt the treasure and hoard it, friend,
For that is the law at the rainbow's end.

*(*GOBLIN *runs quickly in from left.* GIRL *and* SPARROW *from right. All join hands and bow to audience, as the curtain falls.)*

THE END

Pixie in a Trap

Characters

PIXIE
TWO BLUEBIRDS
TWO ORIOLES
TWO WOODPECKERS

TIME: *An autumn day.*

SETTING: *The woods. At left is a large toadstool with an empty suitcase near it. At right is a tree with a trap tied to its trunk with a rope. Bushes and foliage are upstage.* PIXIE's *clothes are scattered about.*

AT RISE: PIXIE *is curled up asleep under the toadstool.* 1ST WOODPECKER *enters left, starts across stage, hopping and fluttering his wings, then notices* PIXIE, *pauses and hurries over to him.*

1ST WOODPECKER:
Pixie, Pixie, why aren't you packing?
Why are you all curled up and napping? (*Shakes him gently*)

PIXIE (*Sitting up and rubbing his eyes*):
What? Which? Where? Who?

1ST WOODPECKER:
They say that the snows will come tonight.

You'd better get packed for your autumn flight.
All of the birds will soon be going . . .

PIXIE (*Suddenly very wide awake*):
Oh, dear me! Is it time for snowing?

1ST WOODPECKER:
Yes, I am flying now to my hole,
To lock up my house in the telegraph pole.
(WOODPECKER *exits right.* 1ST BLUEBIRD *enters left, unseen by* PIXIE.)

PIXIE (*Running about frantically*):
What shall I do? All over the nation
The birds are ready for their migration.

1ST BLUEBIRD:
You'd better pack up. That's *my* advice.
Or you'll be caught by the snow and ice.

PIXIE:
Yes. But my clothes are scattered all over:
Up on the brambles, down in the clover.
Oh, do you think the birds will wait?

1ST BLUEBIRD (*Shaking his head solemnly*):
They just *can't* wait.
You *mustn't* be late! (1ST BLUEBIRD *exits right, and* 1ST ORIOLE *enters left.*)

PIXIE: Why did I leave my things in a scramble?

1ST ORIOLE (*Pointing with a wing*):
There is your hat hung up on a bramble.

PIXIE (*Running to get it*):
Yes. Here is my hat. I'll put it on.
And here is the jacket that I must don. (*He does so.*)

1ST ORIOLE (*Looking around*):
And here is a pair of your pointed shoes.
Those are something you must not lose.

PIXIE (*Sitting down and putting on shoes*):
Oh thank you, thank you! It would be tragic
To lose these shoes. They're green with magic.

1st ORIOLE:

Now you're almost ready for winging
And I must go where my nest is swinging
Just to be sure I've left no trifle
That some too-nosy squirrel can rifle. (1st ORIOLE *exits right.*)

PIXIE (*Picking up suitcase*):

Now I must pack my little suitcase.
My! but it's really a very cute case!
(*He goes about collecting his clothes from the ground, trees, etc.*)
This willow twig will do for a whistle.
A pillow I'll make with the down of the thistle.
And sassafras root is good to munch on,
Just the thing when I can't stop for luncheon!
(*Moves toward trap as he speaks*)
And here are some bright red hawthorn berries.
I'll share them all with the wild canaries.
And what is this thing where the dry leaves flap?
(*He pokes trap with his foot, and it snaps.*)
Oh, oh, *ouch!* It's a trap! *A trap!*
(*He stumbles to the ground and bursts into tears.*)
Boo hoo, boo hoo! Oh what shall I do?
I'm caught by the tip of my pointed shoe.
I can't go South with the birds when they fly.
They're ready to go and they'll pass me by!
(*He wails.* 2ND BLUEBIRD *enters, hopping.*)

2ND BLUEBIRD:

What's that, little Pixie? What is the matter?
Why are you making this terrible clatter?
What made you think we were passing you by?
Why can't you go with us? Why, oh why?

PIXIE: I stepped in a trap and the trap went *snap!* (*He holds up trapped foot.*)

2ND BLUEBIRD:

Why don't you try to hoppity-kick?

It might shake the trap off quick, quick, *quick!*

(*He demonstrates.*)

PIXIE (*Trying it*):

Yes, here is a hop and here is a kick.

(*Rope jerks him down.*)

And bump I go, thump I go, quick, quick, *quick!*

(*He groans. 2ND ORIOLE enters, fluttering.*)

2ND ORIOLE:

What's that, little Pixie? What is the matter?

Why are you making this terrible clatter?

2ND BLUEBIRD: He stepped in a trap and the trap went snap!

2ND ORIOLE (*To PIXIE*):

Why don't you flutter your wings and fly?

Shake the trap off as you mount to the sky!

PIXIE: I'll try. I'll try.

(*He flutters around and is about to "take off" when the rope jerks him back.*)

I can flutter a little. But, oh alack!

That horrid old rope pulls me back, back, *back.*

(*He sinks to the ground and sobs. 2ND WOODPECKER enters.*)

2ND WOODPECKER:

What's up, little Pixie? What is the matter?

Why are you making this terrible clatter?

2ND ORIOLE: He stepped in a trap and the trap went *snap.*

2ND WOODPECKER:

Why don't you let me peck, peck, peck it?

I'll hammer it, break it and wreck, wreck, wreck it.

(*Runs over and pecks at the trap but accidentally pecks PIXIE's foot.*)

PIXIE: No, no, *no!* You're pecking my foot.

2ND BLUEBIRD (*To* WOODPECKER): Stop it!

2ND ORIOLE: Stop it!

2ND WOODPECKER: I didn't mean to bop it.

PIXIE (*Angrily*):

You've torn my shoe.

(*He looks at it closely, then jumps up in sudden glee.*)

I know what to do!

Just take off my shoe!

(*He takes it off and the trap comes with it.*)

BLUEBIRD, ORIOLE *and* WOODPECKER:

He just took off his pointed shoe

And the horrid old trap, it came off too!

PIXIE: Now I can fly to the South with you!

ALL (*Fluttering around the stage*):

Off to the Southland let us go!

Far from the icicle, far from the snow.

Down where the brightest flowers grow . . . go, go, GO!

(*Exit, as curtain falls*)

THE END

Leaf Talk

(Two groups may act this out walking through a pile of leaves as they recite.)

1st Group *(Scuffling through leaves)*:
Scuff, scuff, scuffle through the leaves,
Shuff-shuff-shuffle through the leaves!
  Every leaf's a lisper
  Talking in a whisper—
Scuff, scuff, scuffle through the leaves!

2nd Group:
Crack, crack, crackle go the leaves.
Here comes a grackle through the leaves—
(Grackle enters and frolics through leaves with children.)
  A grack-grack-grackle
  With a cack-cack-cackle
Through the crack-crack-crackle of the leaves!

Big Chief Indian

(BIG CHIEF INDIAN *strides on left, and* NARRATOR *enters right. They meet at center stage, near a tepee.* CHIEF *turns, cups hands to his mouth and with loud Indian call, summons Indian braves from offstage.* FOUR BRAVES *enter, whooping and dancing in circle around stage in traditional war dance style; they then line up in front of* CHIEF.)

NARRATOR:
Big Chief Indian,
With your scarlet feather,
Why is it that you have called
All your braves together?

1ST BRAVE (*Addressing* CHIEF):
Shall we do a war dance
With the tom-toms beating?

2ND BRAVE:
Or smoke a quiet peace pipe
At a council meeting?

(CHIEF *grunts and points at tepee.* BRAVES *begin to rush around as if checking tepee. They shake out fur blankets.*)

NARRATOR:
Big Chief Indian,
Will your pointed tepee
Keep you safe from wind and rain

When at night you're sleepy?
3RD BRAVE (*To* CHIEF):
   Will you dream of hunting
   By a silver stream,
4TH BRAVE:
   And will you track the wild deer
   In your hunter's dream?
   (BRAVES *lead* CHIEF *into wigwam, then tiptoe offstage.*)

Leaf Frolic

(A group of girls in leaf costumes, enter, imitating flutter-ing leaves. As Boy *and* Girl *recite, the "leaves" suit their actions to words.)*

Boy:

    Like little girls in fluttery skirts
      The autumn leaves go by.

Girl:

    They skip, they scoot, they somersault
      Beneath the autumn sky.

Boy:

    The maple leaves are whispering
      Small secrets to the oaks.

Girl:

    The poplars still are tittering
      At summer's breezy jokes.

Boy:

    And all wave colored handkerchiefs
      To passing forest folks.

Girl:

    They are so very gay a crowd
      Of dancers and of skippers . . .

404

Boy:

They'll play until they've mussed their skirts
And worn out all their slippers.

*(Slowly the leaves, one by one, sink to the ground and
go to sleep.)*

Autumn Wind

When autumn wind goes running
  It does some magic things.
It gives the shadows dancing shoes,
  It gives the red leaves wings . . .
When autumn wind goes running.

It curls the bonfire's tail of smoke
And shares a little whispered joke
With cornstalks who delight to prattle.
It turns a seed pod to a rattle.

Oh, autumn days are lots of fun
When autumn wind begins to run!

The Cider Makers

Oh, who is making cider
  In the hills, in the hills?
Working at the presses
  And the mills, and the mills?
Working at the presses—
  (Oh, I'll give you twenty guesses!)
Who is making cider
  In the hills?

The trees are richly appled
  In the hills, in the hills.
The fruit is brightly dappled
  And it spills—rolls and spills—
Through the grasses and the clover,
Turning ever, ever over
Till it reaches mills and presses. . . .
Have you guessed your twenty guesses?
  The Apple Elves make cider
  In the hills.

Magic Carpet

Over the earth's floor the leaves lie down—
Scarlet and crimson, bronze and brown,
Weaving a carpet to cover the town.
Then comes the wind with his noisy throttle,
Fierce as a genie let out of a bottle.
He lifts the leaves without even trying
And the magic carpet goes flying . . . flying. . . .

Huffen Puff

Over the chimney tops Huffen Puff goes—
He is the one who is light on his toes,
He is the one with a smoke-beard that curls
Round him and round him whenever he twirls.
A beard that's as gray and as white as the snows
Huffen Puff grows when he walks on his toes
Over the chimney tops at the night's close.

Out of his chimney top Huffen Puff comes
Pulling himself up with smudgy gray thumbs,
Thick as a dwarf in a muffler and cape
Up he comes, up he comes, changing his shape.
Whether magician or goblin or elf
He changes his shape till he scarce knows himself.

Back to his chimney top, so I suppose,
When the world's bedding down, Huffen Puff goes
Ready to pull himself up by his thumbs
As soon as the dawn of another day comes.

Goldenrod Magic

The goldenrod beside the pond
Is waving like a fairy wand.
It waves above the water, cold,
And turns the blueness into gold.

How Would It Be?

How would it be, I wonder
   To live as squirrels do
Up near the grumpy thunder
   (Skies are not always blue)
Up near the zigzag lightning
   And silver spears of storm;
Oh, would a leaf-house keep one
   Dry and safe and warm?

How would it seem to market
   Far from the leafy hut,
Upon the ground, along the log—
To risk the ever chasing dog
   All for a single nut?

How would it be to race along
   High branches with one's load,
To twist and turn up-sky and down
   Where every bough's a road—
A road that runs through winds and airs
With forks for crossings, twigs for stairs?
This is the life the red squirrel dares!

The Threshing Machine

A funny machine is the threshing machine
  With a neck like a jungle giraffe
And a mouth like an "O" through which he can blow
  The golden-brown dust of the chaff.
Oh, a funny machine is the threshing machine—
  A creature inviting a laugh.

Needle in a Haystack

A country mouse in a haystack burrowed.
Her eyes were anxious. Her face was furrowed.
She said to the farmer, "Sir, good day.
I hear that your needle is lost in the hay;
Oh, how will you ever do any *sewing*
Without a needle? There'll be no growing
Of grain this summer for mice or men
Unless we find that needle again."

(For a country mouse she was not very knowing.
She never had watched the farmer *sowing!*)

The Winter Wizards

Characters

WIND
SNOW
SLEET
BRUIN, *a bear*
RACCOON
PUPPY
BOY

SETTING: *A tall, hollow tree stump is upstage left. A cottage door is upstage right. At left is the entrance to a cave. Dry leaves and wilted flowers are strewn about. There is a backdrop depicting a barren landscape.*
AT RISE: WIND *enters noisily, stamping about and cracking a long whip. He wears a tom-tom around his waist. He circles the stage and comes to center.*

WIND (*Addressing audience with bravado*):
I am the Wind.
This is my whip!
(*Cracks whip*)
See how I make

414

The dry leaves skip!
(*He whisks the dry leaves about.*)
I am the Wind.
I conquer all.
Beware of my wondrous,
Thunderous squall!
(*Beats tom-tom*)
(SNOW *enters on tiptoe, twirling and tossing confetti. She dances to center.*)

SNOW (*Acting out the rhyme as she recites*):
I am the Snow.
I swirl in a tizzy,
Making the whole world
White and dizzy.
I am the Snow.
I quietly heap
Cold and danger
While children sleep.
(*She sprinkles confetti on the wilted flowers.* SLEET *enters, clicking castanets as she comes to center.*)

SLEET:
I am Sleet.
My magic flippery
Makes all the roadways
Slick and slippery.
I am Sleet.
My pellets pound
Like angry fists
On the helpless ground.
(*She tosses rice all about.*)

WIND, SNOW *and* SLEET (*Taking hands and dancing in a circle*):
Here we go, here we go,
Round and round,
Twirling and stamping

And beating the ground.

WIND:
I have stamped out the last of the flowers!

SLEET:
I have put teeth into soft little showers.

SNOW:
I have erased every insect that cowers.

WIND, SNOW *and* SLEET:
Everyone fears such creatures as we—
From crickets in thickets
To Bruin . . . to bee . . .
Everyone fears such creatures as we.
(*They dance wildly.* BRUIN *enters with a fierce growl.*)

BRUIN:
I do not fear you, you big, bad bullies!

WIND (*Turning to look*): What? Who said that?

BRUIN (*With a louder growl*): I said, I am not afraid of you, or you, or you! (*He points to each.*)

WIND: Ah, but have you seen my big stamping feet? (*He stamps about in his boots.*)

BRUIN (*Putting his foot down with a louder thump*): I have big stamping feet, too.

WIND (*Drawing back a little*): Yes, yes, so you have!

SLEET (*Holding up her icicle fingers*): But have you seen my big claws?

BRUIN: They're not nearly as strong as mine. (*He makes a clawing motion in her direction.*)

SLEET (*Shrinking back*): Yes, yes, I see!

SNOW (*Slyly*): But have you seen my beautiful white scarf? I'll warm you with it. (*She steps up to him, flourishing it.*)

BRUIN (*Dodging scarf*): Oh, no, you won't. You'd *smother* me with it. I have a fur blanket of my own and it just fits. It's much warmer than your scarf, too. Would you like to have me hug you with it?

SNOW (*Backing away*): No, no! I don't want a bear hug.

WIND (*Becoming bold again*): See here, Bruin, you may have big, stamping feet, and sharp claws, and a warm fur coat, but you won't be able to stay out all night, every night, the whole winter long, the way we do. You have to eat and sleep. We don't. We'll conquer you in the end.

BRUIN: I wouldn't be so sure about that. See how fat I am? I've been eating enough to store up fat for the whole winter. And now I'm going into a nice snug place to sleep—a place where neither wind, nor sleet, nor snow can get near me.

WIND, RAIN *and* SLEET: What? Which? Where?

BRUIN (*Indicating with a gesture*): In that cave over there. (*He runs toward cave. They run after him but stop at the cave's mouth as* BRUIN *slips into it.*)

WIND: The trickster!

SNOW: The coward!

SLEET: He knew we couldn't get in there.

WIND: Too dark, and stuffy, and ragged with rocks.

SNOW: A safe, safe cave!

SLEET: A hibernating hall!

WIND: Oh, well, let him go. I didn't like his clumsy feet, anyway.

SLEET: And I didn't like his clumsy claws.

WIND: Of course we could have conquered him in time.

SLEET: Of course.

SNOW: But it would have been too much trouble. (*She looks offstage.*) Here comes easier prey. (RACCOON *enters, wearing a mask.*)

WIND (*Rushing up to him threateningly*): Take off your mask, burglar.

RACCOON (*Bravely*): I'm not a burglar. I wear a mask only so folks won't see how fierce I am.

WIND (*Stepping back a little*): How fierce are you?

RACCOON: I'd hate to tell you. (*He shows his teeth and claws.*)

SLEET (*Coming forward*): You aren't nearly as fierce as I am. Look how much bigger *my* teeth and claws are!

RACCOON: But you can't see how fierce my face is behind the mask.

SNOW: Take it off. I dare you to.

RACCOON: Well, if you'll just let me pass, I'll take it off behind that tall tree stump over there. It might be too much of a shock for you if I unmasked suddenly right here.

WIND: Very well . . . don't be long. (WIND, SNOW *and* SLEET *step aside.* RACCOON *dodges quickly behind the tree stump.*)

SNOW (*Trembling*): He must have a terrible face.

SLEET (*Glancing at tree doubtfully*): You don't think he's tricking us, do you?

RACCOON (*From hiding place in tree stump*): Ready! Come and see me. (WIND, SNOW *and* SLEET *tiptoe timidly toward tree. They peek around it, then look at one another in dismay.*)

WIND, SNOW *and* SLEET: He's not there. (*They walk around the tree.*) No, he's not there.

RACCOON (*Poking his head up from the top of the tall stump*): Here I am! (WIND, SNOW *and* SLEET *fall to the ground, startled. They sit with mouths open, looking up at* RACCOON.)

Oh, dear, dearie-oh!

Goodbye and cheerio!

Sorry I startled you into a heap.

I had to climb, you know.

Up here on tippy-toe,

Safe for the winter where I could sleep.

WIND: But you didn't take off your mask!

RACCOON (*Laughing*): It won't come off. It's painted on.

WIND, SNOW *and* SLEET: He's tricked us!

WIND: Well I never! I'll *blow* him out of there. (*He blows and blows on the stump, but the* RACCOON *only huddles down a little more in his hollow.*)

SLEET: He's just too clever! I'll *claw* him out. (*She claws the tree's bark with no results.*)

SNOW: I give up. Even if I piled my white flakes around the tree, they wouldn't touch him.

RACCOON (*Saucily*): That's right. In here I'm snug as a bug in a rug. (*He laughs and withdraws his head into the tree's hollow.*)

WIND (*Angrily*): I suppose he'll sleep safe and sound now for months. I'm sure I don't know why we should let animals get the better of us.

SLEET: We're really much stronger than they.

SNOW: It's just because they're tricky. (PUPPY *enters.*)

SLEET: Look! Here comes a puppy.

WIND: We won't let *him* get away.

SNOW: I should say not! (*They pounce upon the* PUPPY. WIND *blows on him.* SLEET *claws him.* SNOW *throws her white scarf over his head.* PUPPY *whines and whimpers.* BOY *enters, carrying snow shovel*)

BOY: Here, here! What are you doing to a poor helpless puppy? (*He throws the shovel aside, and frees the* PUPPY.)

SNOW (*Turning on* BOY *and tossing confetti over him*): Get out of the way! Don't you dare interfere or I'll—

BOY (*Picking up snow shovel and pushing it toward her*): You'd better look out for your toes. (SNOW *retreats, but* WIND *and* SLEET *rush up and pound and claw* BOY.)

BOY (*Pulling his leather cap down over his ears and putting up his coat collar*): It's no use. You can't hurt me. This coat and cap are windproof and waterproof.

WIND *and* SLEET (*Backing away*): He's a wizard. He's all dressed in black magic.

BOY (*Laughing*): No, just a black Mackinaw. (*He pats the* PUPPY *and leads him offstage, through cottage door, talking to him in soothing tones as they go.*) I'll take you right into my house where neither Wind, nor Sleet, nor Snow can get in. And you and I will lie on a nice thick rug by the blazing fire and Mother will bring you a bone. (*The* PUPPY *yelps and bounces with delight.* BOY *and* PUPPY *exit into cottage.*)

WIND (*Sinking down dejectedly on cottage doorstep*): What's the matter with us? People and animals aren't afraid of us any more.

SLEET: I still think we're stronger than they are.

SNOW: It was all very well when the world first began. They were in our power then. But somehow, over the years, they've learned to get the better of us.

WIND: Yes. While we weren't looking, they dug holes.

SLEET: And built houses.

SNOW: And learned how to hibernate.

WIND, SLEET *and* SNOW: And now *we're* the ones left alone —out in the cold, cold world! (*Curtain*)

THE END

December Twenty-First

(*Four* GIRLS *and three* BOYS *may sit and stand facing fire-place at side, acting out lines and holding up objects indicated.*)

1ST GIRL:
    The shortest day of the year
        Is here.
    The daylight fades and the dark
        Draws near;
    But the singing hearth is a place
        Of cheer.

1ST BOY:
    We sit by the stone while the flame
        Burns gold
    And, oh, the wonderful tales that are told!

2ND GIRL:
    We sit and we sit till the flame
        Burns blue;
    And here are some of the things
        We do:

2ND BOY (*Shaking corn popper over imaginary fire in fire-place*):
    We pop the popcorn and butter it
        Yellow.

3RD GIRL (*Holding chestnuts in one hand and marshmal-*

low on long fork in other):
We roast the chestnut and toast
    Marshmallow.
3RD BOY AND 4TH GIRL (*Holding songbooks*):
We sing old songs till the night
    Is black
And the golden fire-logs sing
    Them back!

Jack Frost

(A little girl may stand on one side of a window, reciting the poem, while JACK FROST *is on the other "painting" a white scene on the windowpane with his brush in one hand. He may also paste cut-out stars or snowflakes on the glass with the other hand so that there is a star and snowflake design on the window at the end of the reading.)*

Jack Frost is looking in at me
And winking through my window-glass.
His silver brush moves busily;
He paints so fast and dizzily
The things that pass
Like stars and clouds and wintry streams.
(He also paints the things in dreams.)

He sketches leaves and shapes of flowers,
But color he has never seen
Because he spends his summer hours
In frozen lands and frosty towers
Where nothing's green.
(He dips his brush in pale moonlight.
That's why his pictures all are white.)

Snowflake Ballerinas

(Little girls dressed in white sparkling ballet costumes may do "snowflake" dance, as NARRATOR *recites poem. Four* BOYS, *labeled* NORTH WIND, SOUTH WIND, EAST WIND, *and* WEST WIND, *may throw white confetti on the* GIRLS *as they dance.)*

NARRATOR:
>Their skirts are made of glittering gauze
>   And sequins glint in their hair.
>They point, they turn, they pirouette
>   All on the empty air.
>
>They have no music save the wind—
>   No flutes, no concertinas.
>Yet rhythmic are the swirling skirts
>   Of snowflake ballerinas.

Remembering the Winter

(*A dramatic reading for two* SOLOS *and a* CHORUS.)

1ST SOLO:
  Remembering the winter, the squirrel goes nutting
  Up where the branches of the hickory are jutting,
  Over where the butternut boughs are tossing . . .
  (The air is a canyon that the squirrel is crossing.)
  Down the oak tree's ladder he hurries to deposit
  All his buried treasure in the earth's safe closet . . .
  Remembering the winter.

2ND SOLO:
  Remembering the winter, the birds go winging,
  (No time for nesting, no time for singing,)
  Sailing to the southward with wings for sails,
  Steering through emptiness with long rudder tails;
  Traveling, traveling, days and days
  With no map to guide them through the wide, wild
    ways.

CHORUS:
  Remembering the winter, the bear finds a hollow
  In a dry cavern where none dares to follow,
  Where even the icicle cannot push its splinter . . .
  Oh, wise are the wild things, preparing for the winter.

Snow

The snow is a bird, soft-feathered and white.
Silent and graceful is her flight
As she swoops to earth and spreads her wings
Over the beautiful unborn things;
Seeds and bulbs that soon will tower
Out of the nest of the ground, and flower.

Sleighs and Horses

Long ago, across the snow,
Sleighs and horses used to go
    To and fro;
And the silver flakes swirled 'round
To the sleigh bells' silver sound
As along the silent ground
    Fast or slow
Sleighs and horses used to skim
    Long ago.

In January

In January I like to go
Out-of-doors where the flakes of snow
Scurry down from a rumpled cloud
And winds go whistling low and loud.

In January when crusts of sleet
Crickle and crackle under my feet,
I climb the hill with my sled drawn after—
And down I go with the storm's wild laughter
Stinging my ears. Oh, this is fun—
Sliding faster than boys can run!

In January I like to go
Into the house and out of the snow
(When I am tired of sliding and coasting)
To sit by a fire that's warm and toasting.

Quietly, Oh, Quietly . . .

Quietly, oh, quietly
   Fall the stars of snow
From a sky of stillness
   To silent earth below. . . .

Quietly, oh, quietly
   As I sit and sew
Little happy, secret thoughts
   Travel to and fro
Through my mind. I cannot find
   How they come and go. . . .

Nothing is more silent than
   Secret thoughts and snow.

The Melting Castle

There once was a fairy who lived long ago
In a castle of ice with a roof top of snow.
Her castle had turrets and icicle towers
Whose windows were curtained with lacy frost flowers;
And the fairy believed there was nothing as nice
As a roof top of snow with a turret of ice.
But, oh, when the winter was over and done,
Her icicle towers all dripped in the sun!
The fairy no longer sat high on a throne.
She splashed in a puddle, afraid and alone.
She cried out for help as she swam through the water.
(How lucky that she was a cloud fairy's daughter!)
Her king father heard her (she shouted so loud),
And he lowered a rainbow right out of his cloud.
The frost fairy laughed, for she couldn't be gladder.
She climbed up the rainbow—it made a fine ladder—
And, safe on the cloud top, she said to her father:
"Ice castles are pretty, but, oh, such a bother!"

After the Sleet Storm

The long twig-fingers of the trees
  Look very smooth and nice.
They've covered knotty knuckles up
  By wearing *gloves of ice*.

Holing Up

The wind is from the north tonight,
   The last, last leaves are scudding.
Soft days have given up the art
   Of flowering and budding.
A dark sky frowns through darkening pines
   And snow lies down in patches.
Oh, bring the last, last autumn torch
   And light the last, last matches—
Wild things are on the run tonight
   And paws pad helter-skelter.
A hollow must be found tonight—
   Or hole, or brushwood shelter.

The bear remembers hollow trees
   As does the masked raccoon.
The bat is looking for a cave
   Far from the frosty moon.
The chipmunk finds a furrow
The groundhog seeks his burrow.
   The skunk, his private den,
The mice will hunt for huddly homes
   Inside the homes of men—
The wind is from the north tonight,
   There's danger in the waiting,
The wild things scatter left and right,
The wind is in the north tonight,
   It's time for hibernating.

First Snowstorm

I saw a little cotton cloud
  Caught high up in a tree.
"I wish he'd toss his cotton down,"
  I said, "on roof and field and town
    And even over me."

I wished aloud, and so the cloud
  (For he was very knowing)
Broke up in little bits that fell
All skitter-scatter, pell and mell,
  And people cried, *"It's snowing!"*

Snowshoes and Skis

When snowflakes fly about like bees
And snowdrifts come up to my knees,
It's time for snowshoes and for skis.

My snowshoes give me just the lift
I need to walk across a drift,
But skis give me a bigger thrill—
They take me coasting down a hill!

Winter Bloom

The red of the maple withers to brown,
The rattling leaf comes tumbling down,
The talking leaf is hushed by the white
Of a winter night;

But see! Indoors the fire is lit
And red and bronze rush out of it,
The fire is lit and talks on the stone
In a voice of its own.

The blue-flag breaks and the petals drop,
The hawthorn apple falls with a plop,
And all that is burning and brilliant must go
Under the snow;

Yet here tonight in this shadowy room
We have planted a tree all bursting with bloom
That we may have fragrance and color and light,
On a winter night.

Production Notes

PRODUCTION NOTES

OUT OF THE CLOCK

Characters: 3 male; 2 female. If desired, animals may be played by either boys or girls.

Playing Time: 10 minutes.

Costumes: Animals wear appropriate costumes, and all should have rope tails. Cat and Mouse have whiskers drawn at either side of the mouth, and the Dog wears a collar. Father Time is an old man with a white robe and beard, and Little New Year wears a white dress and pink bows in her hair.

Properties: Three calendars.

Setting: A living room. A chimney corner and a chair are at right, two chairs are at left, and a grandfather clock is up center. The center panel of the clock is a door through which Little New Year enters. There is an exit at left.

Lighting: No special effects.

Sound: Clock ticking and striking, as indicated in text.

ON NEW YEAR'S EVE

Characters: 2 male; 9 female; as many boys and girls for Hours and Days as desired.

Playing Time: 5 minutes.

Costumes: Boys and Girls wear everyday dress, and Little New Year wears a party dress and gay ribbons, and she carries a wand. Fairies, Hours, and Days wear brightly colored, fanciful costumes. Hours carry trays of flowers, and Days have balls and musical instruments, such as triangles, drums, rhythm sticks, etc.

Setting: A living room with a grandfather clock standing in a corner. The clock may be a folding screen, with the two outer panels turned back, and a clock face painted on the center panel. The center panel should be a door through which Little New Year and others enter, or they may enter from behind the clock. Four chairs are near the clock.

Lighting: No special effects.

VISITORS FOR NANCY HANKS

Characters: 4 female.

Playing Time: 30 minutes.

Costumes: Nancy Lincoln wears a long, dark dress with a full skirt and a small apron and a shawl. The other women are dressed in long, dark cloaks and poke bonnets.

Properties: A workbag, a small basket, teakettle, cups, saucers, spoons, hoecake, shawl, blankets, leaves, twigs, large log, broom, sewing things.

Setting: At the right is a large hearth where a small log burns. At the left stands a table set with rude dishes. Near the hearth is a rough cupboard. On the floor is a large log used as a bench. A teakettle hangs on a crane, swung out, away from the fire. Rough chairs and stools are about the room. A hooded cradle stands to the left of the center of the stage. A door and a window are upstage center.

Lighting: Flashes of lightning are seen through the window.

THE PRINCE OF HEARTS

Characters: 7 male; 1 female.

Playing Time: 15 minutes.

Costumes: The Prince wears a traditional royal costume. His cape and crown are decorated with red hearts. The Groom wears a white apron over his clothes. The Chamberlain wears a dark costume with fancy collar and cuffs. The peddlers may wear working clothes covered by dark aprons. The Princess wears a long flowing cape over a bright dress. The Lion has a lion mask and a yellow or brown outfit.

Properties: Duster, handkerchiefs, bags for the peddlers, helmet, sword, and large heart-shaped shield.

Setting: The throne room of Prince Faintheart's castle in the Kingdom of Hearts. A door up center leads outside and a door at left leads to another part of the castle. There is enough furniture for five people to hide behind; a stool is near the throne.

Lighting: No special effects.

THE LITTLEST ARTIST

Characters: 3 male; 1 female; as many boys and girls as desired for Elves.

Playing Time: 10 minutes.

Costumes: Benjamin and Sylvia are in modern dress. Sylvia wears winter coat when she enters. Jack Frost wears a small child's coat with a red and yellow muffler over a white, elfin costume. King Winter wears a long red cloak trimmed with white and a gold crown. His attendants are dressed in matching shorts and jerkins.

Properties: Workbag filled with sewing things, cardboard heart and paper lace, a small suitcase labeled "Water Colors," filled with paint brushes, pin cushion in shape of heart, a finished Valentine, a frost picture, a silver chain.

Setting: There is a large window upstage center with heavy draperies. A table or a flat-top desk stands to the right. There is a rocking chair at the left. Small scraps of paper are scattered on the floor.

Lighting: No special effects.

A VALENTINE FOR MARY

Characters: 5 female; offstage voice for Mrs. Brown.

Playing Time: 10 minutes.

Costumes: Mary wears an everyday dress. Puss may wear a cat costume—tights, tunic, tail, cap with ears. The Frost Fairies wear silver and white costumes, and silver crowns. Blunt kindergarten scissors are tied to a ribbon and hang at the waist of each fairy.

Properties: Paste, scissors, valentines for Mary; scroll containing cutouts of stars, flowers, lace, etc. for 3rd Fairy; white heart for Puss.

Setting: A living room. At upstage center is a large window. A table and chairs are near the window. Other furnishings may be added as desired.

Lighting: If possible, the lights should dim briefly as indicated in the text. A light might also be turned on behind the window after the valentine is made.

THE FIRST EASTER EGGS

Characters: 4 male; 4 female; extras.

Playing Time: 10 minutes.

Costumes: The barnyard fowl and the little bird have cardboard wings and feathered tails. Rabbit wears patched overalls. The King, the Herald and the Attendants wear court costumes.

Properties: Market basket, large bandanna, trumpet or bell and long scroll for Herald, nests of eggs, toy nest with colored candy eggs, bag of gold.

Setting: The only furnishing needed is a stump. A backdrop of a barn may be used, a fence may run around the stage, and some shrubs and bushes may be placed downstage left and right.

Lighting: No special effects.

GOOD MORNING, MR. RABBIT

Characters: 5 male; 4 female.

Playing Time: 10 minutes.

Costumes: Easter Rabbit wears a white rabbit's suit, a gay-colored coat, and a jaunty hat with holes to let his ears through. He carries a big Easter basket on his arm. The children wear attractive spring outfits.

Properties: Red bandanna, bottle, Easter eggs, and paper grass, for Easter Rabbit.

Setting: A clearing in the woods. Stage may be bare, or there may be trees, bushes, and flowers here and there.

Lighting: No special effects.

THE PLOT

Characters: 6 male; 1 female; as many boys for Guards and boys and girls for Court Attendants as desired.

Playing Time: 10 minutes.

Costumes: All wear appropriate court dress, except Father Perez, who wears a simple dark robe. The King and Queen wear crowns, and the King carries a scepter.

Properties: Letter, scroll, quill pen.

Setting: The castle of Ferdinand and Isabella. There are two thrones up center, and a table is down left, on which are a quill pen and a scroll. Draperies, pictures, maps, etc. complete the setting. An exit is at right.

Lighting: No special effects.

THE SCARECROW AND THE WITCH

Characters: 1 male; 3 female; any number of clowns, sprites, elves, and fairies.

Playing Time: 15 minutes.

Costumes: The elves, fairies, clowns, and sprites are appropriately dressed. The small fairy wears a simple costume so that she can easily slip into a cat costume and mask. The Fairy Queen wears robes and a crown. The witch is dressed in a ragged black cape, pointed hat, and has a grimy appearance. She wears a mask. The scarecrow wears patched and ragged trousers and a shirt, and a straw hat. He wears a grinning mask. Later witch and scarecrow change to better clothes.

Properties: Broomstick, pepper shaker, bags, bundles, and books, for witch; kettle, hawthorn branch, piece of tin for cat; "wings" for Fairy Queen.

Setting: A field, at midnight. There are corn shocks and pumpkins scattered about the stage. A piece of fence or a gatepost is at left of center. A harvest moon is pinned up on the back curtain.

Lighting: The stage lights should be dim, if possible.

Sound: Offstage clock strikes midnight, as indicated in text.

IN THE WITCH'S HOUSE

Characters: 1 male; 2 female.

Playing Time: 10 minutes.

Costumes: The Witch wears a long, black dress. Her hair is straggly, and her face is dirty. The Cat is dressed in long, black pants and a matching jerkin and a mask.

Under this costume the Cat wears modern girl's dress. The Boy wears modern clothes.

Properties: Rain barrel, faggot broom, large bowl, mixing spoon, can of spice, white handkerchief, towel, two combs, mirror.

Setting: The room is dark and dreary. There is a door upstage center, and a window at the right. A rain barrel stands to the left of the door. Downstage left is a large, brick oven with a closed door with a lock and a key. In the center stand a table and a chair. The broom stands in a corner.

Lighting: Dim lights.

THE THREE TERRORS

Characters: 3 male; 2 female.

Playing Time: 6 minutes.

Costumes: Boy and Girl wear everyday clothes. Witch is appropriately dressed, and carries a broom and a wand. Scarecrow has on tattered clothes, and has a big bandanna handkerchief in one pocket. Pumpkin Head wears a large jack-o'-lantern face mask.

Setting: A field on Halloween. There are pumpkins and cornshocks placed about the stage, and a witch's caldron is at center.

Lighting: No special effects.

RUMPELSTILTSKIN

Characters: 3 male; 3 female; Courtiers may be male or female.

Playing Time: 10 minutes.

Costumes: The King wears a long purple robe and a crown. Marion wears a simple, plain long dress in Scene 1. In Scene 2 she is dressed in a long robe and a crown. The servants wear long dark dresses with white aprons and caps. Rumpelstiltskin is dressed all in brown, and has long, tight-fitting pants. He wears

pointed slippers with bells attached to the toes. A little pointed cap completes his outfit. The male Courtiers wear dark-colored knee-pants, and white shirts. The female Courtiers wear long dresses.

Properties: Play money, bills, two brooms, three bales of straw, spinning wheel, stool, necklace, ring, gold coins (paper or foil), pennies, three pails, large book. Note: The closet in which the straw is placed should have two openings: the door in front, visible to the audience, and a dark curtain at the back which may be lifted by a stagehand who exchanges the bales of straw for pails of gold while Rumpelstiltskin is spinning with the closet door shut. The pails may be nearly filled with paper padding which is covered on top with paper coins and pennies, so that the coins will make noise when they are tossed about.

Setting: A room in a castle. There are entrances at left and right. There is a small closet in one corner. The room may be furnished as elaborately as desired. A table and chair are the only necessary furnishings for Scene 1. In Scene 2, a cradle and a chair for the Queen should be added.

Lighting: No special effects.

SNOW-WHITE AND ROSE-RED

Characters: 5 male; 3 female; as many extras for Attendants as desired.

Playing Time: 30 minutes.

Costumes: The girls and their mother wear simple dresses with aprons, and Snow-White carries a roll of bandages and a pair of scissors in the pocket of her apron. The Dwarf wears a bright jacket, and a pointed hat. He has a long, white beard. The prince's bear costume has a hidden pocket for his handkerchief, and under bear costume, he wears a fine, royal suit. Others wear court costume.

Properties: Book, broom, poker, bowls, dishes, pitcher, pot of jam, bread, cheese, bun, bandages, scissors, comb, napkin, purple handkerchief, large sack for Dwarf, cushions, gold cloth, harp, dust cloth, sprays of red and white roses, bunch of flowers.

Setting: The interior of a cottage on the edge of a forest. Up center is a door leading to forest. On either side of the door is a window framing a rosebush. In Scene 1, bushes are covered with snow; in Scene 2, left bush is covered with white roses, the one at right with red roses. A third window for dwarf's exit in Scene 1 is at left, above a table set for supper. Near window is a closet. At right is a large fireplace, with a hanging kettle. A poker and broom lean against fireplace, and nearby are a spinning wheel and a loom. A large chair stands in one corner of the room, and wooden stools complete the furnishings.

Lighting: No special effects.

Sound: Bell, growling and knocking, and music, as indicated in text.

The City Mouse and the Country Mouse

Characters: 3 male; 2 female.

Playing Time: 10 minutes.

Costumes: The Country Mouse is dressed in a plain dress and apron. The City Mouse is dressed in silks and satins. She wears a great deal of jewelry, and she carries a lorgnette. The Cat may be dressed in black trousers and matching jerkin. A mask of a cat's face may be worn.

Properties: Broom, sunbonnet. Scene 2: large trays for serving men.

Setting: Scene 1: a small table on which is spread a simple meal. Two or three chairs are placed about the room. Scene 2: Chairs with fancy pillows on them are placed about the room. A table covered with a white cloth stands in the center. Dishes and food are on the table. There should be a cubby hole with a curtain for a hiding place.

Lighting: No special effects.

The Hare and the Tortoise

Characters: 2 male; 1 female.

Playing Time: 15 minutes.

Costumes: Rabbit suit for Hare; bushy tail suggested for Fox. Tortoise should have dark clothes, possibly fake hump on back, painted to represent tortoise shell.

Properties: Book for Fox.

Setting: There should be a post at one end of stage for a goal and a bush at other end. A hedge would make a good backdrop.

Lighting: No special effects.

The Lion and the Mouse

Characters: 1 male; 1 female.

Playing Time: 10 minutes.

Costumes: The Lion may be dressed in long yellow or tan pants with matching jerkin with long sleeves. A lion's face may be made of cardboard and attached to the player's head. The Mouse is dressed in gray shorts and matching jerkin. A mouse's face may be made of cardboard.

Setting: All that is necessary are some bushes in the background with a net caught in them. A tennis net could be used. If desired, a backdrop of a woody scene may be used.

Lighting: No special effects.

THE BEADED MOCCASINS

Characters: 2 male; 1 female; as many boys and girls for Pilgrims and Indians as desired.

Playing Time: 10 minutes, with additional time required for singing.

Costumes: Pilgrims, including Ruth and Jonathan, wear traditional Pilgrim dress; Ruth also wears an apron and has a cake of soap in one pocket, and both children wear kerchiefs around their necks. Indians are appropriately dressed, and the Indian Boy also wears a necklace of shells around his neck and beaded moccasins. A small tom-tom and a leather pouch are attached to his belt. His hands and face are muddy when he first enters.

Properties: Bundles of twigs, pail containing berries, cake of soap, pail of water.

Setting: A glade in the forest at the edge of a marshland. A few berry bushes are at right, along the edge of the bog, and the trees of the forest are along the back of the stage. Down left is a log, and twigs are scattered about at left. Exits are at right and left.

Lighting: No special effects.

Sound: Offstage sounds as Indian Boy falls, Indian drums, as indicated in text.

FIRE-FACE AND THE INDIANS

Characters: 2 female; as many boys for Indians as desired.

Playing Time: 15 minutes.

Costumes: The girls wear traditional Pilgrim dress. Patience wears an apron. Since only the faces of the Indians are seen, the only costumes they require are feathered headdresses and Indian make-up.

Properties: Two carved jack-o'-lanterns, which contain pencil flashlights, knives, unfinished sampler, musket, ax, ladle.

Setting: The kitchen of a log cabin. A large fireplace is up center, with a kettle hanging in it. At right of the fireplace is a window, and at left is a cupboard and a table on which are several crocks. There are several chairs in the room, and in one corner stand a musket and an ax. A door is at left.

Lighting: No special effects.

THE SHOEMAKER AND THE ELVES

Characters: 4 male; 1 female.

Playing Time: 15 minutes.

Costumes: Shoemaker wears a leather apron over old clothes. His wife wears a long, patched skirt, blouse, and white cap. The Gentleman is richly dressed, with a cape, top hat, and boots, one of which is torn. The Elves wear ragged brown clothes with little green caps and long stockings. Later they put on new clothes—coats, hats, and shoes.

Properties: Shoes, scraps of leather or brown cloth, large needle, thimble, plate, crusts of bread, hammer, candle, purse, gold coins, wrapping paper, tape measure, colored cloth, artificial snow.

Setting: The shoemaker's shop, a poor, bare room. At center are a bench and stool. There are some empty shelves along the back wall, and nearby two three-legged stools. At left is a screen, and near it a window. Doors right and left lead to the rest of the house and to the street.

Lighting: Lights dim, then rise, to indicate evening and passage of time.

Sound: Light elfin music, church bells, lullaby.

PICCOLA

Characters: 2 male; 3 female.

Playing Time: 15 minutes.

Costumes: Snow wears a glittering white gown, and Wind wears tunic, high boots, winged helmet, and carries a whip. Others wear shabby clothes, and Piccola wears wooden shoes.

Properties: Artificial bird, fishnet, candles, kettle.

Setting: A fisherman's hut in Brittany. A fireplace is up center, and to one side of it is a window. Stools are at either side of the hearth, and a broom leans against the wall in one corner. An exit is at right. In Scene 1, there are two candles on the mantel. In Scene 2, mounds of snow (cotton batting) are piled around the room, and the stools are overturned.

Lighting: Red bulbs concealed in the fireplace may be used for the fire and turned on and off as required. In Scene 2, the sun shines in through the window.

Sound: Howling of wind, peeping and singing of bird, as indicated in text.

CHRISTMAS PIE

Characters: 3 male; 1 female; 7 boys or girls for Cooks.

Playing Time: 20 minutes.

Costumes: King and Queen wear appropriate royal dress and crowns decorated with hearts. The Queen wears an apron over her gown. The Page's costume should also be decorated with hearts. Cooks wear white aprons and chef's hats, and each carries a cookbook. The Head Cook's hat is decorated with a large gold star. Jack Horner wears a shabby cloak and hood when he first enters, and under these he is dressed in a fancy costume.

Properties: Pastry dough, tray of unfilled tart shells, cookbooks, rolling pin, pots and pans, bowls of fruit, including plums, flour, spices, etc., large Christmas pie, decorated with holly.

Setting: The kitchen of the King of Hearts' palace. The Queen's work table, with pastry, rolling pin, tray, flour, spices, etc., on it, is down left. Up right is a fireplace, and beside it is an oven with a door that opens and closes. The walls are lined with cupboards containing pots and pans, bowls of fresh and dried fruit, and on the top shelf of one cupboard is a bowl of plums. Two or three chairs complete the setting. A door at right leads to the rest of the palace, and another at left leads outside.

Lighting: No special effects.

WHAT WILL THE TOYS SAY?

Characters: 4 male; 3 female; 3 or more girls for Other Paper Dolls; as many wooden soldiers and other toys as desired.

Playing Time: 10 minutes.

Costumes: Brother and Sister wear night clothes; toys are dressed appropriately, according to their roles; Elf King should wear a red costume, with glittering sequins on it, and carry a wand.

Properties: Two lighted electric candles, Christmas tree, large, fancy box, roll of mending tape, toy bugle.

Setting: A typical Christmas Eve home scene, with comfortable furniture, a fireplace, and a Christmas tree.

Lighting: Lights should be dim before the curtain rises; they go on at rise. There is a sudden flash of light as the Elf King enters.

Sound: Sleigh bells off-stage, clock chiming twelve, crashing noise offstage, with drums and cymbals if possible, tinkling bell, distant sound of cock crowing, carol music at end. "The Parade of the Wooden Soldiers" can be obtained on record.

THE PUDDING-BAG STRING

Characters: 7 male; 2 female; as many boys and girls for Lords and Ladies as desired.

Playing Time: 10 minutes.

Costumes: Appropriate royal dress for all except Cooks, who wear white chef's hats and aprons, and the Cat, who is dressed in a tawny-colored cat costume. The King and Queen wear crowns.

Properties: Book, crystal ball, globe for Advisers, large cloth bag, piece of string, pot, bowl of pudding mixture, bottle of milk, robe, sword.

Setting: The palace kitchen. A cupboard containing bag, string and pot is up left, and a chimney corner is at right. The work table, on which are pots, pans, bowl of pudding mixture, bottle of milk, etc., is down left. There are several chairs placed about the room, on one of which are the King's robe and sword. Exits at right and left lead to the rest of the palace, and a door up center at the back of the stage leads outside.

Lighting: No special effects.

YE OLDEN FESTIVAL OF CHRISTMAS

Characters: 15 male; 2 female; as many boys and girls as desired for Lords, Ladies, Children, Peasants, and Villagers.

Playing Time: 15 minutes.

Costumes: Appropriate medieval dress. The King wears a cape, and carries his shield and his sword when he first enters. Ladies of the Court are dressed in white. The Minstrel's cape is shabby, and he carries a harp concealed under it. Crier has a hand bell.

Properties: Bell, harp, tapestry, yule log, bundles of sticks, evergreen sprays and wreaths, platters and trays holding fruits, meats, pastries, etc., covered platter decorated with holly, plum pudding.

Setting: The throne room of the castle. The throne is up center. A long table is at right, and a fireplace at left. There is a window near the throne, and an exit at right. The room is bare as the play opens, and is later decorated with evergreens, etc.

Lighting: No special effects.

THE SNOWMAN WHO PLAYED SANTA

Characters: 3 male; 1 female.

Playing Time: 10 minutes.

Costumes: Johnny wears winter outdoor clothing. Snowman wears a white costume, well-padded with pillows. Later he wears red coat and hat trimmed with fur. Squirrel and Jackdaw wear appropriate masks.

Properties: Shovel, bags and bundles containing nuts, key, marbles, and other small toys.

Setting: A snowy backyard. Sheets may be spread about to suggest snow.

Lighting: No special effects.

THE CHILD WHO WAS MADE OF SNOW

Characters: 1 male; 2 female; as many boys and girls as desired for Children.

Playing Time: 10 minutes.

Costumes: The Old Man and his Wife wear shabby old-fashioned winter coats. The Children wear winter coats and hats. The Snow Maiden wears a glittering white dress.

Properties: Cardboard ax, bundle of twigs and sticks, wreath, candle, spray of evergreens, lantern.

Setting: The yard in front of the old couple's cottage. At right is a log which the Old Man pretends to chop, and at left on the ground are a few twigs and sticks. Sheets are spread on the stage to represent snow, and at center is a mound of snow, made of a pillow covered by a sheet. Near the mound, white confetti is strewn about on the ground to represent snow. The exit at right leads to the cottage, and there is another exit at left.

Lighting: The stage is in semidarkness for Scene 2, with a white light for moonlight.

Sound: Offstage sleigh bells, clock chimes, and music, as indicated in text.

THE MAGIC WEAVER

Characters: 2 male; 4 female; 10 or more male or female for elves and fairies.

Playing Time: 10 minutes.

Costumes: Traditional elf and fairy costumes, for elves and fairies. Elf King and Fairy Queen wear crowns, and Elf King may wear a cape. Spring wears a flowing pastel dress. Cricket wears a black elf costume and has on his head a black circlet with long antennae wired upright at the front. Spider's costume may be of brown cambric, gathered at the bottom to look like a ball. She wears large, dark goggles, and six false arms, made of stuffed brown stockings, are sewed on her dress,

three at either side. Brightly colored yarn may be wound around her waist.

Properties: Artificial trumpet-flower bugles, fiddle, torn tablecloth and untorn tablecloth, large green leaf with hole in it, green carpet roll and violet carpet roll. If desired, twigs, vase, flowers, etc., may be used to set toadstool table.

Setting: A woodland scene in Elfland, with a toadstool table in the center. The table may be made of a birdbath turned upside down on its pedestal. Other toadstools for seats may be scattered around stage. These may be made of short birch logs turned on end and topped off with a chopping bowl turned upside down.

Sound: Bugle calls and dancing music.

Lighting: No special effects.

SCHOOL FOR SCAMPERERS

Characters: 3 male; 2 female.

Playing Time: 10 minutes.

Costumes: Rabbit costumes. Wiggle-Nose has hair ribbons tied in big bows on her ears. Rover wears a dog costume.

Properties: Carrots.

Setting: A clearing in the woods. A backdrop of trees and bushes may be used, or real greenery may be used. At one side is a hollow log, which may be made of cardboard, and at the other side is a bramblebush, which may be a real bush or may be made of cardboard.

Lighting: No special effects.

THE KING'S HOLIDAY

Characters: 4 male; 2 female.

Playing Time: 10 minutes.

Costumes: Royal robes and crowns for King and Queen. Court costumes for Prime Minister and

Lord Chamberlain. Wizard's robe and pointed hat for Wiseman. Gypsy wears traditional bright gypsy skirt and blouse, gay jewelry, etc.; she carries a pack in which are gypsy clothes for King and Queen to put on over their other clothes.

Properties: Stacks of coins, bread and honey, guitar or lute gypsy pack, two "Do Not Disturb" signs.

Setting: The royal palace. At the right is the countinghouse and at the left is the parlor. They are separated by attractive folding screens, with a gap in between for a door.

Lighting: No special effects.

RAINBOW'S END

Characters: 2 male; 2 female.
Playing Time: 10 minutes.
Costumes: Girl wears dress with pockets and apron with pockets in it. Others wear appropriate costume.
Properties: An earthenware pot filled with gold pieces.
Setting: A meadow. Colored ribbons representing rainbow hang down from tree at one side of stage. A small pile of brushwood is nearby.
Lighting: No special effects.

PIXIE IN A TRAP

Characters: 7 male or female.
Playing Time: 10 minutes.
Costumes: Pixie is dressed in green costume with pointed elfin shoes. Birds should wear appropriately colored costumes (blue for Bluebirds, orange and black for Orioles, black and white for Wood-

peckers), with colored scarves to suggest wings.

Properties: Toadstool, trap with rope attached, suitcase, children's clothes, twigs, berries.

Setting: A woodland scene. At left is a large toadstool with an empty suitcase near it. At right is a tree with the trap tied to its trunk with a rope. Bushes and foliage to suggest woods are upstage.

Lighting: No special effects.

THE WINTER WIZARDS

Characters: 5 male; 2 female.
Playing Time: 10 minutes.
Costumes: Wind wears dark costume, high boots and cylindrical hat. He carries a whip and wears a tom-tom. Snow and Sleet wear white net dresses sprinkled with silver glitter. They carry bags for confetti and rice. Snow wears a white scarf. Sleet wears white gloves with cardboard fingertips that resemble icicles. Bruin wears bear costume. Raccoon also wears animal costume, with mask. Puppy may wear spotted flannel pajamas; he has a floppy tail and floppy ears. Boy wears heavy Mackinaw and leather cap.
Properties: Confetti, for Snow; castanets and rice, for Sleet; snow shovel, for Boy.
Setting: A tall, hollow tree stump is upstage left, with ladder or chair behind it for Raccoon to climb. A cottage door with doorstep is upstage right. At left is the entrance to a cave. Dry leaves and wilted flowers are strewn about. There is a backdrop depicting a barren landscape.
Lighting: No special effects.